# Soviet
# Political Elites

## THE CASE OF TIRASPOL

# Soviet
# Political Elites

## THE CASE OF TIRASPOL

*Ronald J. Hill*

St. Martin's Press · New York

Library of Congress Catalog Card Number: 76–53599
ISBN: 0–312–74846–9
First published in the United States of America in 1977

# Contents

*For my parents*

# Preface

The present study originated as a doctoral thesis and began largely in the Krupskaya Moldavian Republican Library in Kishinev, capital of Soviet Moldavia, where I was fortunate in spending the academic year 1967–68. Living as a lone westerner in that city, I quickly came to recognise that there is rather more to political life in the Soviet Union than what goes on within the red brick walls of the Moscow Kremlin, and that the picture widely held in the West (although admittedly by few serious scholars) of 250 million honest citizens ruled by two dozen somewhat dishonest communist party bosses is a very inadequate caricature.

There has, indeed, been a widespread and growing recognition among western scholars in recent years that this is so, and I am happy to acknowledge the stimulation I received from the published works of writers on Soviet local politics whose names are recorded in the text and notes of this study. This is my own contribution, which I hope will help to restore a little further the balance in our view of the Soviet political system, by demonstrating that there is some sort of political life in the Soviet localities, however circumscribed might be the role of ordinary citizens in their country's social and political existence. I trust it will be of some interest and value to those professional colleagues whose work has been such a stimulus to me.

In preparing this work I have been encouraged and helped by many friends, colleagues and institutions, to all of whom I am extremely grateful, but most of whom I am unable to mention here. However, I wish to record my appreciation of the British Council in London and the Ministry of Higher and Specialised Secondary Education in Moscow for awarding the studentship that allowed me to spend time gathering materials in Moldavia. The staffs of the following libraries deserve thanks for their assistance: the library of the Academy of Sciences, Kishinev; the British Library of Political and Economic Science, London; the British Museum Newspaper Library, Colindale; Essex University Library; the Krupskaya Library, Kishinev; the Lenin

Library, Moscow; and the library of Trinity College, Dublin.

Among personal friends and colleagues, I should like to thank in particular Mr David Shapiro, who first turned my thoughts in the direction of Soviet Moldavia; friends in the Institute of Economics of the Moldavian Academy of Sciences: Dr Ivan Shirshov, and especially Anatolii Gudym, for their warm friendship and generous advice and assistance; Peter Frank, for his unfailingly helpful friendship, encouragement and counsel; and Mr Archie Brown and Dr David Lane, for their invaluable comments on the study in its original form; the final version benefited from the kindly and challenging comments of Professor Jerry Hough. I also thank Hilary Tyrrell for so painstakingly typing the final draft; and finally, my wife, Jackie, for her advice and her good humour and patience in the face of unhusbandly neglect.

To all these and others who have shown interest and encouragement, I willingly concede my debt; however, it goes without saying that the responsibility for everything written here is entirely my own.

*R. J. Hill*
*June 1976*

# Glossary of Russian Terms

| | |
|---|---|
| apparatchik | party bureaucrat |
| buro | executive committee of communist party committee (e.g., gorkom buro, raikom buro) |
| CPM | Communist Party of Moldavia |
| CPSU | Communist Party of the Soviet Union |
| gorispolkom | executive committee of town soviet |
| gorkom | town committee, especially of CPSU |
| gorplan | town planning commission |
| ispolkom | executive committee of local soviet |
| kolkhoz | collective farm |
| MSSR | Moldavian Soviet Socialist Republic |
| nomenklatura | list of posts in the filling of which a particular institution (normally a CPSU committee) has control |
| obkom | provincial committee, especially of CPSU |
| oblast | province (administrative unit below republic; none exist in Moldavian SSR) |
| otdel | administrative department |
| plenum | full (plenary) session of CPSU or other committee |
| politburo | buro of central committee ( = political buro) |
| raiispolkom | executive committee of district soviet |
| raikom | district committee, especially of CPSU |
| raion | district (administrative unit below oblast or, as in Moldavian SSR, below the republican administration; also used of an urban borough within large cities) |
| RSFSR | Russian Soviet Federative Socialist Republic |
| soviet | local council |

ix

sovkhoz          state farm

supreme soviet    republican or all-USSR parliamentary institution

*Note:* Most Russian words form the plural by adding a letter repre-sented in English by -y. Thus, *kolkhozy, otdely.*

# CHAPTER 1

# Introduction

The reorganisation of the Russian Empire in the form of the Union of Soviet Socialist Republics, and its transformation from a relatively unsuccessful power, uncertain of its real position between Europe and Asia, into one of the world's major powers, has been without a doubt one of the distinguishing features of the history of the world in the present century. This transformation has involved a fundamental restructuring of the traditional society and economy; it has meant disruption of the old way of life; it has been accompanied by much cruelty and brutality; it has demanded supreme sacrifice on the part of people and leaders such as has rarely been witnessed in the course of history. So great has been the impact of the Soviet Union on the modern world, and so great the interest added by the ideological dimension, that the literature on the history of the USSR is vast, and spans every aspect of Soviet society, in an effort to understand and explain the nature of the phenomenon being witnessed.[1]

Academic studies of Soviet politics and history, particularly since the late 1930s, have mainly concentrated on the highest levels of political life, that is, on the leaders who have claimed to be directing the construction of the new society, and on the methods they have used in bringing it about. Influenced by the harshness of the form of rule, and encouraged by the attitudes of confrontation between East and West, between 'capitalism' and 'communism', western scholars have produced an extremely unattractive picture of the political process, in which the population are kept in ignorance and at a safe distance, ruled by a bureaucracy that operates in the interests of an elite of desperate politicians perpetually engaged in a power struggle. 'Struggle at the top', 'thirst for power', 'struggle for power': these are the phrases that typify the writings of this long-established school,[2] whose outlook, reflecting its obsession with the comings and goings of the men in the Kremlin, has been aptly named the 'Kremlinological' or (more brutally) the 'Who is doing-in whom' approach.[3] Moreover, the tendency to concentrate on the central institutions and their officers has generally been accompanied by a particular view of the whole system as being characterised by extreme centralisation[4] and by dominance over political life by the communist party.

One important result of this preoccupation with the summit of the system is that local politics have been very largely ignored, or at least their importance has been played down. In the 1930s, it is true, western scholars and others visited the Soviet Union and were favourably impressed by the local government system.[5] However, their generally uncritical acceptance of constitutional norms as a description of how the system might operate in practice led to a reaction by other writers, who tended to discount the importance of local government and politics, and standard textbooks on Soviet government have typically all but ignored the lower reaches of the Soviet power structure.[6]

The reasons for this omission are understandable, and to a considerable extent excusable; they stem in part from certain assumptions that were based on legal norms and on empirical investigation of what seemed to be taking place. It seemed clear for many years that the centre, led by Stalin, was firmly in control of events, so in order to understand the dynamics of the political system we should be best served by concentrating on the Kremlin; it seemed superfluous to study the politics of the Soviet village and provincial town. Moreover, the 'Kremlinological' and 'totalitarian' approaches, particularly fashionable in the fifties and sixties, have at least produced plausible accounts, elements of which have been supported by the testimony of Soviet politicians and others: Khrushchev, in his 'Secret Speech' and purported memoirs,[7] Stalin's daughter, Svetlana Alliluyeva, and the Yugoslav statesman Milovan Djilas.[8]

A further cogent reason for ignoring Soviet local government, and one that is academically more respectable, has been the almost complete lack of access to information on anything in political life below the Kremlin or the republican level of administration. Until very recently, western scholars were not allowed to investigate public organisations in the localities; Soviet researchers were likewise restricted, and their studies tended to be couched in either purely legalistic or propagandistic terms. The social sciences have begun to develop in the USSR only within the past few years,[9] so basic factual information of value to the political scientist is still not available. Furthermore, an export embargo on most local newspapers (which still applies) has deprived students outside the USSR of what might be the richest published source of information on local political life. Without a radical change of attitude on the part of the Soviet authorities, to remedy this situation would require possibly ingenious and necessarily painstaking research, for results that might well prove meagre. As Robert Conquest wrote in justification of his Kremlinological approach,

> My book, and most of the others in the field, seldom descend, and never fully or effectively, below the Presidium, or at most the Central Committee. The provincial secretary level and lower, and even the detailed backgrounds of all the Central Committee membership, are simply impossible without far greater and more widespread time, effort and facilities.[10]

Since then the situation has improved somewhat, in terms of both access to local sources inside the Soviet Union (for both Soviet and foreign researchers), and the ingenuity of research workers in applying new analytical techniques to the Soviet context. In consequence, studies produced since Conquest wrote those words a decade ago have gone some way towards remedying the situation. For example, a set of notes on the backgrounds of all central committee members from 1912 to 1969 – in many cases in considerable detail – is available.[11] The provincial first secretaries have been the object of a number of sociological studies in the past few years.[12] Philip D. Stewart has examined the functioning of the Stalingrad *obkom* (provincial party committee) during the 1950s, while T. H. Rigby's investigation of the membership of the communist party over a fifty-year period is a thorough examination of certain sociological aspects of Soviet politics.[13] The role of the party in directing the economy has been the subject of recent empirical investigation, and attempts have been made to apply functional analysis to the Soviet system.[14] These recent studies of various aspects of the communist party add to the valuable earlier work of Soviet specialists such as Merle Fainsod, whose classic study of the Smolensk province made use of captured archives from the pre-war period, and John Armstrong, who during the 1950s prepared a study of the Ukrainian party apparatus, which has served students as a model for studying Soviet politics through the personnel involved.[15]

There has also been a revival of interest in local soviets in recent years, led by the work of L. G. Churchward.[16] Everett M. Jacobs has performed valuable work in assessing trends in the social composition of local soviets, and has supplemented Jerome M. Gilison's work on local elections.[17] Local elections have also been described and assessed by Max E. Mote and Howard R. Swearer;[18] David T. Cattell prepared an account of the work of the Leningrad city soviet and its executive committee,[19] while a pioneering investigation of the relationship between party and state was made in the early 1950s by T. H. Rigby.[20] More recently, work on Soviet cities and their government has been done by B. Michael Frolic and William Taubman.[21]

These are perhaps among the more valuable studies of local politics in the Soviet Union, and particularly their sociological aspects. However, it is remarkable that there has been no detailed study of political life in the post-war period at the level of the small city.[22] The two major case studies of local politics are of Stalingrad and Leningrad, both of which are of special importance militarily, economically and politically. In 1959 Leningrad had a population of well over three millions, while Stalingrad (now Volgograd) had over half a million; Stalingrad *oblast*, properly speaking the base of Stewart's study, had well over a million inhabitants.[23] Yet the majority of Soviet citizens live in smaller towns, urban settlements and villages, some of them very small. In 1970, 105,728,620 (43.7 per cent of the population) lived in the countryside, and 98,704,917 (40.8 per cent) lived in urban settlements, towns and cities of less than half a million inhabitants. Furthermore, of all the towns, cities and other urban settlements in the country, by far the greater part consist of less than 100,000 inhabitants: 5284 out of 5505 (96.0 per cent) in 1970.[24] The 'typical' Soviet town thus falls into this category; it has been studied in conjunction with larger cities in the work of Frolic and Taubman, but no single study has concentrated on political life at this level.

Yet it is here that the average citizen comes into direct contact with politics. For him Moscow is remote, physically and politically, and he has little influence over the men in the Kremlin; in his everyday life, at work, at leisure, with his family and friends, he is in constant contact with local manifestations of the political system. He may be a member of the communist party, and in any case some of his workmates are; his children belong to the party-sponsored youth organisations; his local newspaper and the radio and television stations abound with references to local political leaders; he may be selected to serve on the town soviet, a body that is responsible for running all aspects of his town, from cinemas and schools to hospitals, roads and trolley-buses. Involvement in either the party or the soviet may be an entry-point into a political career, so for this reason too it is vital for our understanding of leadership recruitment patterns that the more humble levels of administration are not ignored.

What this study attempts to do, therefore, is to examine some aspects of politics at the local level, by taking one of the hundreds of towns with a population under 100,000, and subjecting both its state and party organs to detailed examination. The town selected is Tiraspol, in the Moldavian republic, which was chosen for reasons of both typicality and convenience.[25] The emphasis in the investigation is on sociological and behavioural aspects of the town, rather than on policies, and is further limited to the study of the people who participate in politics, through the state and party apparatus.

The reasons for these limitations are largely concerned with the availability of evidence. In the first place, foreigners are not allowed to undertake attitude surveys in the USSR, among either politicians or the population at large as a means, for example, of identifying the power-holders and evaluating their role; moreover, even if this were possible, the validity of the results could not be guaranteed, as Alex Inkeles has pointed out,[26] in a country that has grown understandably suspicious of questions about political attitudes. Even interviews with local officials in Tiraspol itself proved to be of only marginal value from an academic point of view: those interviewed clearly wished me to come away with the standard, legally based official viewpoint, and all state officials showed a manifest reluctance to discuss relations with the party committee. In general, it proved impossible to penetrate the propaganda facade of the security-minded bureaucrats,[27] so contacts with local political leaders were of little real worth in this study.

Secondly, it seemed impossible to perform a worthwhile study by focusing on policy decision-making without access to local archives and other records, of both state and party organs, and if possible other organisations in the town. Unfortunately such archival material was not made available for inspection, and certain questions could not be approached. The genesis of issues, the channels through which suggestions are passed before being adopted as policy, and the identity of the individuals and institutions active in converting a demand into a policy recommendation; or the provenance of decrees issued by higher bodies, and the discussions that surround their implementation – questions such as these cannot be investigated without either greater access to the records of the institutions involved, or a far more reliable means of eliciting information from local politicians themselves. For instance, I was told that the decision to establish a trolley-bus network in Tiraspol emanated from a session of the town soviet: yet it was not possible to check on who first raised the issue and in what circumstances, how it was initially received, who participated in the discussion, what the various arguments were, and through what channels the matter passed before final authorisation was made and funds for the project included in the town's budget. Details such as these – which may perhaps be regarded as the very stuff of politics – are simply not available to researchers, and one is obliged to use different approaches and perhaps concentrate on slightly different aspects of political life in an individual case.[28]

Eventually, therefore, this study had to be confined to published materials, and the information that they contain on the membership and functioning of the local political bodies. Information, both on individuals and on the composition of various political bodies over the period of the study (1950–1967) was gathered from the local newspaper.[29] From the same source, a limited range of information was gathered on meetings of those bodies, with details of the topics discussed and who participated in the discussions. In this way, trends over time could be identified in the composition of these organs, and the careers of particular individuals could be traced. Further information on subsequent career patterns of prominent politicians was taken from the republican newspaper *Sovetskaya Moldaviya*, published in Kishinev. Using the same information, the degree of overlap over time and across from one body to the other could be quantified and analysed. Similarly, by comparing with information on similar bodies outside Tiraspol (particularly the republican authorities and those at the all-Union level), it was possible to elucidate to some extent the relationship between this level and higher levels: the opportunities that representatives of the town had for presenting local interests centrally, which in turn is an indicator of how effective the political institutions are in carrying out representative functions. Secondary Soviet sources were used to fill in details on organisational aspects of the work of these institutions.

Certain other aspects of local politics are also investigated in this study; for example, the nature of the town's political elite. This concept has been variously and ambiguously used in analysing Soviet politics, indeed in political science generally.[30] Frequently the concept is defined in terms of power and influence: elites are seen as minorities who possess power and wield influence in political affairs.[31] However, as Frederic Fleron has pointed out, it is at present impossible to identify precisely which individuals exercise either power or influence in Soviet politics, since we have no access to records that would indicate which individuals are in fact influential or actually wield power in given situations. To associate power and influence with the tenure of specific offices is largely an assumption whose validity cannot be demonstrated. Fleron therefore suggests that the membership of the elite be defined in 'positional' terms, as 'those occupying leading positions in the formal party and/or government structures'.[32] A problem with this approach, however, is in further defining 'leading positions'. Elsewhere Fleron has suggested a distinction between the 'political elite', defined as all persons holding political office, and the 'party elite', defined as persons holding party or Komsomol (Young Communist League) office, hence forming part of the 'political elite'.[33] But again, what, in the context of Soviet local politics, constitutes a political office?

My usage, while accepting the validity of Fleron's remarks on the advisability of defining the concept in positional terms, combines the essence of his approach with Suzanne Keller's view of elites as 'minorities which are set apart from the rest of society';[34] it refers to all those who have been selected to play an active role in the town's political life through participation in one or both of the major political institutions: the *soviet* (council) and the communist party committee (*gorkom*), which are both legally endowed with decision-making powers within their respective spheres. In later chapters I shall discuss precisely what factors set these political participants apart from the rest of society, and I shall draw distinctions between various sectors of the elite, a concept that, like Rigby, I find it most satisfactory to employ relatively.[35]

Various aspects of the elite thus understood will be investigated: how its members are recruited, its composition, how it changes over time, how it is affected by changes in the political situation. Connected with these questions is the whole problem of relations between the centre and the localities. The period covered in this study spans three leadership regimes: Stalin, Khrushchev, and the Kosygin–Brezhnev collective leadership, with specific phases within the period, and a number of political crises at national level. One aim of this study, in looking at local bodies, is to discover whether these major crises were reflected at the local level, and if so in what way. Did local politics follow the changes at the centre; or did they presage imminent changes at the top? More generally, how far did political customs and habits at this level of administration reflect practices occurring at higher levels? How far did the small city depend on higher levels for policy initiatives, as revealed by the topics that were discussed at meetings? The answers to questions such as these will in some measure help to shed light on the nature of the Soviet political system and how it operates, particularly as it is viewed by Soviet citizens. In short, what this study sets out to do is to investigate certain sociological aspects of a medium-sized town's political institutions, to find whether this confirms the traditional view of Soviet politics derived from different approaches or causes the interpretation to be modified.

In the next chapter there is a brief description of the town of Tiraspol and its institutional framework. Subsequent chapters will attempt to identify the elite of citizens selected to serve in those institutions, and how they performed politically: chapter 3 examines trends in the composition of the membership, and makes comparisons with other studies of Soviet local politics; the following chapter investigates the process of elite recruitment in these bodies, and attempts to identify factors that may lead to an individual's induction into more permanent membership of the elite. In chapter 5, attention focuses on the activity of these politicians in the meetings of their respective institutions, and in chapter 6 relations between the party and the state are examined in greater detail, together with a number of concepts that are seen to have governed the relationship in the past. Chapter 7 extends the discussion to relations with other bodies, and includes an analysis of career patterns among some political leaders in the town; this is continued in chapter 8, where examples of local elite members are presented. The final chapter returns to the traditional view of Soviet politics, and asks whether any modification to it is necessary in the light of the sociological dimension provided in the body of my study.

# CHAPTER 2

# The Setting

In this chapter I set the scene by giving a brief description of the town of Tiraspol and showing how typical it is of Soviet urban communities; the local press – the main source of information for this study – is discussed briefly; and the various institutions that form the town's political structure are described.

## TIRASPOL: A HISTORICAL SKETCH

The Moldavian Soviet Socialist Republic lies in the extreme south-west of the USSR, with Romania to the west and the Ukraine to the north, east and south. The present republic covers most of the territory formerly known as Bessarabia, between the rivers Dnestr and Prut, with the exception of a strip in the south which separates it from the Danube and the Black Sea. Part of the republic lies to the east of the Dnestr however – the *levoberezh'e* (left bank territory) – and it is here that the city of Tiraspol is situated (see Fig. 2.1).

Now the third city in the republic after the capital (Kishinev) and Beltsy, in the north-west, Tiraspol is the largest and most important centre in this part of Moldavia. It takes its name from the river, which was called Tiras by the ancient Greeks and later renamed Danastris by the Romans. Founded by Catherine II in 1792 as a fortress against the Turks, the present settlement quickly attracted immigrants from the surrounding area, and by the beginning of the nineteenth century was the *uyezd* (district) town of the Kherson province, an established administrative centre in that part of the Empire.

By the Treaty of Bucharest (1812), Bessarabia was incorporated into the Russian Empire, and Tiraspol ceased to be a border town. Its growth continued, however, and the town became an important market and commercial centre for the surrounding agricultural area; this also stimulated the establishment of industries for processing primary agricultural produce and servicing the general requirements of the

9

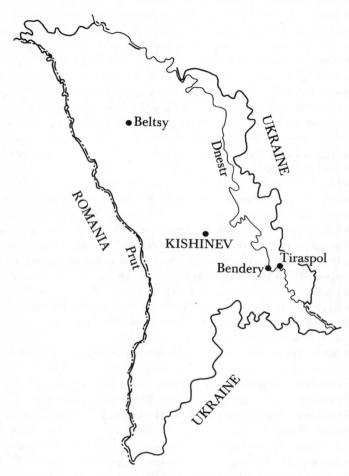

*Figure 2.1  Map of the Moldavian Soviet Socialist Republic*

district. With the extension of the Kiev–Razdel'naya–Odessa railway
to the town in 1867, and the continuation of the line to Kishinev six
years later, industry and trade in Tiraspol flourished, stimulated in
particular by the developing grain exports from Bessarabia through the
port of Odessa. Indeed, it has been stated that the flour merchant and
miller was the town's central figure in the nineteenth century.[1]

Meanwhile, it continued to grow in size: the population of 10,000 in
the middle of the last century had reached almost 29,000 by 1900.[2]
Cultural, medical and service facilities expanded to cater for this
growing citizenry, and for serving the rural population in the
surrounding Tiraspol uyezd. As the most important town in the south-
west of the empire, to which even Odessa was subordinated,[3] Tiraspol
was also an administrative centre of some significance, and this role was
to be enhanced in the Soviet period. The Moldavian Autonomous
Soviet Socialist Republic (MASSR) was formed in 1924, with its capital at
Balta, to the north-east of Tiraspol; however, for geographic and
economic reasons the capital was transferred to Tiraspol on 28 June
1929.[4]

By this time, the town's modern industrial development was under
way: in 1925 alone three factories were established, and now further
development was to be concentrated there, based on the agricultural
produce of the *sovkhozy* (state farms) nearby. With the construction of
the 'Tkachenko' conserving works and the giant '1st May' fruit
conserving factory during the first Five Year Plan (1928–32), fruit and
vegetable bottling and processing became the basic industry; the wine
and cognac works, brought into production in 1940, continued the same
trend; the 'Kirov' machine works produced pumps and other
equipment for irrigation. As capital of the MASSR, the town also
developed further as an administrative and cultural centre for the
Soviet regime. A radio station broadcast from 1930, newspapers were
published in the Moldavian and Ukrainian languages, a national
drama troupe was formed and an educational institute founded.

However, the location of the capital of the republic in Tiraspol was
never intended as a permanent measure. Throughout the inter-war
period Soviet policy was aimed at regaining Bessarabia, annexed by
Romania in January 1918. On 28 June 1940, Bessarabia and Northern
Bukovina were 'liberated' and 'rejoined with the socialist fatherland'. A
Moldavian Soviet Socialist Republic (MSSR) was formed on 2 August
1941, Kishinev was appointed capital, and on 26 August Tiraspol was
given the status of a town subordinated to the republican authorities.[5]

The post-war period witnessed reconstruction, elimination of war damage and the creation of new industrial enterprises, much of this work being done by shock workers along 'Stakhanovite' lines. The fifth Five Year Plan (1951–55) allowed for the re-equipping of the main factories in the town: the '1st May' and 'Tkachenko' conserving works, the wine and cognac works and the brickworks, the 'Kirov' machine works and the two clothing factories. A new fruit-bottling factory was established in 1955; further clothing factories followed, and in 1957 three of these were combined into the 'Fortieth anniversary of the Komsomol' clothing factory, today one of the most impressive factories in the town, whose director, Valentina S. Solov'ëva, has played a central role in the political life of the town and republic, as we shall hear. In the mid-1950s more small factories were combined, and in 1958 the number of industrial enterprises in the town stood at thirty-two; by the end of the decade, 49.7 per cent of the town's workers were employed in industry.[6] In the 1960s industrial expansion continued, and enjoyed considerable success, both in general terms and among individual enterprises, a number of which were given republican and national awards for their achievements.

Tiraspol is thus a flourishing industrial town; it is heavily dependent on agricultural processing, although diversification into clothing manufacture and machine and electrical equipment building has been marked in recent years, partly because of the shortage of local mineral resources, which prevents the development of large-scale heavy industry. The population in 1939 stood at 37,600 and this had risen to 62,700 by 1959 and 105,700 by 1970.[7] The 1959 figure broke down into 69.8 per cent workers, 26.8 per cent employees (*sluzhashchie*: white collar), and 3.4 per cent collective farmers.[8]

To cater for the needs of the population and support the industrial development, there are of course educational and other facilities. The town boasted nineteen schools in 1960 and twenty-eight in 1965, with over 19,000 pupils by the latter date;[9] there is also a pedagogical (educational) institute of considerable renown in the republic, now catering for over 7000 students, in a hostel of which I spent a somewhat uncomfortable month on a field-trip in February 1968. The *sovkhoz-tekhnikum* (agricultural college) named after the military leader Frunze lies on the outskirts of the town, and serves as a training place for agricultural specialists from all parts of the republic. Established in July 1959, this was the first such educational establishment in the whole of the USSR,[10] combining regular production by workers, and practical work in the fields carried on by the students. When I visited this farm in the autumn of 1967 a new complex of lecture halls and student hostels was being built.

In layout and appearance the town is typically Soviet. The centre is built around the '25 October' street, the 'architectural, transport and trading axis of the town',[11] which runs from the Square of the October Revolution, with its obligatory statue of Lenin, up to the town theatre, a not unattractive modern building, painted cream and decorated with a suitably proletarian frieze. The main building on this street is the House of Soviets (*Dom Sovetov*), a huge, impressive Stalinist building, with massive columns flanking the doorway and lots of tiny windows, the whole surmounted by a puny spire with a star at its summit. Throughout the period covered by this study, both the town and rural district were administered from this building: both soviets had their executive offices there, and their various departments. The town and rural district committees of the communist party and the Komsomol were also located in the same building, as were the editorial offices of the local newspaper, *Dnestrovskaya pravda*. This building was the administrative power-house for the town and its surrounding rural district (until the abolition of the latter in June 1971), and in its gloomy corridors there were regular queues of citizens, petitioning local officials on one matter or another.

The majority of the town's inhabitants live away from the town centre, on residential estates consisting of standardised blocks of flats of typical design, while the centre contains small houses of more traditional build, in a few streets grouped round the town's last functioning church. The new estates are not distinctive, and remind one of most other Soviet cities. Facilities for shopping, entertainment, dining out and so forth were in 1968 equally unimpressive: adequate rather than generous. There was one large departmental store in the main street, with intermittent supplies of consumer goods and durables, and other stores on the estates; specialist shops provided food, medical supplies and other daily requisites, and several manufacturing enterprises had their own retail outlets. A peasant market operated on Sundays near to the town centre. For entertainment, apart from the theatre, the town could boast four cinemas, a museum, many libraries and a number of workmen's clubs. There was also an art gallery which arranged to receive circulating exhibitions, and for summer recreation the proximity of the river Dnestr provided a special attraction. The town's own facilities could also be supplemented by visits to either

Kishinev or Odessa, both easily accessible by train or bus. Moreover, a further characteristic feature of the town was the abundance of tall television aerials for receiving both Moldavian and Ukrainian broadcasts.

As a cultural, administrative, service and industrial centre, Tiraspol has an important place in that part of the USSR, serving the local population, the nearby rural areas, and indeed the republic and the south-west Ukraine to some extent with jobs, trading facilities, hospitals, education and entertainment. The inhabitants manifest a certain local pride in their achievements, and in their connections with the country's historic revolutionary past and the world of Soviet science: the fact that the military leader of the Civil War period, Georgii Kotovskii, stationed his headquarters at what is now number 34, Kommunist street, during 1919–20;[12] and the fact that number 44, 25 October street was the birthplace, in February 1861, of the distinguished Russian and Soviet chemist, Nikolai Zelinskii, who died in 1953.[13] A further tremendous source of pride since this study was undertaken has been the award in January 1971 to the citizens of the town of the Order of the Red Banner of Labour, 'for successes achieved ... in fulfilment of the targets of the five year plan for the development of industrial production'.[14]

In short, Tiraspol is a fairly typical Soviet town. A product of the Russian Empire, it has slipped comfortably and successfully into twentieth-century Soviet economic and cultural life. An American expert on Soviet urban geography has classified it as an old regional centre, but basically an industrial centre, the most common type of city in the Soviet Union, which expresses 'the urgent and powerful Soviet drive for industrial development'.[15] It is perhaps more typically Soviet than Kishinev and other towns in the republic. Indeed, it is the only large settlement within Moldavia's present-day borders that has always been within either the Empire or the Soviet Union, and in this sense its development has followed more closely the pattern in other parts of the USSR than have those towns to the west of the Dnestr.

It is interesting to speculate how closely Tiraspol identifies with the right-bank part of Moldavia (Bessarabia proper), and indeed vice-versa. The re-incorporation of Bessarabia deprived Tiraspol of the leading position that she had occupied for a decade, and there may be some regrets at this. Also to be noted is the fact that another major industrial town, Bendery, lies to the other side of the river, immediately opposite Tiraspol, and with the further development of industry and residential districts in both towns, agglomeration will eventually link the two in a large industrial complex.[16] Attitudes could well be affected by this development, but the present study does not seek to illuminate the question, to which a reliable answer will perhaps not be forthcoming.

## THE LOCAL PRESS

The main source of information used in this study was the local newspaper, whose history is somewhat confusing. Over the years, its title changed a number of times, and so did its formal status: for some of the period it was the organ of the town party committee and town soviet executive committee alone; at other times it was also the official mouthpiece of the rural district authorities. Furthermore, it was also published in two editions: Russian and Moldavian, the one being a simple translation of the other.

During the larger part of the period the newspaper was called, in Russian, *Dnestrovskaya pravda* (Truth of the Dnestr), or in Moldavian *Adeverul Nistryan*. Founded in 1941, the Russian edition had in 1950 a circulation of 3000 copies, was published on Sundays, Wednesdays and Fridays, and sold for twenty kopeks. In July 1952, this newspaper was replaced by *Stalinskii put'* (The Stalin Way), which continued publication until the denunciation of Stalin in February 1956, after which (in July) it reverted to its former title, which it retained until 1963. By January of that year, it was publishing 5700 copies, which had increased to 5900 when it ceased publication in March.

It was replaced by *Leninskoe znamya/Drapelul Leninist* (The Lenin Banner), which had been the organ of the Moldavian central committee and council of ministers, and circulated in the Tiraspol and Bendery rural districts; its circulation increased from under 4000 to over 11,000, rising to 15,000 in January 1964, 15,200 in June, and down to 14,415 in December. This situation lasted until April 1965, when the title reverted once again to its original *Dnestrovskaya pravda/Adeverul Nistryan*, organ of Tiraspol town and rural district party and state authorities. It appeared four times a week: on Tuesdays, Wednesdays, Fridays and Saturdays; this remained unchanged until the end of our period. Circulation of the Russian edition rose: it stood at 16,944 copies on 6 July 1966 and about 20,300 during 1967, increasing to 24,000 by early 1968; the Moldavian edition published a relatively insignificant

866 copies on 8 July 1966 – perhaps incidentally a sign of Russification
in that part of the Soviet Union. The newspaper was produced from
offices on the second floor of the House of Soviets, and contained TASS
news agency reports of national and international affairs, in addition to
news and feature items of local interest. Most interesting from the point
of view of this study was the coverage of local political matters: detailed
lists of election candidates were usually carried in advance of the
election date, and subsequently a list of the individuals who had been
successful at the polls; normally the press also carried lists of newly
elected members of the town party committee. Regularly throughout
the year, readers were informed of the business that transpired at
meetings of these two bodies, and often details of the speakers were
given. For the interested reader in Tiraspol and its district, the local
press afforded the possibility of being informed on at least certain
aspects of local political life; this was also its main value for the purposes
of this study.

### THE POLITICAL STRUCTURE

The two major political institutions in the town are the town council, or
Soviet of Working People's Deputies, with its executive committee and
various departments, and the town communist party organisation,
headed by the gorkom, or town committee. This study will concentrate
on these two institutions. Other important political institutions are the
Komsomol, the organs of popular control, and the trade union
organisation; these too will be examined briefly in the course of this
book.

### The town soviet

The soviet is regarded in Soviet legal documents, beginning with the
USSR Constitution (chapter eight), as the organ of state power in the
town. Its formation and functioning are provided for in the republican
constitution and in various statutes, its legal responsibilities being

> ...directing cultural-political and economic construction in the
> territory of the town, fixing the town budget, directing the activity of
> the organs of administration subordinated to them, providing for the
> observance of the law, the maintenance of state order and the rights
> of citizens, co-operating in strengthening the defence capacity of the

country, implementing the leninist policy of the Communist Party of the Soviet Union, and providing for the fulfilment of tasks arising out of decisions of the party and the Soviet government.[17]

It is an elected body of up to 250 representatives or deputies, chosen by ballot according to electoral laws. The electoral process has been the subject of much study by western scholars,[18] and it is not necessary to examine it here. Suffice it to say that the Soviet electors have little real say in choosing their representatives, since the system is supervised and controlled by the political authorities, principally the communist party. More relevant to my purpose is the composition of the soviet when elected, and this question will be examined in chapter 3.

At its first session after the elections, the newly elected soviet deals (often exclusively) with 'organisational questions', a term that refers to the election of the executive committee (*gorispolkom*), the appointment of the heads of the administrative departments, and the assignment of individual deputies to membership of various permanent commissions (see Fig. 2.2). Of these duties, the election of the executive committee is the most delicate, although it seems clear that its membership is largely determined beforehand by the party authorities, exercising their important function of selecting and distributing leading personnel.[19] It is the responsibility of the gorispolkom to run the affairs of the town in the intervals between sessions of the full soviet – a far-reaching duty, which emphasises the importance of careful selection in the committee's membership. The executive is technically subordinated to the full soviet; however, for reasons that will become clear later, the ispolkom is in a position to control the soviet's work, and this too enhances its importance.

In carrying out its wide-ranging functions, the executive committee uses the services of various departments (*otdely*), composed of full-time paid state officials, on the model of a western civil service. These officials perform duties connected with the everyday running of the town's affairs: managing housing lists, appointing school teachers and hospital staff, supervising trade, coordinating industry. The number and scope of these departments is not fixed by law, and varies according to the size of the town, its economic structure and similar factors.[20] However, the most important is the planning commission (*gorplan*), whose rights and functions are legally defined in a separate statute.[21] It coordinates the planning of the other departments and of various industrial and other enterprises, and is generally responsible for

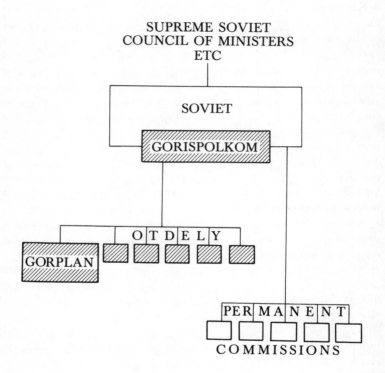

Figure 2.2    Structure of town soviet

devising means of economic development in the town, supervising the allocation and usage of economic resources, and providing statistical and other information for the republican planning authorities.

Key figures in the administration of the soviet's work are the chairman and deputy chairmen of the gorispolkom. The chairmanship will be discussed in detail in chapter 8. It is a post that is often regarded as equivalent to that of mayor of a western city, although in the Soviet context, as Hough has argued, at least some of the functions of a mayor are the responsibility of the chief party official at a given level of administration.[22] There is moreover close personal and institutional connection between the tenancy of this position and involvement in the work of the party, as we shall see. Much of the direct administrative burden is borne by the deputy chairmen, who normally have distinct fields of administration allocated to them (in Tiraspol, of the two deputy chairmen one was usually identified as being responsible for industry), while the chairman is principally concerned with relations with higher authorities.[23]

Although for most of the time the executive committee and its departments carry out the administrative functions of local government, the deputies of the soviet as a whole do have some means of checking on their work. The most effective of these is perhaps that performed by the permanent commissions, the final element in the formal structure. These too are set up at the first session of the newly elected soviet, and consist of deputies, normally under the chairmanship of an expert in the field covered by the commission. The overall function of these commissions is that of a 'watchdog', supervising and checking on the work of the departments and the ispolkom as a whole. These bodies too are established on the basis of statute.[24] They have wide powers of inspection, including the right 'to demand of the relevant leaders explanations and references, and also to acquaint themselves with their orders and other documents necessary for carrying out the check or investigation'.[25] On matters within their area of competence they are required to produce reports, which frequently form an important part of the deliberations of the soviet itself. Thus, the more competently these commissions perform their work, the more effective is likely to be the discussion in the debate of the full soviet. In the recent campaign to improve the work of the soviets, much attention has been focused on these commissions, and a great deal of literature published, to try and raise their efficiency.[26]

Finally, all the deputies meet in regular plenary meetings or 'sessions'. In this capacity the soviet is legally the supreme decision-making body in the town: the deputies may discuss issues and adopt decisions, which then become law within the town's territory, provided they are not rescinded by higher authority.

Such is the broad outline of the structure of a town soviet: I can now add details from Tiraspol during the period covered by this study.

The first feature that is immediately recognisable is the growth in the size of the town soviet from 130 deputies in 1950 to the legal maximum of 250 in 1967 (see Table 2.1). This expansion conforms with the general increase in the town's population, although the scale of individual increases (as in 1955) may be partly due to reorganisations in the republic's administrative structure, or the introduction of

TABLE 2.1    *Growth of Tiraspol town soviet, 1950–1967*

| Date | Number of deputies | Size of executive committee |
|------|------|------|
| 1950 | 130 | 13 |
| 1953 | 138 | Not available |
| 1955 | 165 | 9 |
| 1957 | 183 | 9 |
| 1959 | 188 | 11 |
| 1961 | 202 | 9 |
| 1963 | 223 | 9 |
| 1965 | 249 | 9 |
| 1967 | 250 | 9 |

new legislation. During the period under study, nine sets of elections were held. Apart from a slight delay between December 1952 and February 1953, elections to the soviet were held every two years as prescribed, and in this Tiraspol simply followed all-Union patterns, since elections to all local soviets are now normally held on the same day throughout the USSR.[27] The size of the gorispolkom also varied over the years, but showed a decline towards the end of the period: seen alongside the growth of the body of deputies, this indicates a steady concentration of administrative power.

The number of administrative departments also changed over the years, partly in response to changes in the town's economy, and partly following legal changes (see Table 2.2). Thus, in 1950 there was an agricultural otdel, which subsequently ceased to exist; in March 1957, the local departments of the ministry of internal affairs were

TABLE 2.2  *Departmental structure of Tiraspol gorispolkom*

| Department | | | | | Year | | | | |
|---|---|---|---|---|---|---|---|---|---|
| | 1950 | 1953 | 1955 | 1957 | 1959 | 1961 | 1963 | 1965 | 1967 |
| Finance | *** | | *** | ** | *** | *** | *** | *** | *** |
| Communal economy | *** | | ** | ** | ** | * | * | * | ** |
| Trade | ** | | ** | ** | | ** | | * | * |
| Education | * | | ** | ** | ** | ** | ** | ** | ** |
| Health | *** | **(*) | ** | ** | ** | ** | | ** | ** |
| Social security | ** | | ** | ** | ** | ** | ** | ** | ** |
| General | ** | | * | * | ** | ** | * | * | * |
| Agriculture | * | | | | | | | | |
| Culture-education | ** | | | | ** | ** | ** | ** | ** |
| Planning commission | *** | | *** | *** | *** | *** | *** | *** | *** |
| Personnel sector | | ** | * | * | | | | | |
| Militia | | | *** | *** | *** | ** | ** | ** | ** |
| Local industry | | | | | ** | ** | | | |
| Capital construction | | | | | | * | * | * | * |
| Architecture | | | | | | | * | ** | * |
| Organisational–instructor | | | | | | | | * | ** |
| 'Living' | | | | | | | | | ** |
| TOTAL NUMBER | 10 | | 9 | 10 | 10 | 12 | 10 | 13 | 14 |
| Control committee | | | | | | | | | ** |
| Administrative commission | | | | | | | | | *** |
| Minors' commission | | | | | | | | | *** |
| Observation commission | | | | | | | | | *** |

*Key:* * = such a department existed
** = its head was a deputy of the soviet
*** = its head was a gorispolkom member

transformed into militia otdely of the local soviet executive committees;[28] the formation of a 'department of living'[29] reflects the greater attention that has been paid to the 'quality of life' in recent years. The number of otdely, it will be seen, has shown a tendency to increase, in conformity with the growing needs of society and the economy.

Table 2.2 also shows the degree of overlap between headship of these departments, membership of the soviet, and membership of the executive committee. Thus, in all years the heads of finance, social security, health and the planning commission were deputies; in all years the head of the planning commission was a member of the gorispolkom, as was, in all years but one, the head of the finance department. To some extent, these relationships may indicate the relative importance of various areas of administration.

Information on the permanent commissions is unfortunately incomplete, but what is available is shown in Table 2.3, and it is

TABLE 2.3    *Permanent commissions in Tiraspol town soviet, 1950–1959*

| Commission | Year | | | |
|---|---|---|---|---|
| | 1950 | 1955 | 1957 | 1959 |
| Budgeting-finance | * | * | * | * |
| Economy and construction | * | * | * | * |
| Industry | * | * | * | * |
| Education | * | * | * | * |
| Culture | * | * | * | * |
| Health | * | * | * | * |
| Trade | * | * | * | * |
| Beautification | | * | * | * |
| Housing | | | * | * |
| Inspection | | | * | |
| Transport and communication | | | | * |

sufficient to indicate the kind of fields covered. Thus, the work of both the finance otdel and the planning commission was covered by the one budgeting and finance commission; the health commission covered the work of the health and social security departments. There appears to be a measure of overlapping among the commissions, although whether this is a positive or negative feature cannot be determined on the basis of the limited information available. The press did not publish the names of the members of the commissions, and even the chairmen's names ceased to appear after 1959. This may seem anomalous in view of the importance that attaches to these bodies in Soviet accounts of the local government organs; but it may realistically reflect their importance in acting as a check on the administration.

Two further features merit comment: first, the formation towards the end of the period of special commissions of the gorispolkom, distinct from the departments, to oversee particular areas of administration. I have no further information on the work of these commissions, which were apparently not specifically provided for in law; however, the fact that their chairmen were both deputies and members of the executive committee suggests that they were intended to be of some importance. Finally, in addition to the regular permanent commissions the soviet formed a mandates commission, charged with examining the credentials of all deputies upon election, and disqualifying deputies whose elections were not in accordance with the law;[30] this commission operates throughout the soviet's term of office, to deal with any by-elections (say, following the death of a deputy, or recall by the electors following unsatisfactory conduct of his duties); it also compiles statistics on the social composition and other aspects of the membership. Again, membership of this commission was not made public, although the chairman's name was sometimes published at the time he made his initial report on the composition of the new soviet.

*The town party committee (gorkom)*

Although in terms of the constitution and other legislation the soviets are the political basis of the USSR, it can scarcely be doubted that the local organs of the communist party are of infinitely greater political significance, and enjoy powers of influence amounting to control over the work of local government bodies. Expressing a widely held western view, Azrael declares that 'it can be said both of the Soviet political system as a whole and of each of its constituent territorial units that the "legislative branch" of government is almost completely devoid of effective political power', whereas 'the party *apparat* . . . [exercises] an extensive power-political hegemony'.[31] Any attempt to analyse political activity in the Soviet Union, at whatever level, must therefore devote considerable attention to the communist party and its organs. In the remainder of this chapter, I examine the structure of the party organisation at the level of the town, and specifically in Tiraspol.

The basic structure of the CPSU is defined in party rules (*Ustav*), and the fundamental unit is the primary (or basic) party organisation (PPO), which may be set up at any work place where there are three or more party members (Rule 54/53).[32] These bodies are responsible for the actual implementation of party policy, through a kind of division of labour: each member of the organisation is given regular 'party assignments', ranging from simple propaganda work, the delivery of lectures and so forth, to more demanding duties, including membership of public bodies such as the soviets. The highest formal decision-making organ at this level is the monthly meeting; here the ordinary members may discuss a variety of questions concerning the organisation's political work and its work in stimulating the operations of the institution in which it is situated.[33]

Once a year, normally in the autumn, the members meet to hear the committee's report on the work of the organisation, and to elect officers and a committee of eleven to seventeen members (in the case of larger organisations) or a *buro* of three to nine members.[34] This meeting must take place in the presence of a representative of a higher party committee, who does not take part in the voting, but is present 'to ensure strict observation of the demands of the party rules', and he usually also attends the first meeting of the new buro or committee.[35] It seems most probable that his presence is mainly to ensure that an acceptable individual is elected to the important post of secretary: as a recent party handbook puts it, this representative is there 'to ensure proper control over the course of the reports and elections' and he 'may, of course, express the opinion of the party organ which he represents on individual candidates and recommend one or another communist to membership of the party buro or committee. There is nothing in this to contradict the principles and norms of party life.'[36]

The same meeting elects delegates to a town party conference, the highest organ of the town party organisation, which is required to take place biennially (annually under the 1952 rules) or may be convened on the demand of one third of all party members in the town organisation (Rule 49/48). This conference is discussed in detail in chapter 7; for the moment I will note that one of its major functions is to elect the town party committee, or gorkom.

The general functions of gorkomy are defined in the party rules, and include organising and confirming the work of primary party organisations, exercising leadership in their work, receiving regular reports from them, and keeping records on individual party members in the town party organisation (Rule 51/50). Some of these activities are subsumed under the general heading of 'party accounting' (*partiinoe khozyaistvo*), referring to the issue of party membership cards, receiving members' subscriptions, and maintaining records of members, meetings, decisions and other documentation.[37] These activities may be regarded as strictly intra-party; party committees also engage in more public activities, including political work among the population (agitation, propaganda, political education), and the selection of 'leading personnel' for lower positions in the party's own apparatus and in other public bodies, including the soviets. This is regarded as one of the chief ways in which the communist party plays its leading and guiding role in society, and it extends to the selection not only of party members, but also of other persons approved by the party. In this particular aspect of the party committee's work the important principle of *nomenklatura* is in operation, a term that refers to a list of posts in the administrative apparatus, many of which are formally elective but which are by custom staffed by nominees of the party.[38]

A further activity of local party committees – one that also impinges fundamentally on the work of other institutions, and specifically local soviets – is debating issues of national and local interest. It is the duty and obligation of all the committee members and all members of the party organisation to obey decisions on these issues. This means that topics may be discussed by the gorkom, whose members are then bound to strive for the implementation of any decision by other bodies of which they may be members, including the soviet: this question will be more fully explored in chapter 6.

The general position of party organs in Soviet society is thus clear: the local committee plays a central part in the party's guiding and controlling activity, strategically positioned between higher committees, where wider, more fundamental decisions are reached, and primary organisations, where these policy decisions are translated into action and reality. As Avtorkhanov has put it,

> District committees and town committees are considered the most important detachments in the party apparatus because they have direct control over the primary party organisations, which, in turn, put into effect the highest party directives.[39]

Moreover, in the party hierarchy, they can serve as an important stage in the career structure of politicians.

Structurally, the gorkom consists of two categories of member: members proper, and so-called candidate members, both groups comprising only full members of the party (candidate, or probationary, party members are not eligible for election to such committees). The major difference between these two categories appears to be that only the full members have a vote, the candidate members being allowed only a 'consultative voice'.[40]

In common with the soviet, the gorkom elects an executive committee, known here as the *buro* (for a diagram of the structure see Fig. 2.3). This consists of secretaries (one of whom is usually designated first secretary) and members; formerly, candidate buro members were also elected, but all buro members and candidates were chosen from among the full members of the gorkom. The gorkom also, like the soviet, carries out its work through a number of departments, here too called otdely, although they are generally fewer in number than those of the gorispolkom, and their range varies from one town to another. Politically, the most important is the otdel named variously 'department of party, trade union and Komsomol organs', 'organisational department', and 'department of organisational–party work' (see Table 2.5, p. 31). Its major function is to supervise the staffing of various branches of the administrative and political apparatus, largely through the nomenklatura system, but it also performs the vital functions of supervising the work of PPOs, training party workers, and coordinating the work of the gorkom with that of other institutions, from the soviet and its executive committee to the Komsomol committee, trade union council, and control organs.[41]

The political role of this department, and that of the propaganda and agitation (agitprop) department, is clear; indeed, all party committee otdely appear to have a considerable political, rather than administrative, role: organisation, education, exhortation and inspection. It seems likely, therefore, that the heads of the departments are selected with care, most probably in consultation with the next higher party committee, which in the case of Tiraspol is the Moldavian central committee and its departments. Other councils, committees and commissions may also be set up, some staffed by party workers, others by leading party members, drawn from among the gorkom membership on a more or less voluntary basis. This is one aspect of the system of assignments mentioned earlier; they have special responsibility for stimulating a response to party policy in a specific area of administration (1961 Rule 52): a sub-committee to organise the May Day parade might be an example, or one to make arrangements for the Lenin *subbotniks*, Saturdays when all workers are strongly encouraged to do a day's work without pay for the good of the country.

There is one further arm to the party's structure at every level: the auditing commission (*revizionnaya komissiya*), which is elected by the

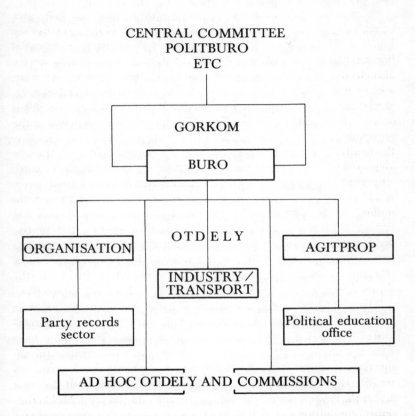

*Source:* Adapted from *Kommunisticheskaya Partiya Sovetskogo Soyuza – naglyadnoe posobie po partiinomu stroitel'stvu* (compiler: V. I. Strukov) Moscow, 1973, p. 62.

*Figure 2.3 Structure of gorkom*

area party conference at the same time as the committee. In political terms, this body is of lesser importance than the committee, and it is responsible (by analogy with the central auditing commission at the all-Union level of administration) for watching over the speedy and correct execution of the party committee's business by primary organisations, and examining the party's accounts, with particular reference to the regular payment of membership subscriptions.[42]

Finally, I must mention the so-called party *aktiv*, a rather nebulous body consisting of 'leading' party workers in the town organisation. Its formal membership is not defined, but varies according to the question under review; invitations are issued by the gorkom,[43] for debating 'the most important decisions of the party' and working out measures for achieving them, and also for reviewing questions of local life (Rule 27/29). The importance of this gathering is said to be that it gives the party committee a chance to find out opinion in the party's ranks, with a view to developing the principle of 'criticism and self-criticism';[44] whether there is a need for such a body, in view of the way in which party committee plenary sessions have been run, at least in the 1960s, is open to question,[45] but the fact is that such meetings are regularly held in town and other party organisations.[46]

In the whole of the USSR there were, in 1968, 747 town party organisations; in 223 of them there were also rural organisations, and in 417 of the larger cities there were urban district party committees (called, as are the rural district committees, *raikomy*).[47] Tiraspol town party organisation was a simple one, with neither rural nor district infrastructure.

In common with developments elsewhere in the Soviet Union, the size of the organisation has grown considerably over the past two decades. Figures for party membership as such are hard to come by, but it was revealed in 1966 that there were about 6000 party members in the town, compared with 1429 in 1953.[48] The 1966 figure represents about 6.7 per cent of the town's population (about 90,000 at that time), or 6.3 per cent of the total membership of the Moldavian communist party, given as 94,574 in 1966.[49] They belonged to over 140 primary party organisations, which compares with a mere twenty in 1945 and eighty in 1953.[50] These 140 organisations varied considerably in size: they included two of over 300 members, while over a quarter of them had fewer than fifty members – 363 communists were in such small organisations. It is interesting that, in giving these figures for 1966 in an article on *small* party organisations, Ya. Fomenko is writing about a mere 5.2 per cent of the town's party members: most were in larger units.

These figures indicate the structure of the party organisation in the town, and its size in relation to the population as a whole: whereas the town soviet has formal responsibilities towards the total population of the town, the party committee is directly responsible for a much smaller number, and can thus be considerably smaller itself. In fact, as the figures in Table 2.4 show, it grew steadily over the period under review:

TABLE 2.4    *Growth of Tiraspol gorkom, 1950–1967*

| Date | Number | Members | Candidates | Size of buro |
|---|---|---|---|---|
| Jan 1950 | XI | 57 | 9 | 10* |
| Feb 1951 | XII | 57 | 9 | 9 |
| Aug 1952 | XIII | No full list published | | 7 |
| Oct 1953 | XIV | 57 | 9 | 9 |
| Jan 1954? | XV | Not available | | |
| Nov 1954 | XVI | 59 | 9 | 9 |
| Oct 1955 | XVII | 61 | 15 | 9 |
| Dec 1956 | XVIII | 66 | 15 | 9 |
| Nov 1957 | XIX | 69 | 17 | 9 |
| Nov 1958 | XX | 73 | 19 | 9 |
| Nov 1959 | XXI | 76 | 19 | 9 |
| Jan 1961 | XXII | 79 | 19 | 9 |
| Sep 1961 | XXIII | 80 | 21 | 9 |
| Dec 1962 | XXIV | 83 | 21 | 7 |
| Dec 1963 | XXV | Not available | | |
| Jan 1965 | XXVI | 87 | 21 | 9 |
| Jan 1966 | XXVII | 89 | 23 | 9 |
| Dec 1967 | XXVIII | 89 | 23 | 11 |

*Includes 2 buro candidate members.

from fifty-seven full members and nine candidates in January 1950 to eighty-nine full and twenty-three candidate members in December 1967. The auditing commission grew from five to twenty-one members in the same period, while the buro stood at nine members for most of the time, occasionally declined to seven, but rose in 1967 to eleven. The departmental structure also altered over the years, perhaps in response to needs perceived at a higher level, but which are not immediately apparent. The information is not complete, but such as was published is summarised in Table 2.5. In no year do there appear to have been more than four otdely, and sometimes only three: agitprop, industry (normally combined with transport), and the politically crucial organisational department. Some of the apparent structural changes may in fact be purely changes of name: the different titles of the 'organisational' department have already been mentioned; similarly, the so-called ideological otdel mentioned in the case of the xxvi gorkom probably refers to the agitprop department: this reference was taken from the Moldavian-language newspaper *Drapelul Leninist* (19 January 1965), in the absence of the Russian *Leninskoe znamya* for that period. Other similar changes can be seen in the table. However, one significant change appears to be the discontinuation of the department for work among women some time after the xviii gorkom's term of office expired, in 1957.[51]

In all cases departmental heads were full members of the gorkom, suggesting that this is normal practice. Nothing has come to light to suggest the size of departmental staffs, nor was anything revealed about the formation of special commissions. Occasionally, however, reference was made to individuals who held posts that had not been explicitly mentioned in reports of appointments to gorkom positions. Thus, at a plenum on 3 February 1955, reported in the newspaper *Stalinskii put'* three days later, one of the speakers was referred to as head of the gorkom department for schools, although no such appointment had been made after the party conference of the previous November; nor was the individual involved, a certain Grekul, either a member or candidate member of the gorkom, and he never became one, or a deputy of the soviet. This instance shows the limits of the press as a source of information on Soviet local politics, as it is impossible to estimate how much information is hidden in this way. The picture that emerges from this study is thus not necessarily the whole truth; but it is at least part of the truth.

## Other political institutions

Apart from the town soviet and its apparatus and the party gorkom and its apparatus, with which this study is mainly concerned, at least three further national structures of considerable political relevance exist, which must therefore be brought into the discussion: the Komsomol, the trade unions, and the control organisation.

The Komsomol, or All-Union Leninist Communist Union of Youth (vlksm), with membership open to young people aged between

TABLE 2.5 *Departmental structure of Tiraspol gorkom: selected years*

| Department | Number of gorkom | | | | | | | | | | | |
|---|---|---|---|---|---|---|---|---|---|---|---|---|
| | XI | XII | XIII | XIV | XVI | XVII | XVIII | XXIII | XXIV | XXVI | XXVII | XXVIII |
| Party, trade union and Komsomol organs | * | * | ? | * | | | | | | | | |
| Propaganda and agitation | * | * | * | * | | * | * | * | * | | * | * |
| Industry and transport | * | * | * | * | * | * | * | | | * | * | * |
| Work among women | * | * | * | * | * | * | * | | | | | |
| Organisational | | | | | * | * | * | * | * | * | | |
| Ideological | | | | | | | | | | * | | |
| Organisational–party work | | | | | | | | | | | * | * |

fourteen and twenty-eight, is very much like a youth version of the communist party, and indeed its rule book and formal structure are virtually identical with those of the CPSU.[52] It too is based on primary organisations, which elect delegates to an area (town) conference, which in turn elects a committee (also called a gorkom[53]), headed by a buro and secretaries. The Komsomol in Tiraspol had 7036 members in 92 primary organisations in 1960; comparable figures for 1965 were 11,703 and 102 respectively.[54] Although formally an independent organisation, the Komsomol operates in close collaboration with the party, which sees itself as 'the organiser and leader of the Komsomol', and the latter as its own 'active helper and reserve'.[55] The links between the two institutions are close, with young party members frequently serving as officers in the junior organisation, and the Komsomol representing an important source of recruitment into the party: indeed, according to the prologue of the Komsomol rule book, the highest honour for a Komsomol member is to transfer to party membership when old enough. A significant political function of this institution is that of giving experience of political administration to future party and state leaders: this question will be discussed further in chapter 7.

Less overtly political than the Komsomol is the trade union movement, whose role is more specialised. Its membership is much wider, embracing practically the whole work force of the USSR,[56] and its responsibilities towards most of these members (totalling 71,229,000 in mid-1964 and 98 millions by the spring of 1972[57]) are concentrated on the field of production, labour relations, conditions of work, pensions, vacations and similar welfare activities. However, the unions do have their political connections: members and officials are elected as deputies to the soviets, and there are firm links with the party. Party leadership has been described as 'the basis of the successful activity of the trade unions', and this leadership is achieved 'above all by the communists who work in the trade unions'.[58]

Like the communist party and the Komsomol, the trade union structure is based on branches in the individual productive enterprises and other institutions, linked at the level of the town through a town committee for each union. The various unions are linked at a higher level through the oblast (provincial) trade union council (*sovet professional'nykh soyuzov*) or (in the case of Moldavia) the republican council of trade unions.[59] The chairmen of the town committees of the individual unions enjoy a modicum of prestige and possibly influence through involvement in the work of directly political institutions, including the soviets and the party. However, despite the political relevance of the higher positions in the trade union movement, and unions' general significance as political organs, my study revealed little direct information on the details of the union organisation in Tiraspol, and this may be a fairly accurate indicator of the *political* importance of the unions at local level; in industrial management their importance, and the influence of their officials, may be somewhat higher.

A further important all-USSR structure is the popular control, which replaced the party–state control in the post-Khrushchev period.[60] Its aims, as defined in the Statute of the Popular Control (confirmed on 19 December 1968), consist in checking that party and state decrees are fulfilled, further perfecting the leadership of communist construction, struggling to raise the economy by every means, and strengthening state discipline and socialist legality (article 1 of the Statute). The structure is similar to that of party, Komsomol and trade union organisations. Headed by an all-Union committee, with local committees at each administrative level (including the town), the structure penetrates other institutions with its basic units, known as 'groups' and 'posts', whose 7–50 members are elected by representatives of trade union, communist party, Komsomol and other bodies.[61] The popular control is technically subordinated to the state structure,[62] whereas its predecessor was fundamentally a party-controlled institution.[63] Its significance appears to be greater in the economic sphere than in the political, and its major effort is directed towards reporting and eradicating irregularities in economic life: for example, in February 1966 it was revealed that controllers in Tiraspol had unearthed eighty-seven cases of illegal price adjustment among metal-goods and television repair workers.[64] Little information is published on the personnel aspects of this institution, although the chairmanship of the town committee carries a degree of responsibility, and the post was reserved for individuals of some prominence.

Finally, there are in the USSR a number of other institutions and societies which, although not overtly political, do have political overtones, in that all organisations in the Soviet Union are to some extent controlled by the party, which has a strong influence in the selection of officers; this is a further extension of the party's role in supervising the selection and distribution of cadres. These organisations include the town's Red Cross society, the sports council and other bodies. Their officers are chosen with care through the system of nomenklatura, and, as with the trade unions, holding such an office occasionally involves the incumbent in more directly political activity.

## CONCLUSION

The above description of the political structure of Tiraspol is typical of similar communities all over the country. It can be seen that the communist party is in a central position, playing a 'leading and guiding' role. This confers great importance on the gorkom, which will be given special attention in this study as I attempt to identify the body of individuals who held a measure of responsibility and power through membership of the committee. It will be examined as a body in its own right, and also in relation to other political bodies in the town, especially the soviet, to explore the nature of its relationship with them. What is the measure of overlapping membership, among both ordinary members and officers? How far does the gorkom control the functioning of the soviet, and in what ways? Is the relationship two-way?

These are some of the questions with which this study is concerned. Before answers become available, however, it is necessary to examine the operations of the main political structures, the town soviet and the town party committee, and a descriptive analysis of their composition and functioning appears in the following chapters.

# CHAPTER 3

# Trends in the Elite

In this chapter, I examine patterns in the membership of the town soviet and the town party committee, with the emphasis on trends in their composition over time. During the period of almost eighteen years, certain tendencies can be identified in the membership of these bodies, which disclose both features of stability and continuity and also points of change, which I argue are responses to changes in policy.

One question with which this chapter is concerned is the level at which policies on the desired social composition of these local bodies are decided, and in this I extend the work of Everett Jacobs, who has identified patterns in the social composition of local soviets. Jacobs established that certain 'norms' for the representation of sociological characteristics are evidently set on an all-Union basis, while 'norms' for representation of other variables are decided at a lower level, probably that of the republic, and reflect the social and economic structure of the area concerned.[1] This interpretation, based on an analysis of official statistics, to some extent supports Azrael's view that 'the soviets are composed so as almost perfectly to replicate the ethnic, sex, and other demographic differences in society'.[2] Elsewhere I have further analysed the implementation of these 'norms' in an attempt to identify their nature.[3] As far as the strength of women's, party and Komsomol representation is concerned, and also the age distribution among deputies, the degree of uniformity observed does suggest that these 'norms' are fairly strictly applied; however, data from Tiraspol, which will be recorded below, also imply that the local authorities have the freedom to take specific conditions into account in their selection policies. The body of individuals that ultimately constitutes the local soviet can thus be seen as the product, on the one hand, of central directives on a 'desired' composition, and on the other, of local perceptions about specific requirements and the available candidates.

The same may also apply to the communist party structure, where the principle of centralism (although referred to as 'democratic centralism') is formally incorporated into the rule book. The degree to

35

which changes in the composition of the gorkom are made in response to major changes in the centre of the political system may be used as an indicator of how far the structure is in fact centralised. In trying to assess this question, however, the western student of Soviet politics has a number of special problems, greater than those encountered in the case of the soviets. First of all, the party committee is structurally complex, consisting of two categories of membership, full and candidate; the executive buro in the past also had a category of 'candidate' members. This complicates the problems of analysing trends in the composition. A more serious difficulty is the lack of published information on gorkom members. Officially the party is regarded as a voluntary, exclusive, private organisation, which is not required to publish information about its internal affairs, including the identity of members of its organs (even though in practice their impact on local life may be more fundamental than that of the soviets). The press publishes at most a list of names, and if this were all the information available, together with lists of some or all office holders, little of value would be forthcoming from this kind of study.

However, it so happens that there has been a considerable degree of overlap between gorkom and soviet membership, so that many of the gorkom members were identified in the lists of newly elected deputies, together with brief biographical details. By transferring information from one context to the other, I have been able to build up a file on a fair proportion of gorkom members; further members could be identified from press reports and articles in which their names appeared. However, it must be stressed that for all years information on gorkom membership is incomplete, and in three cases even membership lists were not published.

Two further points must add to our caution in dealing with this information on gorkom members. First, the dates of party conferences and elections to the soviet did not coincide precisely. Hence, I have had to make the assumption that the information published at the soviet election nearest in time to the party conference is sufficiently accurate for direct transfer to the gorkom. Secondly, when an individual was elected to the soviet, his or her published occupation was not necessarily the qualification that merited his or her election to the gorkom. For instance, part-time trade union committee chairmen, and party or Komsomol organisation secretaries would normally be identified in the election data by their main employment, whereas the part-time occupation – politically the more relevant – would doubtless be the factor that qualified them for selection. This factor, the incidence of which cannot be estimated, must be borne in mind when analysing the available data.

I now proceed to the analysis, based on information available in the published record. For each variable examined, the soviet will be considered first, followed by the gorkom.

## SOCIAL COMPOSITION OF SOVIET AND GORKOM

*Party membership*

This variable is dealt with first because it is the only one where it is sufficient to examine merely the soviet, since gorkom members must be full members of the party. I found that there was always a majority of party members among the deputies. Even in the years 1950–55, when data are missing in a substantial number of cases, a majority of full members of the party has been identified (see Table 3.1, which shows the strength of representation among various classes of party affiliation). There was a tendency during the 1960s to increase gradually the proportion of non-party deputies, although the strength of 'committed' deputies (full and candidate party members, and

TABLE 3.1  *Tiraspol soviet: distribution of deputies by party membership status*

| Date of soviet | Non-party | | Full | | Candidate | | Komsomol | | Not available |
|---|---|---|---|---|---|---|---|---|---|
| | No. | % | No. | % | No. | % | No. | % | No. |
| 1950* | 40 | 30.8 | 68 | 52.3 | 5 | 3.8 | 5 | 3.8 | 12* |
| 1953 | 29 | 21.0 | 74 | 53.6 | 0 | 0.0 | 2 | 1.4 | 33 |
| 1955 | 26 | 15.8 | 93 | 56.4 | 0 | 0.0 | 0 | 0.0 | 46 |
| 1957 | 49 | 26.8 | 118 | 64.5 | 4 | 2.2 | 12 | 6.6 | 0 |
| 1959 | 47 | 25.0 | 128 | 68.1 | 3 | 1.6 | 10 | 5.3 | 0 |
| 1961 | 52 | 25.7 | 126 | 62.4 | 5 | 2.5 | 19 | 9.4 | 0 |
| 1963 | 65 | 29.1 | 123 | 55.3 | 7 | 3.1 | 28 | 12.6 | 0 |
| 1965 | 73 | 29.3 | 129 | 51.8 | 11 | 4.4 | 35 | 14.0 | 1 |
| 1967 | 87 | 34.8 | 147 | 58.8 | 0 | 0.0 | 16 | 6.4 | 0 |

*Dnestrovskaya pravda*, 4 January 1951, gives the following figures for party membership of the 1950 soviet: non-party – 48; party – 82. These figures represent 36.9% and 63.1% respectively.

Komsomol members) was always well over one half: in 1965, when only 51.8 per cent were full party members, the strength of these formally 'committed' deputies rose to 70.2 per cent of the soviet's membership. During the later years of the study (1959–67), the strength of the communist party was consistently higher than the all-Union level for urban soviets, and also higher than in urban soviets in Moldavia as a whole. Average figures for those years were as follows: Tiraspol town soviet – 61.6 per cent; Moldavian urban soviets – 56.7 per cent; USSR urban soviets – 51.8 per cent.[4] In conformity with the overall rule that 'the more important the local Soviet, the more demanding are the criteria for selection of deputies to that Soviet',[5] the party strength in Tiraspol was also higher than the average for all local soviets, which includes the scores of village soviets where the party is normally in a minority.[6] Thus, in 1959 there was a difference of over 30 per cent between the Tiraspol figure for party strength (69.7 per cent) and the Moldavian figure for all local soviets (39.0 per cent).

These figures show in some measure how far Tiraspol was out of line with general trends in this respect, and it calls for some comment. There are several factors that may have been at play. The first is that Tiraspol is the longest-sovietised town in present-day Moldavia, so that its party organisation became well established in the inter-war period when the rest of the republic was under Romanian rule. Tiraspol is, too, one of the most industrialised towns in Moldavia: doubtless this fact has also contributed to party strength when compared with other towns, such as Kagul and Rybnitsa, which are rural rather than industrial,[7] and where the party's traditional weakness among the rural population is probably evident.[8] Finally, the town's former status as capital of the Moldavian ASSR may mean that there are still substantial numbers of retired and serving officials of various kinds in the town, most of whom would be party members.

In common with trends elsewhere,[9] Komsomol strength in the soviet increased markedly during the 1960s. This implies an enhanced role for young people in the soviet's affairs, and might influence the general level of energy and enthusiasm with which the deputies carried out their work. Their presumed desire to be eventually admitted to the ranks of the CPSU might also spur them on to perform their duties competently, as well as effectively bringing them under party discipline.

To sum up, party control over the soviet was always very firm. It is perhaps irrelevant to speak of majorities and minorities in the context of Soviet local government, yet the case remains that even if the formally uncommitted deputies (that is, excluding full and candidate party members and Komsomol members) had in fact been anti-party, rather than simply non-party,[10] their concerted effort would at no time have been sufficient to thwart any party-approved policy. This is one of the realities of Soviet political life.

*Sex*

The degree to which women were brought into the activity of the soviet over the years is indicated by the data in Table 3.2. It is clear that men were dominant: of the 1728 places on the nine soviets, 1081 (62.6 per cent) went to males; their mean strength was 63.1 per cent. While the

TABLE 3.2    *Tiraspol soviet: distribution of deputies by sex*

| Date of Soviet | Male | | Female | |
|---|---|---|---|---|
| | No. | % | No. | % |
| 1950 | 84 | 64.6 | 46 | 35.4 |
| 1953 | 83 | 60.1 | 55 | 39.9 |
| 1955 | 111 | 67.3 | 54 | 32.7 |
| 1957 | 123 | 67.2 | 60 | 32.8 |
| 1959 | 131 | 69.7 | 57 | 30.3 |
| 1961 | 135 | 66.8 | 67 | 33.2 |
| 1963 | 124 | 55.6 | 99 | 44.4 |
| 1965 | 140 | 56.2 | 109 | 43.8 |
| 1967 | 150 | 60.0 | 100 | 40.0 |

*number* of women ranged between 46 and 109, the pattern of development was not steady, as both number and proportion varied from year to year. When the figures are compared with wider trends, we see that Tiraspol was generally behind all-Union levels in urban or all local soviets, with the exception of 1963 and 1965; moreover, Tiraspol was generally behind Moldavian trends too, although performance was somewhat erratic, indicating a measure of local influence in the selection of deputies with respect to this variable.[11]

Turning to the party committee, we find that here too men always enjoyed a majority, and their strength was much greater than in the soviet. In both categories of membership, the strong position of males is evident (see Table 3.3) and this is consistent with wider trends, both in Moldavia and elsewhere.[12] There appears to be a slight difference in the strength of women among full as opposed to candidate members of the committee, as is revealed by both the percentage figures for each category year by year, and also by the overall figures: in the fifteen committees for which information is available there were 1082 places taken by full members and 249 by candidate members; of these, at least 864 (79.9 per cent) of the full member and at least 168 (67.5 per cent) of the candidate member places went to males, while 12.8 per cent and 12.9 per cent respectively went to women. These figures are statistically inconclusive, but it seems likely that women succeed less regularly in winning the status of full membership, with the voting rights that that would accord them.

TABLE 3.3　*Tiraspol gorkom: distribution of members by sex*

| Number of gorkom | Male | | Female | | Not available | |
|---|---|---|---|---|---|---|
| | No. | % | No. | % | No. | % |
| XI | 47 | 71.2 | 6 | 9.1 | 13 | 19.7 |
| XII | 48 | 72.7 | 13 | 19.7 | 5 | 7.6 |
| XIV | 50 | 75.8 | 11 | 16.7 | 5 | 7.6 |
| XVI | 55 | 80.9 | 8 | 11.8 | 5 | 7.4 |
| XVII | 63 | 82.9 | 10 | 13.2 | 3 | 3.9 |
| XVIII | 68 | 84.0 | 11 | 13.6 | 2 | 2.5 |
| XIX | 72 | 83.7 | 8 | 9.3 | 6 | 7.0 |
| XX | 74 | 80.4 | 7 | 7.6 | 11 | 12.0 |
| XXI | 85 | 89.5 | 8 | 8.4 | 2 | 2.1 |
| XXII | 85 | 86.7 | 9 | 9.2 | 4 | 4.1 |
| XXIII | 86 | 85.1 | 8 | 7.9 | 7 | 6.9 |
| XXIV | 71 | 68.3 | 14 | 13.5 | 19 | 18.3 |
| XXVI | 70 | 64.8 | 22 | 20.4 | 16 | 14.8 |
| XXVII | 83 | 74.1 | 17 | 15.2 | 12 | 10.7 |
| XXVIII | 75 | 67.0 | 18 | 16.1 | 19 | 17.0 |

It is hard to believe that these trends are the product of pure chance, and without necessarily implying a deliberate policy of discrimination against women, there are one or two factors that probably contribute towards the situation. One is the tendency of many Soviet women still to regard their child-rearing and family role as proper and adequate. The 1959 Moldavian census reveals (Table 13) that there were 283,998 urban-dwelling females aged ten years and over, yet only 127,712 (45.0 per cent) in that age group had a job (Table 33). It is inconceivable that the remainder were all 10–16-year-old schoolgirls, hence a substantial proportion of them must have been unemployed and probably married women; most of them would be ineligible to join a party organisation, since these are normally attached to places of work. Secondly, even for those women who do work, old attitudes towards the appropriate feminine occupations die hard, and in employment women are evidently discriminated against.[13] Again taking the data in the 1959 census, we find that of the 791,819 employed women in Moldavia, only 882 were in political administrative posts, and only 666 in industrial or agricultural administrative positions (Table 43); yet these are the very positions from which party committee members tend to be drawn, as will become clear later. In other words, as other writers have commented, women tend to be less strongly represented in the party than do men; and they tend to be appointed to 'line' or career posts in government, party, or industrial administrative hierarchies in fewer numbers than men.[14] Obviously these two factors are not unconnected, since party membership is widely accepted as a necessary qualification for appointment to positions of responsibility in Soviet society.

It is striking that the strength of women on the gorkom was significantly lower than on the town soviet, and this has its implications. In Soviet legalistic interpretations, the comparatively high representation of women in the 'organ of state power' in the territory concerned attests to their political equality, and it is certainly true that the level of female membership of government bodies is generally higher than in western systems of representative government.[15] However, given the influence of the CPSU, the exercise of genuine power and authority by any social group depends less on that group's strength in the organs of state than on its representation within the party, and particularly its organs; on this showing, women in Tiraspol as elsewhere were in a politically weak position compared with men.[16] I do not deny the outstanding role played by a few women in the political life of the town, and of the country; nevertheless, the limited strength of women in even the lower committees of the country's most important political institution suggests that in practice they are unlikely to achieve the full equality that Soviet legislation guarantees.

## Age

Figures showing the age distribution of deputies over the period of this study are presented in Table 3.4. An interesting feature of the trends is the fluctuation in the strength of younger members: the early sixties

TABLE 3.4 *Tiraspol soviet: distribution of deputies by age*

| Date of soviet | Under 30 No. | Under 30 % | 30–39 No. | 30–39 % | Age group 40–49 No. | 40–49 % | 50–59 No. | 50–59 % | Over 60 No. | Over 60 % | Not available No. | Mean age (years) |
|---|---|---|---|---|---|---|---|---|---|---|---|---|
| 1950* | 25 | 21.7 | 31 | 27.0 | 42 | 36.5 | 13 | 11.3 | 4 | 3.5 | 15 | 38.9 |
| 1953* | 14 | 16.1 | 26 | 29.9 | 32 | 36.8 | 11 | 12.6 | 4 | 4.6 | 51 | 40.4 |
| 1955* | 9 | 8.9 | 30 | 29.7 | 40 | 39.6 | 17 | 16.8 | 5 | 5.0 | 64 | 42.7 |
| 1957 | 26 | 14.2 | 62 | 33.9 | 68 | 37.2 | 21 | 11.5 | 6 | 3.3 | 0 | 40.1 |
| 1959 | 29 | 15.4 | 50 | 26.6 | 77 | 41.0 | 26 | 13.8 | 6 | 3.2 | 0 | 40.6 |
| 1961 | 34 | 16.8 | 50 | 24.8 | 84 | 41.6 | 27 | 13.4 | 7 | 3.5 | 0 | 40.5 |
| 1963 | 56 | 25.1 | 76 | 34.1 | 70 | 31.4 | 18 | 8.1 | 3 | 1.3 | 0 | 37.4 |
| 1965 | 62 | 24.9 | 90 | 36.1 | 71 | 28.5 | 25 | 10.0 | 1 | 0.4 | 0 | 37.2 |
| 1967 | 43 | 17.2 | 81 | 32.4 | 95 | 38.0 | 28 | 11.2 | 3 | 1.2 | 0 | 39.3 |

*Percentage figures for these years are based on *known* deputies only.

were marked by the sudden influx of young deputies – in 1965 deputies under 40 formed a two-thirds majority. This deserves comment, since it seems to be an obvious reflection of deliberate policy. Thus, Lepëshkin wrote in 1967 that 'enlisting youth for participation in the work of the soviets has important political significance from the viewpoint of the prospects for state development in our country'. He added, 'It would be desirable for the number of young persons in the local soviets to grow with each new set of elections, which without doubt would lend them the energy and Komsomol-style "bite" which is sometimes lacking in our soviets in the localities'.[17] This desire to tap the energy and enthusiasm of young people has already been mentioned in my discussion of Komsomol representation, and there appears to have been a drive to bring young people to serve in local soviets all over the country in the 1960s.[18] A further explanation for this might be a desire to win over the younger generation, whose dissatisfaction at this time has been commented on,[19] by drawing them into the political system and involving them in public life, rather than alienating them from it by excluding them. Another factor may have been a desire to sponsor a more positive role for the Komsomol, following the adoption of the new party Programme in 1961, which announced that that organisation 'will play a greater role' in assisting the party 'in the practical job of building the new society'.[20] An influx of Komsomol members would obviously imply an influx of younger members. Whatever the explanation, Tiraspol followed the new policy in 1963 with apparent enthusiasm, increasing its representation of young deputies more than elsewhere. In 1967, however, when the policy was temporarily reversed, Tiraspol followed this reversal with equal enthusiasm, removing large numbers of young deputies and replacing them with older representatives, so that the decline in the strength of those under thirty was of 7.7 percentage points, compared with 4.3 in Moldavian urban soviets as a whole, and 3.0 in all urban soviets. If we can assume that the town authorities have a say in the selection of deputies for the soviet, this particular response to externally devised policy may indicate the level of political sophistication among the town's politicians: they clearly did not believe in the golden mean, or even in moderation in applying such a policy, but were anxious to demonstrate their loyalty in following generally expressed guidelines.

A further aspect of the age structure becomes apparent when the distribution of individuals' ages is considered separately, rather than in classes. The typical age distribution, shown in Fig. 3.1 (referring to the deputies elected in 1961), showed two peaks: a main one in the late thirties and early forties, and a secondary peak in the very young age categories. This pattern persisted in subsequent years, the peak showing no tendency to move steadily upwards, which reveals one aspect of the deputy selection process. Clearly the large number of younger deputies are not allowed to mature as deputies; instead they are removed and replaced by a further group of equally young deputies. It thus appears that youth debars deputies from re-election, so that the potential for long-term participation by an individual fortunate enough to be selected at an early age is severely reduced, except perhaps in individual cases where personality and capabilities lead to a young deputy's retention.

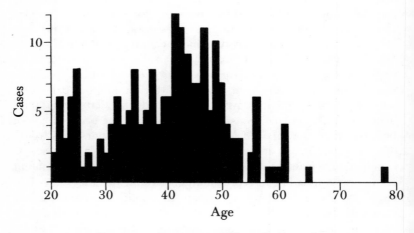

*Figure 3.1    Age structure of Tiraspol soviet, 1961*

In the gorkom, we find a rather different situation. The average age seems again to have been in the early to mid-forties, as the figures in Table 3.5 suggest; but the number of really young members was always very small, and the proportion of elderly members comparatively high; there was also a slight distinction between full and candidate members, with the older generation more strongly represented among the full members. This generally conforms to one's intuitive expectations, the more prestigious and influential positions, which bring voting membership of the gorkom, being filled by more mature individuals. It also points to the presence in Tiraspol of a phenomenon of widespread

TABLE 3.5 *Tiraspol gorkom: distribution of members by age*

| Number of gorkom | Under 30 | | 30–39 | | Age group 40–49 | | 50–59 | | Over 60 | | Not available | |
|---|---|---|---|---|---|---|---|---|---|---|---|---|
| | No. | % | No. | % | No. | % | No. | % | No. | % | No. | % |
| XI | 0 | 0.0 | 7 | 10.6 | 26 | 39.4 | 3 | 4.5 | 0 | 0.0 | 30 | 45.5 |
| XII | 1 | 1.5 | 11 | 16.7 | 22 | 33.3 | 7 | 10.6 | 1 | 1.5 | 24 | 36.4 |
| XIV | 4 | 6.1 | 8 | 12.1 | 20 | 30.3 | 6 | 9.1 | 2 | 3.0 | 26 | 39.4 |
| XVI | 1 | 1.5 | 8 | 11.8 | 23 | 33.8 | 6 | 8.8 | 3 | 4.4 | 27 | 39.7 |
| XVII | 1 | 1.3 | 13 | 17.1 | 25 | 32.9 | 7 | 9.2 | 3 | 3.9 | 27 | 35.5 |
| XVIII | 2 | 2.5 | 18 | 22.2 | 30 | 37.0 | 9 | 11.1 | 4 | 4.9 | 18 | 22.2 |
| XIX | 1 | 1.2 | 18 | 20.9 | 29 | 33.7 | 13 | 15.1 | 3 | 3.5 | 22 | 25.6 |
| XX | 0 | 0.0 | 17 | 18.5 | 28 | 30.4 | 14 | 15.2 | 3 | 3.3 | 30 | 32.6 |
| XXI | 0 | 0.0 | 15 | 15.8 | 29 | 30.5 | 14 | 14.7 | 3 | 3.2 | 34 | 35.8 |
| XXII | 3 | 3.1 | 15 | 15.3 | 35 | 35.7 | 14 | 14.3 | 4 | 4.1 | 27 | 27.6 |
| XXIII | 1 | 1.0 | 17 | 16.8 | 36 | 35.6 | 7 | 6.9 | 5 | 5.0 | 35 | 34.7 |
| XXIV | 6 | 5.8 | 23 | 22.1 | 24 | 23.1 | 3 | 2.9 | 1 | 1.0 | 47 | 45.2 |
| XXVI | 5 | 4.6 | 27 | 25.0 | 23 | 21.3 | 10 | 9.3 | 3 | 2.8 | 40 | 37.0 |
| XXVII | 3 | 2.7 | 26 | 23.2 | 32 | 28.6 | 10 | 8.9 | 2 | 1.8 | 39 | 34.8 |
| XXVIII | 3 | 2.7 | 15 | 13.4 | 40 | 35.7 | 12 | 10.7 | 2 | 1.8 | 40 | 35.7 |

significance in the USSR: a possible split between the younger mass membership, recruited from the Komsomol a decade or less previously, and an older (and ageing) leadership, occupying positions of power and delaying the career development of the younger generation. A number of western commentators have pointed out that, whereas the general age of party membership is fairly young, those appointed to positions of authority, particularly at the top, tend to be of an older generation, which may be out of touch with the young recruits and the younger generation of established party members and officials, whose impatience to experience genuine power could lead to a violent political clash in the foreseeable future.[21] There is strong evidence that the introduction of a new rule on turnover among party officials and committee members at the XXII CPSU Congress in 1961 was an attempt to deal with precisely this problem in the party apparatus.[22] Soviet comment on the abandonment of the rule in 1966 refers to the resultant excessively high level of turnover and consequent lack of continuity;[23] the frustration among party workers deprived of their positions of responsibility may also have contributed to the reassessment of the rule. Whatever the explanation, it is clear that the phenomenon was not unknown in Tiraspol, and it will be viewed from a slightly different angle in the next chapter.

*Occupation*

I turn now to what is perhaps the most fundamental social characteristic in the Soviet Union: occupation. It is fundamental at least in the sense that the Soviet political system is dominated by an ideology that places great stress on social class, defined in economic and occupational terms. The Constitution, introduced in 1936, opens with the words, 'The Union of Soviet Socialist Republics is a socialist state of workers and peasants' (Article 1). In 1961, the new, third Programme of the CPSU continued to stress the significance of the working classes in Soviet society and for the future of the world. It is therefore of considerable importance to examine the extent to which these particular social groups are represented in political bodies. The soviets are seen as 'organs which are situated in direct proximity to the population' and which 'dispose of enormous possibilities for drawing the toiling masses into state management, and for their daily participation in directing state and public affairs in the localities'.[24] How far do selection practices conform with this official view of the

TABLE 3.6  Tiraspol soviet: distribution of deputies by occupation

| Sector | | 1950 | 1953 | 1955 | 1957 | 1959 | 1961 | 1963 | 1965 | 1967 |
|---|---|---|---|---|---|---|---|---|---|---|
| Industrial | No. | 64 | 56 | 69 | 88 | 95 | 115 | 156 | 168 | 163 |
| | % | 49.2 | 40.6 | 41.8 | 48.1 | 50.5 | 56.9 | 70.0 | 67.5 | 65.2 |
| Of whom: | | | | | | | | | | |
| Production | | 43 | 31 | 41 | 49 | 61 | 71 | 123 | 132 | 127 |
| Management | | 21 | 25 | 28 | 39 | 34 | 44 | 33 | 36 | 36 |
| Administrative | No. | 23 | 34 | 35 | 33 | 40 | 40 | 33 | 39 | 42 |
| | % | 17.7 | 24.6 | 21.2 | 18.0 | 21.3 | 19.8 | 14.8 | 15.7 | 16.8 |
| Of whom: | | | | | | | | | | |
| Party officials | | 6 | 13 | 14 | 13 | 9 | 11 | 8 | 8 | 10 |
| State officials | | 15 | 14 | 14 | 14 | 19 | 18 | 12 | 19 | 20 |
| T.U., Komsomol | | 1 | 2 | 2 | 2 | 5 | 5 | 1 | 3 | 2 |
| Law | | 1 | 0 | 2 | 1 | 3 | 3 | 1 | 1 | 3 |
| Security | | 0 | 5 | 3 | 3 | 4 | 3 | 11 | 8 | 7 |
| Facilities | No. | 30 | 41 | 44 | 45 | 39 | 33 | 31 | 39 | 44 |
| | % | 23.1 | 29.7 | 26.7 | 24.6 | 20.7 | 16.3 | 13.9 | 15.7 | 17.6 |
| Of whom: | | | | | | | | | | |
| Trade | | 4 | 2 | 3 | 4 | 5 | 6 | 4 | 9 | 9 |
| Education | | 19 | 26 | 32 | 32 | 24 | 18 | 19 | 18 | 22 |
| Medicine | | 5 | 9 | 7 | 7 | 7 | 7 | 6 | 10 | 9 |
| Communications | | 2 | 4 | 2 | 2 | 3 | 2 | 2 | 2 | 4 |
| Others | No. | 0 | 0 | 1 | 4 | 2 | 7 | 3 | 3 | 1 |
| | % | 0.0 | 0.0 | 0.6 | 2.2 | 1.1 | 3.5 | 1.3 | 1.2 | 0.4 |
| Not available | No. | 13 | 7 | 16 | 13 | 12 | 7 | 0 | 0 | 0 |

Date of soviet

soviets? And is there any discrepancy between their strength on the soviet and on the gorkom, where their presence is a surer guide to the political status of the various social groups?

As a fundamental requirement, if either of these bodies is to fulfil broadly representative functions, we should expect their social composition to reflect the various facets of the town as an industrial, administrative, cultural and service centre.

Taking the soviet first, the dominating position of industry is striking (see Table 3.6), a clear reflection of the importance of industry in the town's economy. This dominance increased in the 1960s, to the detriment of other sectors, although the balance between sectors did fluctuate.

Certain patterns can be discerned when deputies are considered in terms of their precise occupation, rather than sector. In the sector headed 'facilities', the weakness of the retail trade is striking, and probably in part reflects the extremely low status of trade: 'shop assistant' featured seventieth in preference out of seventy-four occupations presented in a survey questionnaire,[25] which suggests that the bright, dynamic individuals who might merit selection to serve as deputies are not likely to be found among the workers in that sphere. This weakness applies all over the USSR: in 1965, for instance, a mere 3.8 per cent of all local deputies were engaged in trade and service to the population, a weakness that causes Lepëshkin to comment, 'it is extremely desirable that there should be among the deputies more representatives of people working in the sphere of service for the population than there are now'.[26] This can be seen as part of a much wider policy of stimulating the growth of service facilities for the population, which began in the mid-sixties.[27]

Workers in education were usually more numerous on the soviet, with school teachers especially strong among them, but also including some students, headmasters, lecturers and officials of the pedagogical institute, and others. However, educationalists never accounted for as many as 20 per cent of all deputies, and their relative strength declined after 1960, falling to a mere 7.2 per cent in 1965. This reduction in their relative strength took place at a time when the number of schools and pupils in the town rose considerably, as did, presumably, the number of teachers and headmasters. The figures for Tiraspol suggest that the occupational group with perhaps the highest general academic and educational standards to its credit plays a comparatively minor role in the work of the state institutions. It may be of relevance to note that the

| Sector | | XI | XII | XIV | XVI | XVII | XVIII | XIX | XX | XXI | XXII | XXIII | XXIV | XXVI | XXVII | XXVIII |
|---|---|---|---|---|---|---|---|---|---|---|---|---|---|---|---|---|
| | | | | | | | | | | *Number of gorkom* | | | | | | |
| Industrial | No. | 14 | 13 | 14 | 20 | 21 | 30 | 26 | 21 | 25 | 33 | 24 | 21 | 26 | 38 | 33 |
| | % | 21.2 | 19.7 | 21.2 | 29.4 | 27.6 | 37.0 | 30.2 | 22.8 | 26.3 | 33.7 | 23.8 | 20.2 | 24.1 | 33.9 | 29.5 |
| Of whom: | | | | | | | | | | | | | | | | |
| Production | | 4 | 4 | 4 | 3 | 3 | 6 | 6 | 3 | 3 | 4 | 1 | 5 | 5 | 12 | 8 |
| Management | | 10 | 9 | 10 | 17 | 18 | 24 | 20 | 18 | 22 | 29 | 23 | 16 | 21 | 26 | 25 |
| Administration | No. | 20 | 17 | 22 | 23 | 21 | 19 | 18 | 26 | 25 | 26 | 22 | 23 | 44 | 32 | 36 |
| | % | 30.3 | 25.8 | 33.3 | 33.8 | 27.6 | 23.5 | 20.9 | 28.3 | 26.3 | 26.5 | 21.8 | 22.1 | 40.7 | 28.6 | 32.1 |
| Of whom: | | | | | | | | | | | | | | | | |
| Party officials | | 11 | 7 | 11 | 12 | 10 | 11 | 10 | 12 | 12 | 15 | 12 | 10 | 28 | 19 | 22 |
| State officials | | 7 | 7 | 6 | 6 | 6 | 5 | 6 | 6 | 5 | 5 | 4 | 5 | 9 | 7 | 5 |
| T.U., Komsomol | | 1 | 1 | 2 | 2 | 2 | 1 | 0 | 2 | 3 | 3 | 2 | 2 | 2 | 1 | 2 |
| Law | | 0 | 1 | 1 | 1 | 1 | 0 | 0 | 3 | 3 | 1 | 2 | 1 | 1 | 2 | 2 |
| Security | | 1 | 1 | 2 | 2 | 2 | 2 | 2 | 3 | 2 | 2 | 2 | 5 | 4 | 3 | 5 |
| Facilities | No. | 6 | 6 | 7 | 8 | 8 | 10 | 9 | 9 | 7 | 6 | 8 | 3 | 3 | 9 | 11 |
| | % | 9.1 | 9.1 | 10.6 | 11.8 | 10.5 | 12.3 | 10.5 | 9.8 | 7.4 | 6.1 | 7.9 | 2.9 | 2.8 | 8.0 | 9.8 |
| Of whom: | | | | | | | | | | | | | | | | |
| Trade | | 0 | 0 | 0 | 0 | 0 | 1 | 1 | 1 | 0 | 0 | 0 | 0 | 0 | 1 | 2 |
| Education | | 5 | 5 | 5 | 6 | 4 | 6 | 6 | 6 | 5 | 4 | 5 | 2 | 3 | 7 | 6 |
| Medicine | | 0 | 0 | 1 | 1 | 2 | 1 | 1 | 1 | 1 | 1 | 2 | 0 | 0 | 0 | 1 |
| Communications | | 1 | 1 | 1 | 1 | 2 | 2 | 1 | 1 | 1 | 1 | 1 | 1 | 0 | 1 | 2 |
| Others | No. | 0 | 0 | 1 | 0 | 1 | 0 | 0 | 1 | 1 | 1 | 3 | 2 | 2 | 3 | 3 |
| | % | 0.0 | 0.0 | 1.5 | 0.0 | 1.3 | 0.0 | 0.0 | 1.1 | 1.1 | 1.0 | 3.0 | 1.9 | 1.9 | 2.7 | 2.7 |
| Not available | No. | 26 | 30 | 22 | 17 | 25 | 22 | 33 | 35 | 37 | 32 | 44 | 55 | 33 | 30 | 29 |
| | % | 39.4 | 45.5 | 33.3 | 25.0 | 32.9 | 27.2 | 38.4 | 38.0 | 38.9 | 32.7 | 43.6 | 52.9 | 30.6 | 26.8 | 25.9 |

majority of teachers in the Soviet Union are women, and that the teaching profession has a low status in society;[28] their modest participation in Tiraspol town soviet is probably a reflection of this. The same applies to the medical profession, which also enjoys low status in society, and is likewise staffed largely by women.[29]

A similar pattern can be identified among the gorkom members (see Table 3.7). There too, in the 'facilities' sector, education is the strongest represented, trade the weakest, with medicine also fairly weak. Their general level of representation was even lower than on the soviet, but again we see an improvement in the 1960s, attributable partly to the policy of stimulating the services sector, and partly to a revival of interest in recruiting representatives of education.

In general, it can be said that the low representation in the political institutions of those sectors of the work force engaged in providing various facilities for the population is part of a much broader phenomenon, reflecting the low status of the services professions compared with the ideologically-endowed high status of industrial production. As such, Tiraspol was strongly in line with trends right across the USSR.

I have already drawn attention to the dominant position of the industrial sector in the two institutions. It is among industrial employees that the most marked trend is evident, and here we see a contrast between the soviet and the gorkom. In the soviet, the representation of production workers increased dramatically during our period, so that they came to form by far the biggest occupational group. This was to some extent due to a central committee decision that preceded the 1957 elections, and led to increased worker representation throughout the USSR.[30] The strength of industrial management, by contrast, remained much more stable, and declined proportionally (along with other non-worker groups) during the sixties. This would appear to signify an impressive gain for the workers, in line with the ideological predilections of the regime. Whether this is in fact so depends however on many factors, some of which will be further considered below. One such factor is their strength on the gorkom, and on that basis a rather different conclusion might be drawn.

On the party committee, the strength of workers fluctuated, but never reached more than twelve individuals identified, less than 11 per cent of that gorkom (xxvii). True, the large numbers of missing data may include some workers. Yet if they are absent on anything like a random basis, production workers are far outnumbered by managerial staff in every committee for which information is available. This coincides with Stewart's findings of 'underrepresentation of workers and peasants and the overrepresentation of white collar workers on the local Party committees'.[31]

White collar workers include, of course, administrators of all kinds. On the soviet, they accounted for an average of 18.9 per cent of deputies over the nine terms of office, but there were differences between categories: more state than party officials, a modest sprinkling of trade union and Komsomol officials and lawyers, and slightly more security officers. On the gorkom, administrators formed the strongest group. Party officials were predominant – gorkom officers and officials, party secretaries from lower, primary organisations. In view of the high level of missing data, even the comparatively high strength of administrators in most years may underestimate the true strength of this class. A further point to note is that in some cases – particularly of members recruited from industry – the individuals concerned may have also held political office, which would have qualified them for inclusion in this category.

In both bodies, these officials formed a substantial block, and this is in tune with wider trends. For example, in the 1963 Moldavian central committee, only 38 per cent of members did not hold some high political office in the republic,[32] while as a general rule the central committees in the republics include, apart from 'prominent workers, peasants and key administrators', 'the most important officials in the area',[33] who form the bulk of the membership. In 1961, the rural raikomy and gorkomy together contained 26.3 per cent party and soviet officials.[34] In the Stalingrad obkom, the proportion ranged from 64.9 per cent in 1954 to 56.2 per cent in 1956 and down to 51.9 per cent in 1957 and 1960.[35] For the CPSU central committee elected in 1966, the total for those groups included in my 'administrative' sector was 72.3 per cent.[36] These figures, taken in conjunction with my own, support a staffing model for party committees whereby the higher the level, the greater the proportion of administrators in the committee membership, with in any case a relatively high proportion at all levels in comparison with other occupational groups. In the state apparatus, at the higher levels at least, there is always a sizeable number of such officials, although 'the proportion of Soviet and party personnel slumps considerably at the lower levels of Soviets'.[37]

To sum up this discussion of the composition of the soviet and the gorkom. The membership of the soviet reflects its role as a representative organ: its composition adheres to some extent to the economic and social balance of the town's population, with its high representation of industry, and especially production workers. It is also clear however that its composition, judged by occupation, varies according to social attitudes and political criteria decided elsewhere, and certain sectors were consistently under-represented. This obviously affects the adequacy with which it might play its constitutional role of a representative and deliberative organ, and I shall return again to this question.

The make-up of the gorkom, by contrast, points to its function as a party body, rather than one which aims at broad representation of all social and occupational groups. The general composition shows a bias towards men, older members, and administrators, especially party administrators. However, most other groups were also present, and, as Stewart has pointed out, this gives other, non-party interests an opportunity of expressing themselves, so that the party committee can act in some sense as a 'representative' body. Representation here means that a social group has an opportunity of putting forward its views based on its particular expertise or interests, rather than being included in numbers proportional to its strength.[38] The gorkom can serve several functions: it can take decisions on specialised questions more competently than it might otherwise be able to do; it can ensure that its decisions, once taken, are transmitted back to the bodies responsible for implementing them, through the PPOs in the individual enterprises, whose 'representatives' sit on the committee; it can give party and state functionaries an opportunity of hearing a wide range of professional opinion on a variety of issues; similarly it can give the representatives of various groups in society an insight into the political requirements that lead to particular decisions; the gorkom can serve as a means of rewarding active and deserving party members – perhaps the small number of ordinary workers fall mainly into that category – and at the same time it can serve as a career grade for party officials, for whom gorkom membership represents one step on a career ladder that may lead to higher party committee membership and party apparatus positions, possibly coupled with membership of other political bodies, such as the town soviet, the supreme soviet, and so forth – this aspect of committee membership will be further discussed in chapters 7 and 8 below. The gorkom is thus seen as a multi-purpose organ, whose membership reflects the various facets of its existence.

## TURNOVER

My discussion of trends in the membership of the two main political institutions concludes with an analysis of patterns in turnover, defined as the proportion of members of any particular soviet or committee who were not re-elected at the end of the term of office. In both institutions, we find a fairly high level of turnover, but with major fluctuations from year to year that suggest political significance in some cases.

Taking the soviet first, we find that in only two years were less than half of the deputies dropped; in 1965 almost three-quarters of the deputies elected in 1963 failed to be re-elected, as the figures in Table 3.8 show. One general trend is towards a higher level of turnover in the

TABLE 3.8   *Tiraspol soviet: deputies not re-elected for a further term*

| Date of soviet | Deputies not re-elected at end of term | |
|---|---|---|
| | No. | % |
| 1950 | 71 | 54.6 |
| 1953 | 68 | 49.3 |
| 1955 | 89 | 53.9 |
| 1957 | 81 | 44.3 |
| 1959 | 99 | 52.6 |
| 1961 | 132 | 65.3 |
| 1963 | 167 | 74.9 |
| 1965 | 157 | 63.1 |

1960s than in the 1950s. This may be in response to the proposal, contained in the 1961 party Programme, that at least one third of the deputies should be elected anew each time.[39] Although turnover levels in Tiraspol were always much higher than this minimum level, the inclusion of such a 'norm' in the party Programme may have had the political aim of suggesting that more citizens in general should be brought into the task of governing through the soviets, and the authorities in Tiraspol enthusiastically took up the proposal.

It is tempting to try and connect the fluctuations with national political events, although this is not easy to do with certainty. Thus, one might wish to link the unusually high rate of turnover from the 1963 soviet with the removal of Khrushchev from power five months before the elections of March 1965. This is perhaps the most plausible interpretation, and it supports the notion of a highly centralised political system, where the effects of changes at the top penetrate to the very foundations of the structure. It also suggests that the regime takes these local soviets seriously as *political* bodies, not regarding them simply as rubber stamps; after all, any body of deputies can competently act as a rubber stamp, so there would be little need to change them for political reasons.

However, even if we could ascribe the high turnover of 1965 to Khrushchev's downfall, the fluctuations of previous years are not easy to account for. This is especially true of the relative stability between 1957 and 1959, a period that covered the politically crucial crisis of the 'Anti-Party Group', when Khrushchev's political career was at stake.[40] The issue was over the position of the party vis-à-vis the state apparatus, so one would definitely expect to find the resolution of the crisis reflected in the turnover rates in the soviet. In fact, this is not the case, and one has to search for reasons why. Had perhaps the higher turnover in the election immediately before the crisis (in March 1957: the crisis was at its peak four months later, in June and July) been a preparation? Were the ninety-four new deputies who entered the soviet at that time Khrushchev supporters? Was the Khrushchev 'lobby' already preparing the ground at the grass roots in preparation for the showdown? Or is one to conclude that the local soviets were less important at that time than they had evidently become by 1965, and that the intervening period had witnessed a development in their political significance? Was there a change in official views of the local soviets that affected their role, such that the Khrushchev 'ouster' was reflected in turnover patterns, but earlier leadership crises were not? At this level of discussion one is reduced largely to speculation, and the evidence is ambiguous: to 'solve' one case means to raise problems in others, so that attempts to connect the local soviets with high politics are fraught with difficulties. I shall present some of the relevant evidence in chapter 6.

Turnover patterns in gorkom membership are more complex, owing to the existence of two categories of membership, full and candidate. An individual full member might be re-elected to full membership, demoted to candidate membership, or expelled from the committee; a candidate might retain that status, be promoted to full membership, or leave the committee entirely. These considerations might affect one's definition of turnover. For our purposes, turnover is defined as *departure from the committee as a whole after one term of office*. A further complication is brought about by the absence of membership lists in some cases, which means that turnover levels cannot be calculated for all years; however, I have attempted to overcome this difficulty by looking at *attrition* (i.e. cumulative turnover) over two conference elections, which gives a further perspective on change in membership. Despite these complicating factors, the figures for turnover in the gorkom are less puzzling than those for the soviet, and it is clear that turnover patterns here do reflect leadership crises outside the town. The relevant statistics are presented in Table 3.9.

TABLE 3.9  *Tiraspol gorkom: members not re-elected for a further term*

| Number of gorkom | Date | Number dropped after one term of office | | | | | | Number dropped after two terms | |
| | | Full | | Candidate | | Total | | Total | |
| | | No. | % | No. | % | No. | % | No. | % |
|---|---|---|---|---|---|---|---|---|---|
| XI | Jan 50 | 26 | 45.6 | 4 | 44.4 | 30 | 45.5 | – | – |
| XII | Feb 51 | – | – | – | – | – | – | 44 | 66.7 |
| XIV | Oct 53 | – | – | – | – | – | – | 26 | 39.4 |
| XVI | Nov 54 | 17 | 28.8 | 4 | 44.4 | 21 | 30.9 | 39 | 57.4 |
| XVII | Oct 55 | 22 | 36.1 | 9 | 60.0 | 31 | 40.8 | 42 | 55.3 |
| XVIII | Dec 56 | 17 | 25.8 | 9 | 60.0 | 26 | 32.1 | 37 | 45.7 |
| XIX | Nov 57 | 13 | 18.8 | 7 | 41.2 | 20 | 23.3 | 37 | 43.0 |
| XX | Nov 58 | 21 | 28.8 | 10 | 52.6 | 31 | 33.7 | 47 | 51.1 |
| XXI | Nov 59 | 21 | 27.6 | 13 | 68.4 | 34 | 35.8 | 60 | 63.2 |
| XXII | Jan 61 | 38 | 48.1 | 11 | 57.9 | 49 | 50.0 | 83 | 84.7 |
| XXIII | Sep 61 | 61 | 76.3 | 18 | 85.7 | 79 | 78.2 | – | – |
| XXIV | Dec 62 | – | – | – | – | – | – | 73 | 70.2 |
| XXVI | Jan 65 | 38 | 43.7 | 15 | 71.4 | 53 | 49.1 | 67 | 62.0 |
| XXVII | Jan 66 | 39 | 43.8 | 16 | 69.6 | 55 | 49.1 | – | – |

One or two general comments are in order to begin with. Note first the comparative stability in membership in the 1950s, and the general increase in the turnover level in the 1960s, a feature that I also identified in the soviet. This too can be linked with the new party Programme (1961), which regulated the turnover at 50 per cent (and incidentally implied that committee members should not be elected solely on merit, but in part on the basis of the length of their previous service).[41] Tiraspol adhered to this rule, but interestingly enough largely at the expense of the candidate members, who dropped out at a far higher rate than the full members. The attrition rates over two terms of office also show a marked increase during the 1960s, emphasising that decade as a period of change. However, although we can see this general trend, fluctuations in turnover rates throughout the period under study can be confidently linked to political crises at the top.

Information is unavailable on the very early part of this period. However, in comparison with later levels, the drop-out rate of 45.5 per cent in February 1951 (from the gorkom elected in January 1950) stands out as fairly high, and is most likely one effect of a purge of the Moldavian apparatus following a cpsu central committee declaration of 5 June 1950 criticising the Moldavian central committee. This declaration specifically censured the republican party leadership for 'mistakes in the selection and placing of personnel'. The committee accepted the criticism and 'obligated the CC buro of the CP(b)M and the council of ministers of the republic, gorkomy and raikomy of the party to eliminate the mistakes and deficiencies which had been revealed. . . .' Furthermore, in consequence of the declaration the then first secretary of the Moldavian central committee was shortly replaced by 'the experienced party worker' L. I. Brezhnev, for whom tenure of this Moldavian position was an important step on the road to the cpsu general secretaryship.[42] Further effects of this purge on the political elite in Tiraspol will be seen later in this study.

Following the death of Stalin, in March 1953, there was a relatively high level of attrition between February 1951 and October 1953, again probably prompted from outside, followed by a period of stability. This was broken during 1956 with a dramatic increase in turnover and attrition levels from the xvi and xvii gorkomy, at a time that coincided with the manoeuvrings of Khrushchev against the 'Anti-Party Group': it seems probable that the increase in replacement was in anticipation of the coming crisis. Once the crisis had passed (and been resolved, at least temporarily, in Khrushchev's favour), the process was completed at the election in November 1957: thus, we see a fairly low level of direct turnover from the xviii (December 1956) gorkom, but still a comparatively high level of attrition from the previous committee. A plausible interpretation of this is that a 'mopping up' operation was being carried out – expelling the old anti-Khrushchev forces from the committee, and consolidating the position by augmenting the new members brought in at the previous election. This crisis was therefore reflected at the grass-roots level in two stages: a preparatory influx of supporters before the crisis broke, followed by a second, clearing up operation after it had been resolved. Had the crisis been settled to Khrushchev's disadvantage, we might have witnessed a higher turnover, but lower attrition in November 1957.[43]

The committee then reverted to its more normal stability until 1961, when the Soviet Union experienced a further leadership crisis.[44] A purge of the apparatus after the XXII Party Congress (October 1961) extended down to the level of the gorkom, and perhaps went to the very roots of the party structure, the PPOs. The turnover and attrition rates in December 1962 rose to their highest ever level during our period, indicating that the challenge to Khrushchev's leadership at that time was perceived as a major threat, greater even than that of 1957: certainly, after his victory in 1961 Khrushchev seems to have felt a greater need to purge the apparatus. Information is missing that would enable us to identify the direct effects of Khrushchev's eventual defeat in October 1964. The level of attrition between December 1962 and January 1966 stands at 70.2 per cent – not very high for such a lengthy period; the 84.7 per cent attrition between the earlier XXII and XXIV conferences covered a mere twenty-three months. However, turnover and attrition fell after this; perhaps Khrushchev's successors had also felt a need to make a thorough change in the membership of the party apparatus.

### CONCLUSION

In this chapter I have presented a statistical description of the changing profile of Tiraspol town soviet and party committee over the period 1950–1967. One feature that became clear is that, although similar general trends on, for example, turnover were apparent in both institutions, the party committee seemed to be more closely supervised and controlled than the state body. Overall changes in the composition of the soviet were in line with wider trends, but in some cases there was considerable divergence from patterns identified elsewhere, pointing to limits in the extent of centralisation in the state apparatus. In the party committee, however, we find very close adherence to wider trends, and rapid responses to political changes at a higher level. This attests to the greater political significance of the gorkom, a fact that is also reflected in the quality and character of its membership: compared with the soviet, the gorkom is more powerful in terms of its male bias, its generally mature age structure, and above all its occupational composition. Because of its political importance, the gorkom is more vulnerable to policy changes than is the soviet: in the party apparatus, purges are certainly not restricted to the more influential levels of the party apparatus, but pervade the whole structure, sometimes in anticipation of a crisis, and sometimes to regulate the situation after a crisis has been resolved. In either case, the political careers of local administrators can be abruptly halted, or given a sudden uplift, since the beneficiaries of purges at higher levels may be officials from the lower levels; in chapter 8 I shall present examples of individuals who were affected in this way. To some extent this applies to the soviet, where changes also take place in response to promptings from outside; however, although officers and officials can be removed or promoted at a moment's notice, and ordinary deputies may be recalled by their constituents, in principle the term of office is fixed, and elections take place more regularly than in the party. The available evidence from Tiraspol suggests that the soviets have been less vulnerable than party organs to the influence of high politics. It is perfectly clear, nevertheless, that the selection process in both party and state is broadly in accordance with national policies, and in the next chapter I examine the patterns of service on these bodies in greater detail, to see how individual elite members were affected by some of the trends I have identified and analysed.

# CHAPTER 4

# Elite Recruitment in Party and State

In chapter 3 I considered the deputies and committee members as occupiers of places on each soviet or gorkom for a term of office. I now look at them as individuals, and examine their various social characteristics. Turnover also is given greater consideration, to help identify characteristics that promote prolonged membership of these bodies, in order to shed further light on recruitment practices at this local level. I commented in the previous chapter on what seemed a relatively high level of change in the membership of these bodies: this high rate is also manifested in the *number* of individuals who participated in their work. On the soviet, a total of 1013 individuals occupied 1728 places; on the gorkom, in the fifteen cases for which information is available, 1331 places (1082 full and 249 candidate member places) were taken by 600 individuals. The subject of this chapter is the identity of these individuals and the length of service they enjoyed.

## LENGTH OF SERVICE

For purposes of discussion, I propose to consider the members of each body in terms of three categories of membership: short, medium and long service, which will have to be defined independently for each institution in view of the different length of a term of office. Among soviet deputies, I consider short-term service as a membership of one or two terms only; medium-term includes deputies who served three, four or five terms (6–10 years); long-term refers to the smaller number of deputies who sat for over a decade. For gorkom members, where the nominal term of office is of one year's duration, the categorisation is as follows: short-term – those who served between one and five terms; medium-term – six to ten terms; and long-term – eleven or more terms. In approaching this question, however, one must ensure that analysis is based on those members whose length of service is known with a fair degree of certainty, and this involves some kind of selection process.

## The soviet

In most cases the careers of deputies before 1950 and after 1969 are not known: even though in 1950 it was revealed that forty-six deputies had just been elected for the second or third time,[1] they were not identified, so cannot be included in the study as far as selecting short-term or medium-term deputies is concerned. These two groups must be selected from among those with finite careers within the period under study, that is from those who entered the soviet in 1953 or later, and left in the

TABLE 4.1   *Length of service of 655 deputies*

| Length of service | Number | % |
|---|---|---|
| Short-term | 568 | 86.7 |
| Of whom: | | |
| 1 term | 463 | 70.7 |
| 2 terms | 105 | 16.0 |
| Medium-term (3–5 terms) | 65 | 9.9 |
| Long-term (over 5 terms) | 22 | 3.4 |

elections of 1967 or earlier. However, this restriction need not apply when selecting long serving deputies, and this group will contain all those who are known to have served six or more terms of office at any time in the period 1950–69.

On this basis, after eliminations, we are left with 655 individuals. Of these, 568 (86.7 per cent) served short terms, including 463 who sat for a single term of office: the full figures are included in Table 4.1, which shows the number and proportion of individuals who served short, medium and long terms as deputies. A little over one-eighth served for more than two terms. This means that once they have served their one or two terms the overwhelming majority of deputies are dropped, in most cases for good: the chances of a former deputy returning to the soviet after a period away, although not entirely negligible, are small, and may be connected with progress in his non-political career. Further discussion below will attempt to identify factors that may influence an individual's career on the soviet.

*The gorkom*

The period here covered eighteen terms of office, and complete information is available on the membership of fifteen committees. In making my selection, I eliminated those members who served on the first and last (xi and xxviii) gorkomy, and a small number from intermediate committees where information is lacking on immediately

TABLE 4.2 *Length of service of 439 gorkom members*

| Length of service | Membership category | | | Total | |
|---|---|---|---|---|---|
| | Full | Candidate | Full & candidate | No. | % |
| Short-term | 260 | 112 | 30 | 402 | 91.5 |
| Of whom: | | | | | |
| 1–2 terms | 205 | 107 | 13 | 325 | 74.0 |
| 3–5 terms | 55 | 5 | 17 | 77 | 17.5 |
| Medium-term | | | | | |
| (6–10 terms) | 17 | 0 | 7 | 24 | 5.5 |
| Long-term | | | | | |
| (over 10 terms) | 12 | 0 | 1 | 13 | 3.0 |
| TOTALS | 289 | 112 | 38 | 439 | |

previous or subsequent gorkomy; the major exceptions, as with the soviet, are again those who served long terms of office. On this basis, 439 individuals were finally selected, of whom 402 served for a short period only (including 325 for one or two terms of office), twenty-four served terms of medium length, and thirteen served for eleven or more terms of office (see Table 4.2, which also breaks down service according to membership status – full or candidate committee membership, or both – and gives percentage figures showing the balance between the various categories). As with the soviet, the overwhelming majority of gorkom members served for only short periods before being dropped. Again, this is consistent with the high level of turnover that was identified earlier, and points to constant change in personnel in the party apparatus.

## FACTORS AFFECTING LENGTH OF SERVICE

### Party membership

The question of party membership status applies of course only in the soviet, where there does appear to be a relationship between re-election and party status on entry: a person who was already a party member or candidate member when first elected was more likely to be elected for

TABLE 4.3    *Mean length of service on soviet and gorkom enjoyed by various social categories*

| Variable | Category | Mean soviet service (2-year terms) | Mean gorkom service (1-year terms) |
|---|---|---|---|
| Sex | Males | 1.75 | 2.63 |
| | Females | 1.41 | 2.03 |
| Age on entry | Under 30 | 1.41 | 1.41 |
| | 30–39 | 1.78 | 3.49 |
| | 40–49 | 1.80 | 3.39 |
| | 50–59 | 1.88 | 3.52 |
| | Over 60 | 2.67 | 4.00 |
| Occupation on entry | Industrial production | 1.37 | 1.71 |
| | Industrial management | 2.06 | 3.49 |
| | Party officials | 2.00 | 3.36 |
| | State officials | 2.35 | 2.82 |
| | T.U., Komsomol officials | 2.17 | 2.00 |
| | Law | 1.60 | 3.40 |
| | Security | 1.29 | 1.70 |
| | Trade | 1.29 | – |
| | Education | 1.91 | 2.95 |
| | Medicine | 1.67 | 3.50 |
| | Press, communications | 1.17 | 1.60 |
| | Others | 1.40 | 1.00 |
| Party membership on entry (deputies) | Non-party | 1.41 | |
| | Full members | 1.92 | |
| | Candidate members | 1.44 | |
| | Komsomol members | 1.33 | |
| Average for all deputies/members | | 1.61 | 2.30 |

further service than one who was not or who was a Komsomol member. A higher proportion of non-members and Komsomol members served only short terms (91.0 and 93.2 per cent respectively) than did either category of party affiliates (79.3 per cent of full and 88.9 per cent of candidate members), while a majority of medium- and long-term deputies were already party members when first elected (70.8 per cent of medium- and 77.3 per cent of long-termers). It is interesting that Komsomol membership was no help in securing re-election, and in fact was probably outweighed by the age factor. The mean length of service for the various categories of party membership confirms this interpretation. Figures for mean length of service related to a number of categories are presented in Table 4.3.

*Sex*

As figures given above show (p. 53), there was an extremely high turnover rate for all deputies, regardless of sex. Only a handful of deputies, of either sex, were privileged to serve for a decade or more; most were soviet members for only a couple of years. Yet there is an observable difference between the sexes, with males serving on average longer than their female colleagues. Whereas 316 (83.4 per cent) of males dropped out after only one or two terms of service, the rate among women was 91.3 per cent (252 out of 276); a single term was served by two-thirds of the men, but over three-quarters of the women. At the other end of the scale a mere 1.1 per cent of the women (three individuals) served long terms, whereas men did rather better: nineteen individuals, or 5.0 per cent. Thus, not only did men outnumber women in the initial selection process, as their numerical strength among deputies shows; in addition they were favoured by a higher level of re-election, and indeed repeated re-election.

We see a similar situation in the party committee: there was a high attrition rate for both sexes, but this was slightly less marked in the case of the males than of the females: 89.5 per cent of males, against 91.2 per cent of females served short terms; 6.3 per cent of males and 8.8 per cent of females served medium terms; all thirteen long-serving members were male. There is a measure of missing information, particularly among the short-termers, but taken as a whole the data do tend to support my contention that men are favoured in the re-election process.

These results are supported too by figures for the mean length of service in Table 4.3. On the soviet, male deputies served an average of

1.75 terms, compared with 1.41 for females; on the gorkom women members sat for 2.03 terms of office, against 2.63 for men.

Women are clearly at a disadvantage in local politics: they are initially selected for office in fewer numbers than men, and are less likely to be recruited for continued service.

*Age*

Although in crude actuarial terms younger politicians might be expected to serve longer in office than older men and women, in practice it seems that this is not so as far as the deputies are concerned, and it is doubtful among the gorkom members. I found that over 90 per cent of deputies aged under 30 on entry served for short terms only, and the proportion declines as entry age rises, to 82.9 per cent in the 30–39 age group, 80.0 per cent for those aged 50–59 and 66.7 per cent for those who entered in their sixties. By contrast, 15 per cent of those who entered aged 50–59 served for medium terms, as did 13.3 per cent of the 40–49 age group, and only 9.1 per cent of those under 30 on entry. One individual (0.6 per cent) among the under-thirties on entry served a long term, compared with about 5 per cent for the next three groups, and one of the three whose age on entry was 60 or over. Similarly, the mean length of service rises steadily with age on entry, so that deputies entering under 30 served an average of 1.41 terms, those in their forties – 1.80 terms, and those aged 60 and over – 2.67 terms. We can thus conclude that in general terms the older an individual when first recruited to the soviet, the greater his chances of re-election for continued office.

The results in the case of the gorkom are not so clear-cut, owing mainly to lack of information on the age of members. However, among those whose age is known, all twelve under-30 entrants served only short terms, while three-quarters to four-fifths of all other groups did so; medium terms were served by 14.3 per cent of the 30–39 group, 11.3 per cent of the 40–49 group, and 17.6 per cent of the 50–59 group; 6.5 per cent of the 30–39 group served long terms, as did 8.5 per cent of the 40–49 group, 5.9 per cent of the 50–59 group (one individual), and 20.0 per cent of the over-60 group (again, one individual). There seems to be a relationship between age on entry and length of service similar to that found in the soviet, and average service figures tend to support this, with the youngest members serving very short terms (see Table 4.3). However, the absence of data may have distorted these results, so it is wise to conclude that the relationship is not demonstrated with certainty, although it is probable that it exists.

## Occupation

The final sociological variable for which information is available is occupation, and substantial differences among the various groups can be identified, suggesting that occupation is of relevance in determining a person's career in local politics; it may indeed be the most crucial factor in re-election, as it has been shown to be in the USSR supreme soviet, the CPSU central committee, and the republican central committee.[2]

The results of the analysis of the 655 selected deputies are presented in Table 4.4. It will be seen that over half of the short-term deputies were production workers, and that 93.1 per cent of production workers served for short terms. In a variety of other occupations – security, trade, the press and communications – more than nine-tenths of the representatives served for only one or two terms, while only seven of the

TABLE 4.4    *Occupational distribution of 655 deputies*

| Length of service | Industrial production | Industrial management | Party officials | State officials | T.U., Komsomol officials | Law | Security | Trade | Education | Medicine | Press, communications | Others | Not available |
|---|---|---|---|---|---|---|---|---|---|---|---|---|---|
| Short-term | 285 | 63 | 17 | 21 | 3 | 5 | 23 | 17 | 51 | 20 | 11 | 9 | 43 |
| Of whom: | | | | | | | | | | | | | |
| 1 term | 235 | 48 | 15 | 19 | 3 | 2 | 18 | 15 | 38 | 17 | 9 | 7 | 37 |
| 2 terms | 50 | 15 | 2 | 2 | 0 | 3 | 5 | 2 | 13 | 3 | 2 | 2 | 6 |
| Medium-term | 17 | 12 | 4 | 10 | 3 | 0 | 1 | 1 | 12 | 3 | 1 | 1 | 0 |
| Long-term | 4 | 8 | 2 | 3 | 0 | 0 | 0 | 0 | 2 | 1 | 0 | 0 | 2 |
| TOTALS | 306 | 83 | 23 | 34 | 6 | 5 | 24 | 18 | 65 | 24 | 12 | 10 | 45 |

twelve occupational groups had members surviving for six or more terms on the soviet. In numerical terms, the longest-serving group were those who entered as industrial managers: eight out of eighty-three survived six or more terms. Four deputies who came in as production workers survived six terms or more, but one of these had been promoted to minor managerial rank after two terms. These distinctions in length of service among various occupational groups are confirmed by reference to the mean length of service (Table 4.3), which varied from 1.17 terms for press and communications representatives, to 1.37 for industrial workers, 2.00 for party officials and 2.35 for state officials; these are measured against an average figure of 1.61 for all 655 deputies.

Analysis of the gorkom membership is complicated by two factors that I have commented on before: lack of information, and the fact that some gorkom members held more than one office – their regular employment, and simultaneously a party, trade union or Komsomol post, which is probably of much greater significance in determining the course of an individual's career on the committee. In preparing my tables, such overlapping has been eliminated.

TABLE 4.5　*Occupational distribution of 439 gorkom members*

| Length of service | Industrial production | Industrial management | Party officials | State officials | T.U., Komsomol officials | Law | Security | Education | Medicine | Press, communications | Others | Not available |
|---|---|---|---|---|---|---|---|---|---|---|---|---|
| | | | | | Occupation on entry | | | | | | | |
| Short-term | 31 | 46 | 59 | 20 | 11 | 4 | 10 | 17 | 3 | 5 | 3 | 193 |
| Of whom: | | | | | | | | | | | | |
| 1–2 terms | 25 | 35 | 46 | 14 | 8 | 2 | 8 | 9 | 1 | 4 | 3 | 170 |
| 3–5 terms | 6 | 11 | 13 | 6 | 3 | 2 | 2 | 8 | 2 | 1 | 0 | 23 |
| Medium-term | 1 | 9 | 5 | 2 | 0 | 1 | 0 | 3 | 1 | 0 | 0 | 2 |
| Long-term | 0 | 4 | 8 | 1 | 0 | 0 | 0 | 0 | 0 | 0 | 0 | 0 |
| TOTALS | 32 | 59 | 72 | 23 | 11 | 5 | 10 | 20 | 4 | 5 | 3 | 195 |

Although in all occupational categories a large majority of identified members served for only short terms (see Table 4.5), there do appear to be differences among the various groups, indicating that occupation is of relevance in determining a person's career on the gorkom. Most industrial workers, for example, served only short terms; but long periods on the committee were enjoyed by identified members of three groups: state officials, industrial managers and party officials. However, comparisons of the mean length of service (Table 4.3) lead towards a different conclusion, with medical workers, industrial managers, lawyers and party officials serving longer than the average, and industrial production workers, security officers, communications workers and members of the residual group serving for comparatively short terms.

These figures may have been distorted by missing data, yet it is interesting to make a comparison between the results for the soviet and those for the gorkom. Thus, we find that industrial managers and party officials tended to serve long on both bodies; industrial production workers, security officers, and workers in press and communications served for short periods on both; trade workers served for short terms on the soviet, and were not mentioned in the case of the gorkom; educational workers served for average terms on both. These similarities may reflect the political status of these occupations: the fact that security officers served for only short terms on both bodies is probably because they are posted to the town for short tours of duty and quickly moved on. However, there are striking differences between state and party institutions: state officials, the longest-serving group of deputies, served for only average terms on the gorkom; so did trade union and Komsomol officials. Lawyers, by contrast, served on average more terms on the gorkom than on the soviet (and, in fact, with an average service of 3.2 years – 1.60 terms – on the soviet, and 3.4 nominal years on the gorkom, their actual mean length of service there was greater). Medical workers, too, appear to have served longer on the gorkom than on the soviet, although the number of cases is small, and so the figure is not necessarily reliable. It is interesting to note that industrial management appeared to be a 'safer' recruiting ground than party office-holding: this reflects rapid turnover among lower party officials, many of whom enjoyed a brief period of prominence, during which they were elected to the gorkom for one or two terms, before disappearing from the political scene into obscurity.

### Gorkom candidate membership

There is one further characteristic of recruitment into the gorkom that must be considered: the relationship between full and candidate membership of the committee. The question is whether there is much transfer from one category of membership to the other. According to Cattell, 'Candidacy is usually a stepping stone to full membership' of the Leningrad gorkom.[3] However, he provides no evidence of this, and his assertion may be based on the fact that candidate membership of the *party* is a period of probation, which does usually lead on to full membership. Certainly candidate membership is not probationary in this sense in the Moldavian central committee: a mere fourteen of the ninety-nine full members of the 1963 committee were identified as having served as candidate members, and in one of those cases this followed a term as a full member.[4] Similarly with the CPSU central committee: Gehlen and McBride have indicated that 'Some particular types of specialists may consistently be given candidate status',[5] suggesting that an individual's position in society, rather than previous central committee history, influences the committee status he is given; any 'stepping stone' phenomenon would be the result of an individual's specific career pattern, not of a policy towards candidate membership. What was the situation in Tiraspol?

The answer appears to be that candidate membership was not used in a probationary sense, although there was movement between the two categories. In the fifteen committees for which information is available, there were, as we have seen, 1331 places, filled by 600 individuals. Of these, 404 (67.7 per cent) served only as full members, without going through a prior stage of candidate membership; 134 (22.4 per cent) served as candidate members only, and were never promoted to full membership; a mere fifty-nine individuals (9.9 per cent) served on the committee in both categories. Moreover, in some of those cases candidate membership followed a spell as a full member, and some returned to full membership even after that. The number of individuals for whom candidate membership can be regarded as a 'stepping stone' to full membership is thus reduced to forty-one, or a mere 7.1 per cent.

It is thus clear that candidacy was not usually a stepping stone to full membership. I would suggest that an individual's political career progresses more or less regardless of any experience as a gorkom candidate member. The fact that this coincides with the findings of studies at other levels leads me to conclude that this is normal party practice.

## WHO ARE THE ELITE MEMBERS?

In previous sections, I have tried to identify patterns in the recruitment of soviet and gorkom members that might point to factors influencing the selection process. The following points stand out clearly: men are re-elected in greater proportion than women; there is greater stability (in the soviet) among party members than among non-party deputies; there is greater turnover among the young than the older; and there are considerable differences in turnover between the various occupations. These characteristics of elite recruitment lead to a particular kind of membership structure at any one time, and I will identify this with reference to the soviet, where the information at our disposal is fuller.

Among the deputies, two groups can be identified: those with a clustering of what one might term 'weak' characteristics (low-status occupation; youth; lack of party membership; female sex), and those with 'strong' characteristics (responsible, high-status occupation; maturity; party membership; and male sex). This division can be demonstrated by simple bi-variate analysis of the various characteristics. For this, I return to the approach adopted in the previous chapter, and look at the kind of persons who occupied places on the soviet. In view of repeated election and the possibility of changes in some variable (party membership status, occupation and, of course, age) it is not appropriate to look at one point in time, and the aggregate pattern is more reliable.

There were, as we saw, 1728 positions on the soviet over the nine terms of office; 1081 of these were taken by men and 647 by women. Among the places taken by men, 823 (76.1 per cent) went to party members, 24 (2.2 per cent) to Komsomol members, and 181 (16.7 per cent) to non-party males; among the places taken by women, however, 102 (15.8 per cent) were taken by known Komsomol members, 287 (44.4 per cent) by non-party women, and only 218 (33.7 per cent) by party members and candidates. In terms of other variables, too, women tended to be weaker: 255 women (39.4 per cent) were under 30, and 419 (64.8 per cent) under 40; for males the comparable figures were 73 (6.8 per cent) and 375 (34.7 per cent); the mean average age on election was 34.8 years for places taken by women and 42.6 years for places taken by men. In terms of occupation, 568 men (52.5 per cent) and 406 women (62.8 per cent) were engaged in industry; 274 men (25.3 per cent) were in the administrative sector, compared with 45 women (7.0 per cent); 157 men (14.5 per cent) were engaged in the provision of facilities, against 189 women (29.2 per cent). These figures show differences between the sexes in overall occupational groups; but even within those broad groups there were further distinctions. Thus, in the industrial sector, of the 568 places taken by men, 253 (44.5 per cent) were reserved for managerial staff, whereas out of the 406 places that went to women, only 43 (10.6 per cent) went to managers; in this sector, women production workers actually outnumbered men (363 places taken by women workers, against 315 by men).

From this it is clear that women deputies were in a generally weaker social position than their male colleagues: they tended to be younger, not to be party members, and to come from the less prestigious occupations. Male deputies tended to be older, party members, and employed in the more responsible and prestigious occupations.

Soviet writers have also paid some attention to this kind of analysis, and produced results that show that Tiraspol is far from untypical. An Armenian study, for example, revealed that six out of ten deputies under 40 years of age were women, while among the over-forties men accounted for 85 per cent.[6] This study, which was aimed at measuring the effectiveness of local soviets as representative organs, took as its basic premise the idea that 'deputies of local soviets should, as representative organs of the whole people, reflect the structure of the population'. The authors found significant discrepancies, and concluded that 'this composition should be corrected with regard to both age and sex. This applies in particular with respect to deputies aged over thirty-five.' They pointed out that in other republics, including Moldavia, the role of women in local soviets was greater, judging by their greater numerical strength. I have no figures on which to assess how closely the composition of Tiraspol town soviet corresponded to the composition of the adult population: however, it can confidently be said that the sociological characteristics of the population are unlikely to be clustered quite so dramatically as those of the deputies in this study.

These correlations can be expressed another way, using different basic variables; the same clustering effect becomes apparent, as the following figures demonstrate. First, taking party membership as the base, we find the following:

| *Non-party deputy places (468)* | | *Party member deputy places (1041)* |
| --- | --- | --- |
| % | | % |
| 61.3 | Women | 20.9 |
| 63.7 | Under 40 | 35.0 |
| 69.4 | Industrial production workers | 21.0 |
| 5.8 | Industrial management | 24.2 |
| 23.5 | Facilities sector | 18.3 |

Hence we can conclude that non-party deputies tended to be women, younger, and employed in the less prestigious occupations; party member deputies tended to be men, older, and engaged in the more responsible and prestigious occupations.

Taking age as the base, we find similar results:

| *Under-40 deputy places (794)* | | *Over-40 deputy places (804)* |
| --- | --- | --- |
| % | | % |
| 52.8 | Women | 23.1 |
| 37.5 | Non-party | 21.1 |
| 45.8 | Party | 78.9 |
| 58.4 | Industrial production workers | 22.6 |
| 9.4 | Industrial management | 25.2 |
| 12.5 | Administration | 23.6 |

These figures lead towards the conclusion that the older deputies tended to be male, party members, and with considerable strength in the more responsible occupations; the younger deputies tended to be women, with a high proportion of non-party deputies, and a high proportion of workers in less responsible jobs.

Similar results apply with occupation taken as the base: the places taken by representatives of the less prestigious jobs tended to be also younger, not party members, with greater female representation, while the more prestigious jobs tended to go to men, who were older and usually party members.

The turnover and re-election patterns I identified earlier add a further dimension to this clustering, so that the situation is perpetuated and enhanced. The 'strong' deputies gain the possibility of becoming entrenched in the soviet, while the 'weak' are not generally there long enough for their individual impact to develop. Soviet writers have shown themselves aware of this problem, and a longer term of office has been suggested in order to permit the new recruits to make a positive contribution after they have learnt procedures and so on. A writer quoted by Frolic has stated that 'Only after one year is a new deputy ready to do anything significant ... the average term should be four years'.[7] Frolic also quotes a Moscow official who also recommended doubling the term to four years: 'there is so much for them to learn, so many problems to deal with, that two years just aren't enough.'[8] One might add the comment that, in comparison with these 'weak' recruits, how much stronger is the position of the deputy of several years' standing. Moreover, the differentiation in election patterns has also been identified at the USSR supreme soviet level,[9] so it is not unreasonable to conclude that it is a general phenomenon in the Soviet political system.

The absence of crucial data on sex, age and occupation on a significant scale renders this kind of analysis impossible to repeat for the gorkom. However, the results of the single-variable analysis that was performed in previous sections, and the differences in average length of service of various groups, do support the proposition that similar factors applied there too; and individual cases can be found to illustrate the point (see chapter 8). The general characteristics of the gorkom membership are such that it can be seen as a far more prestigeful body than the soviet, and more tightly controlled in its membership. The proportions of women, young persons, and representatives of the low-status occupations are far smaller than among the deputies, giving the committee a much greater appearance of an 'elite'. The gorkom may indeed be considered as a separate section of the town's political elite, and one that is more exclusive, hence perhaps less representative of general interests than is the soviet. It must be borne in mind, however, that membership of one body does not exclude membership of the other, and this further important dimension of the town's political elite will be extensively investigated in chapter 6.

## THE EXECUTIVE MEMBERS

I have now identified patterns in the personal characteristics of deputies and, to a limited extent, gorkom members, that permit me to characterise individuals as 'strong' and 'weak'. When I similarly analysed the members of the two executive bodies – the gorispolkom and the gorkom buro – I found that both tend to be composed of individuals with 'strong' characteristics.

Over our eighteen-year period, membership details were published on eight of the nine gorispolkomy: a total of seventy-eight places, which were filled by forty-seven individual deputies. This information permits one to make a number of generalisations. First, note a preponderance of *men*: barely a quarter were women – twelve of the forty-seven, indicating further apparent discrimination against them, already more weakly represented in the body of deputies than were men (although in the executive committee, too, they are probably more strongly represented than in most western countries).

Secondly, all but three gorispolkom members were *full or candidate members of the party* by the time they became executive committee members, and one of those three, a woman, later joined the party. This too is a higher level of representation in the executive committee than in the full soviet, even though party membership there involved a majority of deputies.

The *age* at which members first joined the gorispolkom varied from 29 to 57, although the majority were under 45: the average age on election for those who entered after 1950 was 41.7 years. This suggests that the really young deputies are discriminated against, presumably because of their inexperience, as are older deputies, perhaps because they are regarded as having passed their peak.

The *occupational* breakdown of members tends to support this: the majority (thirty-five individuals) were active politicians at some time in their careers: some currently held state and party office (officers of the gorispolkom itself, gorkom secretaries, Komsomol gorkom secretaries, chairman of the town party–state control committee); others attained such a position before, after or during their gorispolkom membership; four served as permanent commission chairmen. The remaining eight included a surgeon, a research station head, an industrial management official, and two skilled workers.

Finally, ispolkom members on average *served longer* as deputies: the average length of service for all deputies in the selected group was 1.61 terms, but for those who rose to membership of the gorispolkom it was 3.6 terms; eleven were deputies for three terms, nine for four terms, and eight for six terms; two served for eight terms.

All these characteristics point to the strength of the gorispolkom as a body of individuals: these factors set them apart from the ordinary deputies, and give the executive committee prestige and probably political influence beyond that conferred on it by statute. A final observation: most ispolkom members achieved that position as soon as they entered the soviet, or after only one term as deputy. This, no doubt, reflects the fact that the posts occupied by most gorispolkom members are governed by nomenklatura, and their executive committee membership is tied to their position; in other words, gorispolkom membership is 'ex officio', and this concept will be further explored below.

The same applies also to the gorkom buro, which had a similar composition: headed by gorkom secretaries and otdel heads, its membership also included the gorispolkom chairman, usually the editor of the town newspaper, the Komsomol gorkom first secretary, and a security officer; these numbers were filled out by occasional industrial managers and workers, ppo secretaries, and others. Stewart found a similar balance at the obkom buro level.[10] Analysed in detail, of the fifty-six known buro members, only three were women (and on half of the buros no woman was present); eighteen members served as gorkom secretary, five as Komsomol gorkom first secretary, six as gorispolkom chairman and six in industrial management; five edited the local newspaper, two were chairmen of the popular control town committee, and seven were security officers. There is some overlapping among these, since individuals moved around while remaining on the buro; but the dominance of the 'strong' occupations is in evidence. As with the soviet, most came into the buro on their first or second term of gorkom office (twenty-six immediately on election, ten after one term on the committee); one individual had served seven terms, and another eleven, but these are the exception rather than the rule, and membership is in most cases linked with 'nomenklatura' positions in the town. The buro thus seems deliberately composed to create an effective decision-making unit, with all the most responsible officials in the town present.

The true significance of this lies in the fact that appointment to these nomenklatura posts is the prerogative of authorities outside the town. The opportunities for locally trained politicians to achieve buro and gorispolkom membership, and thereby influence decisions in matters affecting the town, thus depend not on how effectively they can impress the electorate, the broad party membership, or even the ordinary membership of the gorkom and soviet; rather these groups are at the mercy of the central republican authorities, who may select any individuals from within or outside the town for nomination to those positions. There is therefore little local control over the composition of the executive organs, and the elective principle in their formation is drastically reduced. The town is governed by nominees of the central authorities, who may have little commitment to the town, its problems and needs. How far local interests can be articulated and taken into consideration by those with power to reach decisions must partly depend on two sets of personal relations: those among executive committee members; and those between them and the wider membership of the elective bodies, together with the heads of various administrative departments and of institutions and enterprises in the town.

## 'Ex Officio' Elite Membership

This principle can be extended to the ordinary membership of the soviet and the gorkom, for it is clear that there is a relationship between the tenancy of specific positions in the town and membership of either or both of those bodies. Such a relationship exists at other levels, as several studies have firmly established. Gehlen and McBride identify a number of appointments that seem to carry CPSU central committee membership with them, virtually on an 'ex officio' basis;[11] the main conclusion of my study of the Moldavian central committee was that the tenancy of specific posts in the administration of the republic carries with it membership of the committee;[12] Stewart's discussion of the Stalingrad obkom implies that such a system was in operation there too.[13] These studies all apply to the party apparatus. It is not certain that one would expect to find the same in the soviets, although strong evidence from Soviet sources indicates that the practice has been widespread in the past. Thus, a CPSU central committee resolution of 1957 criticised the fact that some election candidates were put forward 'simply on an occupational basis';[14] the fact that the same point was repeated in articles written in 1967 and 1970[15] shows that the phenomenon had generally still not been eradicated. On this basis at least, we should expect to find the same in Tiraspol.

In fact, in addition to the executive committee membership, a number of specific posts (the list is not necessarily complete) can be identified as being related in this way to political institutions. The incumbents are automatically selected for membership of the town soviet or party committee; if they are removed from the post, and not transferred to a post of equivalent political relevance, they do not retain membership of the soviet or gorkom, but their successors are admitted. In the soviet, the gorkom first secretaryship was normally such a position, as we might expect; similarly, from 1959 at any rate, the first secretary of the Komsomol gorkom was also elected a deputy following election to that post. Other gorkom secretaries were also members of the soviet, perhaps automatically; so was the editor of the local newspaper, formally a joint organ of the soviet and the gorkom. In the opposite direction, it can be said that the gorispolkom chairman was always a member of the gorkom; however, apart from possibly the militia department, none of the headships of gorispolkom departments appears to have carried automatic membership of the party committee. Industrial posts did bring such political responsibilities, although it is not easy to determine which individual plants or their precise number. (One reason for this is that factories were amalgamated, or their names changed, or other organisational changes intervened, making it impossible to trace directorships accurately.) In the soviet, nevertheless, the 'Kirov' mechanical works, the '1st May' fruit and vegetable conserving works, the bread combine, and the 'Fortieth anniversary of the Komsomol' clothing factory all appear to be such enterprises, along with probably one or two other industrial units such as the railway station: the director of each was normally elected to a place on the soviet.

This process can be illustrated by tracing the history of the directorship of the '1st May' works. The director in 1950, I. F. Kotlyarov, was a member of the soviet elected in that year. By 1953 he had been replaced by D. M. Zvegintsev, who entered the soviet in 1953 and served only one term; two years later, I. M. Dryagin had been appointed director, and he entered the 1955 soviet. He too served for only one term, and was replaced as director by F. D. Shtan'ko, who came into the soviet in 1957. The promotion to director of the factory's chief engineer, N. P. Bushtyan – already a deputy – brought Shtan'ko's membership of the soviet to an end, and Bushtyan retained his position and his place on the soviet until the 1963–65 term of office. From June 1964 or earlier he was replaced by V. I. Panasevich, and he left the soviet; Panasevich came in and was re-elected in 1967, still holding the post of works director. Here the association between soviet membership and tenancy of the factory directorship is clear. In other cases, factory managers occasionally served on the soviet, perhaps not of right, but possibly on a rota basis, although the evidence is not strong enough to confirm this.

The case of the '1st May' conserving works directorship is interesting since the same example can be used to show the same phenomenon in the gorkom. Thus, Kotlyarov served as a member of the xii committee (and possibly of the xiii); Zvegintsev was on the xiv; Dryagin served on the xv and xvi; Shtan'ko on the xviii; Bushtyan, who had already served on the xi and from the xvii, continued to serve until and including the xxiii; and Panasevich came in at the xxvi (possibly the xxv) conference and served until the end of the period. Gorkom membership appears also to be associated with the directorship of the 'Tkachenko' works, and the directorship of the 'Kirov' works seems to have carried gorkom full membership as well as soviet membership. This connection shows the *political* nature of these ostensibly *economic* positions in the town.

The secretaryships of the major ppos also probably carried such automatic, 'ex officio' gorkom membership. Thus, five incumbents of the post of party secretary in the 'Kirov' works have been identified, and in all cases election to the gorkom followed their appointment; in four identified cases the party secretary of the '1st May' works was also subsequently appointed to the gorkom (such ppo secretaryships are, of course, on the gorkom's own nomenklatura list). The Komsomol gorkom first secretaryship normally brought party gorkom full membership (and membership of the buro as well), along with soviet membership, and the same applies to the key legal post of town procurator.

## THE ELITE SELECTION PROCESS

In the foregoing sections I have demonstrated several important aspects of elite recruitment, even though in the absence of certain data I could not quantify some factors exactly. It should be borne in mind, however, that the selection of personnel – whether for political or ostensibly economic posts – is a complex procedure, involving, it is assumed, personal characteristics and qualities, as well as professional competence and political reliability, any of which might be dominant in a given case or situation. An individual might be selected for the soviet and the gorkom because he holds a particular managerial post; yet conversely, a person might be appointed to a managerial position if he has shown sufficient political merit to have already been selected for gorkom or soviet membership. Thus, in one of the cases cited above, N. P. Bushtyan was appointed director of the '1st May' works not only after a number of years as the factory's chief engineer (during which he had demonstrated his professional competence), but also after service on both the soviet and the gorkom (in 1950), when he had no doubt shown his political reliability; full membership of the Moldavian central committee came later, in 1961.

Obviously, the factors that I have identified as relevant to the selection process would need careful examination if I wished to establish why particular individuals were elected, re-elected or dropped at a particular time. A further factor to be added is political loyalty and reliability, as perceived by the appropriate authorities within the town or outside it. However, the materials examined in this chapter reveal further dimensions in the task of selecting elite members, in both party and state, so it becomes possible to make certain generalisations and tentatively put forward a model. It is clear that any model of the selection process must be relatively complex. Neither the general public (for the soviet), nor the party conference (for the gorkom), nor officials at any one level make the total selection of members for these bodies. Instead, the selection processes in each case probably take place at several levels and in several stages.

First of all, there are a number of official appointments that are the prerogative (i.e. are on the nomenklatura list) of the republican authorities: key administrative posts in the gorkom and soviet apparatus. It is possible too that the central, all-Union authorities are consulted in the appointment of individuals to such posts, which take up a fairly small number of places on each body. Next come other positions, such as I have identified, which carry 'ex officio' membership of either the soviet or the gorkom, or both. It is impossible to identify, on the basis of the available information, at what level these nominations are made. It seems reasonable to assume that the republican authorities have at least a consultative voice in the initial appointment; it is less certain that they decide which posts are to carry automatic membership of one or both of the town's main political institutions. This may depend on the size of the enterprise or institution, its production turnover, the size and importance of its party organisation, and similar features, including even tradition and prestige in the case of certain long-established industrial works. Thirdly, there may be a group of responsible officials whose positions do not automatically qualify them for a political position, but may do so intermittently, possibly even on a rota basis: a number of incumbents of such positions serve at any one time, perhaps for only one or two terms of office, after which a second set from the group are selected for political service; the original incumbents may return at a later date. A fourth group might consist of individuals with no special occupational position to qualify them for repeated election, but whose personal merit brings them to the attention of the selectors. Then, finally, there is a fifth group in each institution consisting of 'ordinary' deputies or party members, who are selected in order to balance out the membership in accordance with norms on the desired composition, which are defined at the republic or all-Union level.

The selection process might then take place in several stages. First, the nomenklatura officials would be allocated their places, followed by the 'ex officio' members; the 'rota' members would similarly be chosen and allocated to their constituencies, or allotted their gorkom positions; the next group, consisting of particularly meritorious individuals, would follow. In the soviet, arrangements would be made for all the individuals concerned to be adopted by an appropriate nominating body; for the gorkom, officials could ensure nomination at the town party conference.

It is at the next stage – in both party and state – that the element of choice built into the Constitution and party rules might come into play. For elections to the soviet, individual production units in the town would be allocated a constituency or ward for which they might nominate election candidates; informal soundings might take place beforehand, and these nominating bodies might be given a hint as to the kind of candidate whom they should put forward. A fairly wide spectrum of candidates might be nominated at that stage, consisting – apart from individuals whose candidature has been sponsored by the authorities – of potential deputies with 'weak' characteristics who would serve in most cases for only a comparatively short period; they could also include candidates who had already served on the soviet. At the stage of final selection, under the guidance of the gorkom's organisational department, attention would be concentrated on this group, and the choice from their number made in accordance with the desired composition, bearing in mind that a number of places are already filled, and quotas on particular variables already partly – possibly wholly – taken up. As the process nears completion, social characteristics would tend to become more relevant than merit in individual cases, and a final category might stipulate five female Komsomol members in industrial production jobs, in order to fill norms on several characteristics at once.

The process is probably less clearly defined in the party committee, where the size of the body is not fixed, and the selectors have consequently more room to manoeuvre. Nomination procedures are not published, but are regulated by a special central committee Instruction, entitled 'On Carrying Out Elections to Leading Party Organs'. According to this Instruction, as expounded in the book *Raionnyi komitet partii*,[16] representatives of delegations to the conference may (at the discretion of the conference presidium) meet for preliminary discussion and nomination of candidates, although this is supposed not to prejudice the rights of conference delegates to make further nominations and reject agreed nominees. Each individual candidate is to be discussed, prior to secret ballot in closed conference session, attended by only the voting delegates; the results are announced to all delegates. These procedures, if adhered to, give some discretion to the local officials who control the conference, and doubtful cases can be sanctioned by the republican representative who is always present on such occasions. As a general rule the composition of a party committee (as of a soviet) is expected to contain representatives of all branches of the economy. As *Raionnyi komitet partii* expresses it:

> If in a *raion* there is a preponderance of industrial enterprises, then into the composition of the *raikom* are elected predominantly worker communists, engineering and technical workers, economic leaders, and leading specialists. At the same time representatives of other branches of the economy and institutions should not be forgotten: schools, institutions of public service, trade and catering. If in a raion's economy the main position is occupied by agricultural production, then into the party organ are elected collective farmer communists, farm machinery workers, agronomists, farm managers, leading specialists in agriculture. It is extremely important that into the new composition should go the most capable and authoritative communists.[17]

Many of these 'most capable and authoritative communists' are, of course, selected in advance, so the final selection may consist of rather less authoritative individuals whose presence on the gorkom, like that of the 'weak' deputies on the soviet, is comparatively short-lived. Soviet comment on party elections in an article published in 1973 tends to support my broad interpretation: although referring specifically to elections in primary organisations, it speaks of a distinct tendency in recent years to confirm (re-elect) party cadres who know how to do their job skilfully, while at the same time bringing in fresh, young persons, drawn from among production workers; moreover, the article states that 'There is no doubt that this is the correct line'.[18]

## CONCLUSION

Concentrating on the individual participants in the town's political institutions, I have in this chapter examined more closely some of the principles that became evident in my earlier discussion of trends in the composition of those bodies. I noted that the overwhelming majority of members served for short periods only – most for a single term of office. I noted too that the personal characteristics of members fell into distinct patterns, so that two kinds of deputy, and I believe gorkom member, could be identified: the 'weak' and the 'strong' – the younger, non-party members, women, in unspectacular jobs, against the older, party member males in prestigious occupations. I discovered that not only did such a pattern apply at any one time, but it was also superimposed on the selection process, so that the 'weak' tended to serve for short terms, and the 'strong' for longer terms. Further investigation of the identity of the leading politicians – specifically members of the two executive bodies – revealed that a system of 'ex officio' membership is in operation, which at this level can be connected with the nomenklatura system. However, the same practice applies outside the executive bodies: a number of posts in the town carry with them, more or less automatically, membership of either the town soviet, or the gorkom, or both. Their total number cannot be identified, but sufficient cases were identified to establish the point.

This led me, finally, to suggest a possible model for the selection of elite members, whereby members are chosen in several stages, and according to different criteria. It is impossible to check the validity of such a model at the present stage of our knowledge: we have no means of knowing how the electoral commissions operate, or even the nature of the 'norms' handed down by the central authorities.[19] The model fits the known facts on composition and turnover patterns in Tiraspol, and accords with what is known of procedures elsewhere. But until local archives become available to western scholars, or it becomes feasible for Soviet scholars to examine these questions openly, it seems unlikely that it will be possible to confirm it.

These limited conclusions permit one to make some judgement on the efficacy of these institutions. First, as Soviet commentators have pointed out, a two-year term does not give the inexperienced deputy enough time to learn his job and then use his skills to benefit his electors, nor would a single term of office – possibly of less than a year – on the gorkom permit the ordinary member to have much impact on the course of debates. The high level of turnover is partly designed to give as many citizens or party members as possible a chance to take part in public life, and hence perhaps satisfy some of their ambitions. However, if most are allowed to remain in office for only a short time, such a policy cannot meet this particular aim in the long term. Giving ambitious men and women a brief taste of political participation and influence as a deputy or a gorkom member might simply whet their appetite and increase the sense of frustration when their services are no longer required.

When we recognise the division into 'strong' and 'weak' members, the political implications of such a structural feature are immediately apparent. The 'strong' possess such great prestige that they could conceivably dominate the workings of the two institutions; and their repeated re-election gives them experience, familiarity with pro-cedures, and a whole background of information that places them in a different political category from the 'weak'. These suffer the difficulty of having to overcome their initial inhibitions, and by the time they are perhaps feeling at ease in their new role, a new election comes up and they are replaced, in all likelihood by someone just as inexperienced as they were two years previously. In this situation, it would not be surprising to find evidence of domination by the 'strong': this question will be examined in the next chapter.

Finally, I may remark that the discussion in this and the previous chapters points to a dilemma for Soviet local politics (and, indeed, it is not unique to that system: Kazimirchuk and Adamyan refer to the work of Duverger in this context[20]). This is, how to combine expertise and continuity with the broadest, fullest involvement of the masses in local government, a question that reflects on the system's capabilities. And there is a further problem: how to ensure that these local political structures provide an adequate vehicle for a career in public life, not only for those who have already established themselves, but also for those who aspire and are striving to do so. Patterns in the composition of both the soviet and the gorkom over time, and interpretations of the selection process, suggest that both institutions have their limitations in this respect; in the context of Soviet society, the alternative channels for participation in public life – where they exist – are severely restricted. If the population show signs of cynicism and frustration with politics, as has been suggested,[21] this may be one reason for it.

# CHAPTER 5

# The Elite in Action:
# Soviet and Gorkom Meetings

In this chapter I examine the formal meetings of the gorkom and soviet: how often did they take place? what topics did they discuss? who participated in the discussions? were there any observable patterns in the public behaviour of the deputies and gorkom members?[1]

Discussion has to be limited to the information available in newspaper reports, because of the lack of access to local archives containing fuller accounts of the proceedings. The published record is known to contain gaps,[2] and there are limitations in the accounts that appear. Nevertheless, an examination of the press reports does permit some judgement on the work of the elite members, particularly in the later years when the record was fuller. For this reason, my analysis is based largely on reports published in the years 1964–67, with further comparative references to earlier years.

## THE FREQUENCY OF MEETINGS

According to the Statute on Town Soviets (Article 28), sessions are to be held at least six times a year; they are normally called by the executive committee.[3] In most years, Tiraspol town soviet adhered to its legal requirements, holding six sessions in 1960, 1964, 1966 and 1967; in 1965 it met only five times, however. In earlier years, when legislation required monthly sessions,[4] the soviet met only eleven times in 1955 and 1950. The party rules are less demanding, requiring that plenums be held once every three months (1961, Rule 51), a reduction from the monthly meetings prescribed by the previous rules (Rule 52). During 1964–67 sixteen plenums are known to have been held, so that the committee on average precisely filled its norm.

However, in both institutions, the sessions were held *irregularly*. For the soviet, the period between sessions varied from three weeks (7–28 July 1965) to nineteen weeks (18 July–29 November 1967); in the gorkom, the interval ranged from three weeks (28 January–18 February 1967) to twenty-six weeks (20 July 1964–17 January 1965, assuming no unreported plenums took place in the interim).

Thus, in practice the letter of the law was broadly adhered to, while the spirit of regularity was infringed. This is a widespread and long-standing problem that has been critically commented on by Soviet writers. Surilov, for example, discussing the work of the Moldavian local soviets elected in December 1950, writes that 'as before there were flagrant violations in the regularity with which sessions were called';[5] for Barabashev this practice is a 'crude infringement of socialist legality';[6] and Kozlova states categorically that mere adherence to the letter of the law, while infringing its spirit, is not satisfactory.[7] In recent years stress has been placed, too, on regularly holding party committee plenums: D. A. Kunaev, Kazakhstan central committee first secretary, clearly indicating official policy, wrote in 1966 that 'The role of party committee plenums has also been significantly raised. They are *convened regularly*, are better prepared, and take place in a businesslike atmosphere.'[8] The evidence of Tiraspol shows that both institutions were infringing the accepted interpretation of party and governmental statutes; yet equally clearly, Tiraspol was not unusual in this respect, as these Soviet writers testify.

In view of this irregularity, is it possible to identify factors that prompt the calling of meetings? For example, does the pattern of topics discussed suggest that they are convened at the request of higher bodies, to discuss items of burning national importance? Does it indicate careful and systematic planning of these organs' work over a term of office? Does it reflect problems that arise within the town itself? Is there anything in the pattern that might indicate a possible division of functions between the two institutions? Indeed, what topics were debated in the soviet sessions and the gorkom plenums?

## THE BUSINESS OF THE MEETINGS

A recurrent item on the agenda of both the soviet and the gorkom was 'organisational questions', that is personnel appointments, especially to the executive bodies. Apart from the initial allocation of portfolios at the first post-election meeting, further adjustments become necessary during a term of office, due to transfers, promotions and demotions, and occasionally deaths, and these are formalised by a full meeting of the appropriate body. Thus, both the soviet and the gorkom met in February 1967 to approve a complex set of changes involving key posts in the political apparatus – the gorispolkom chairmanship, a gorkom secretaryship, and the popular control gorkom chairmanship, among others.

An important point of interest in these 'organisational questions' is that in perhaps most cases the changes have already been enacted by authority of the appropriate executive body, most likely in response to orders from a higher level, through the nomenklatura system. The full plenary session of the soviet or gorkom is then required simply to endorse the executive's action; if the change has already been implemented, obviously the full meeting can do very little to reverse the situation, particularly when ultimate responsibility lies elsewhere. If, say, the soviet refused to uphold a gorispolkom dispensation, the soviet's decision would simply be countermanded by the republican authorities. So the executive body's action is normally endorsed retrospectively; hence the full session performs a 'rubber stamp' function. This is standard procedure in the Soviet legislative process, and is occasionally carried to lengths that would be contrary to legal principles in most western parliamentary systems. For instance, the Moldavian supreme soviet elected in June 1971 ratified decrees issued by the presidium of the *previous legislature*, including some relating to the appointment of ministers to the pre-election government. Since these changes had been effective for over four months, and had in any case formally ceased to be valid following the intervening election, the supreme soviet could not but concur.[9] This practice of government by decree followed by retrospective legislative formalisation obviously gives the executive bodies and higher authorities great power and freedom of initiative.

This is an example of a political practice that the town authorities 'borrow' from higher levels. 'Organisational questions' provide us with another example, where an unclear point in legislation is overcome by adopting practices established centrally: at a plenum on 17 July 1965 a gorkom member transferred to another town was relieved of office, and his place filled by promoting a candidate member. This is sanctioned at the cpsu central committee level by Rule 32/33, but the obscurity of the legal position at local level is reflected in an enquiry to the journal *Partiinaya zhizn'* (Party Life) from the head of a gorkom organisational department, who had found no guidance in the literature as to the correct procedure for this kind of promotion.[10]

Organisational questions took up a fair amount of the available time, but it was unusual for a whole meeting to be devoted to them. Normal business sessions covered a fairly wide range of topics, varying between the two institutions, and were reported in the local and, occasionally, republican press, with some detail about who participated and what was said.

*The soviet*

An important item here is the annual budget debate, normally held in December. The term 'budget debate' may be misleading, and it should be noted that the soviet local government body differs markedly in its fiscal arrangements from its typical western counterpart. This is because the centralised planning system regulates its economic life, and coordinates it with that of the republic and the whole ussr. Major capital expenditure has to be sanctioned by higher authority and incorporated into the town's economic plan, and this restricts the power of the local soviet in financial matters. The soviet itself is largely confined to making proposals, debating them, and passing them on to the planning authorities (through gorplan, the town planning commission) for further consideration; the proposal may eventually be incorporated into a plan, after which the necessary capital would be allocated through inclusion in the town's budget. The allocation might need to be supplemented by other means, as with the new trolley-bus system: much of the installation was done by unpaid voluntary labour, so we might conclude that the budgetary allocations were inadequate and required extra, locally organised measures. The town soviet is not authorised to decide on a project and make independent arrangements for implementing it; this places it in an ostensibly dependent and vulnerable position, as was recognised in the early 1970s.[11]

The role of the deputies in their· annual budget debate is also naturally affected by this arrangement. The plan and its financial provisions are presented to the soviet in the form of a detailed breakdown of the town's economic plan for the next twelve months, accompanied by a budget to make the allocations necessary for its completion. The same session also hears a report on the execution of the budget provisions during the previous full fiscal year, ending approximately twelve months before. This is normal practice in soviets at all levels, and the planning commission and finance otdel heads play a leading part in the debate.

Another session each year is normally devoted to the report of the gorispolkom and its departments, presented by its chairman. A copy of the report is also sent to the republican authorities for their consideration.

A further regular duty of the full soviet session, but one that in Tiraspol rarely – if ever – involved debate, was the approval of regulations to control specific aspects of life in the town: the use of the trolley-bus system (November 1967); cycling (May 1960); control of dogs (May 1965); buses (May 1965); and so forth. These sets of rules, and others, passed as a matter of routine at the end of a session, were valid for two years, after which they were either renewed or allowed to lapse.

The remaining sessions debated a range of subjects; however, matters of particular concern appeared on the agenda more than once a year, and other topics had to be neglected. In the four years 1964–67, twenty-three sessions were held, but after the regular annual debates only nineteen sessions were left for other topics, and one of these dealt solely with organisational questions. Details of the agenda were not published in every case, and several sessions debated two substantive matters. Among the various topics that were publicised, education was discussed at three sessions, and town improvement and sanitation at four; at two more sessions, the preparedness of the town's economy for working in winter conditions was discussed (and found wanting); two meetings dealt with cultural facilities, one with facilities for sport, two with the role of deputies, and one with the work of the permanent commissions; service facilities were debated in July 1965, while the session of 24 December that year discussed plans for celebrating the fiftieth anniversary of the revolution, in November 1967; the general long-term development plans for the town were explored in September 1965, along with preparations for winter.

We can see that certain topics – education, preparedness for winter, culture, and sanitation – cropped up repeatedly; questions such as trade, service and sports facilities were raised only infrequently; and important matters such as medicine and social security were not debated at all in these years. Not once during the term of office from March 1965 did the press report a session where the heads of the health and social security departments had to account directly for their work, although they did occasionally speak in debates. The repetition of a restricted number of themes is by no means unusual, however, and Tiraspol is again showing how typical it is; hence the periodic calls for soviets to extend the range of questions discussed at their sessions.[12]

The issue of sanitation and hygiene provides an interesting example where the soviet reacted to pressures from the electors. This question, together with the related one of town beautification, was discussed four times between 1964 and 1967, revealing one of the persistent problems facing Tiraspol deputies and their constituents: one session in 1967 expressly debated the question 'bearing in mind the requests of the voters'. Even earlier, a session in March 1960 had featured 'the battle with flies' in the title of the main report (reported in *Dnestrovskaya pravda*, 18 March 1960), while a letter published shortly afterwards (*Dnestrovskaya pravda*, 6 April 1960) complained that private house-owners could not obtain garbage bins, and there were no arrangements for regularly emptying them. This problem was not peculiar to Tiraspol, and one might observe that anyone who has suffered the problems of inadequate sanitary arrangements in the provincial parts of the USSR (and even in major cities) will appreciate the preoccupation of the Tiraspol soviet with this vexed question.

## The gorkom

Whereas the soviet is essentially concerned with administrative questions, the gorkom is more an interpreter of policy. This permits greater latitude in the questions it chooses to discuss, and the different role is reflected in the range of topics in our review period. In 1964–67, organisational questions concerned six plenums, as did political work; agriculture was discussed three times, and industry, construction and the economy once; two other topics were discussed. This list is interesting, in that it shows that the kind of substantive issue debated most frequently concerned broadly political work, referred to variously as 'party-organisational work', 'personnel selection', or 'work among young people'. The range of topics was broadened to include economic issues; however, perhaps curiously, in view of the town's industrial economy, industry as such was debated only once (in January 1964), and then with specific reference to the chemical industry. By contrast, agriculture was discussed more than once, even though the town had little direct connection with that sector, and it was never a matter for the soviet's concern. In this field (as, for example, in March 1964) it was largely a question of what support the town's industrial enterprises could give to the drive for increased mechanisation in agriculture. We can see how far the committee was involved with the pressing problems facing the whole country, rather than simply the town. Although on the face of it the industrial town is remote from the needs of agriculture, in fact so serious was the situation on the farms that the gorkom members – and specifically the buro, whose members drew up the agenda – found it either necessary or politically expedient to devote time to examining the implications for the town of national issues, frequently taking a cpsu central committee resolution as their starting point. To that extent, at least, the local party committee depends on the initiative of higher bodies: even if explicit orders were never issued *requiring* the gorkom to raise these particular matters, the local party leaders considered it sufficiently urgent to take central committee resolutions as a basis for their own discussions. This was common in the obkom too, as Stewart has pointed out.[13]

This is a further dimension of relations between the town and other levels of administration, which is even more eloquently demonstrated by an occasion in May 1953. The republican central committee debated a report from Tiraspol gorkom, noted that this committee 'gives a weak lead to the industrial enterprises and building organisations', and ordered it to improve its work of leading the local party organisations. Back in Tiraspol, the party organisation could not but discuss this question, first in the gorkom buro, then at a plenum, and in a host of other meetings as well.[14] During 1964–67 seven plenums debated current topics that had been dealt with at higher levels, and especially by cpsu central committee plenums; the remaining topics may have been selected on local initiative.

In the main, the gorkom seems to have been concerned with questions of high current political priority, rather than a systematic examination of issues facing the town. This supports the notion of a division of functions between the gorkom and the soviet: the former debates and interprets political issues, and these may then be taken up by the soviet and its executive arm, which concentrate on the administrative tasks involved in running the town.

### THE ORGANISATION OF MEETINGS

In assessing the role that these meetings might play, one must look at not only what questions they discuss, but also the form of discussion, the organisational arrangements, which might encourage or frustrate participation by a wide circle of members. It is clearly impractical for 250 elected members to speak at every session, or even all members of a much smaller party committee; the time available would preclude that in any local government system. The question is, how far *could* these institutions go in that direction, and how far *did* they in practice?

In both institutions, debates followed normal Soviet procedures. At a soviet session, after the election of a chairman and secretary for that session and agreement of the agenda, a *doklad* (report) was delivered, often by a departmental head, followed by a critical co-report, generally by the relevant permanent commission chairman; a gorkom plenum usually opened with a single report, normally delivered by a secretary. The meeting then proceeded to the discussion (*preniya*), in which ordinary deputies and members could speak, and at the end of the debate the members present voted on a resolution. These are drafted by the executive organ, and may or may not be circulated in advance – a question that can obviously profoundly affect how competently members can comment on the issues at hand. In this connection, the Soviet political scientist A. A. Bezuglov had identified two specific situations that are widespread and that affect the role of individual deputies in sessions: *under-preparation*, when deputies are not forewarned of the content of reports, and have to react spontaneously in the session; and *over-preparation*, 'when everything is written down beforehand in its petty details: it is known who will speak and what they will say. In this case the sitting bears not a business-like, but a parade-like character. In such sittings many deputies restrict their participation to attendance and voting.' These factors lead, in his view, towards the creation of two kinds of deputy: *active* and *passive*.[15] I shall discuss this question with reference to Tiraspol below. It remains to be seen what will be the effect of Article 11 of the 1972 Statute on the Deputy's Status, which makes prior circulation of documentation mandatory.

Another factor is the duration of the session, a question that Soviet writers have discussed in general terms. Yu. A. Tikhomirov mentions two to three hours as the norm in many soviets, which in his view is too short: in some oblast soviets, he adds approvingly, the session lasts two whole days.[16] This obviously affects the chances of holding a full debate, with maximum participation of members. So does the length of permitted speech, which is decided at the beginning of each session. It may be approximately as follows, based on figures given by Vasenin for oblast and village soviets:[17] main or co-report – thirty minutes to one hour; speeches in the debate – ten to fifteen minutes; similar rates may apply in the gorkom too. One of the most thorough and complex studies of deputies' activity, combining materials from Estonian and Armenian research, reveals that in town soviets subordinated to republican authorities (such as Tiraspol), the average duration of speeches was 14.3 minutes.[18]

Details for Tiraspol are not available, but one thing is clear, and it applies to all local soviets and party committees: in a meeting lasting two sittings (morning and afternoon) at most about twenty discussion speeches could be made; even if there were twelve sessions in the term of office, some deputies would have no chance at all to speak; if there were even the slightest tendency for certain groups to speak more than once, the time constraint would make wide participation impossible. This is one of the likely factors behind Vasenin's complaint that 'in the practical work of the soviet, many deputies, particularly ordinary workers, still poorly make use of the session as a speaking-platform'.[19]

The same is true of party committees elsewhere: I found that out of 140 Moldavian central committee members who served between December 1963 and March 1966, fifty-two full and twenty-nine candidate members failed to speak at a single plenum;[20] Stewart too gives figures that suggest a large proportion of committee members failed to contribute to the Stalingrad obkom debates.[21] A *Pravda* editorial on 21 November 1966 emphasised that poor attendance and low levels of participation in plenums cannot be accepted as the norm, and added that the principle of collective leadership requires that the opinion of each committee member be known. Yet whatever *Pravda* may regard as acceptable, the observed result seems to be the consequence of such large committees holding such infrequent meetings, which inevitably degenerate into mini-conferences.

Other writers have suggested further factors influencing the level of participation, especially among deputies: Vasenin sees shyness as a major inhibiting factor,[22] while Bezuglov stresses the individual's level of experience, knowledge, breadth of vision, and similar personal qualities.[23] Other studies have correlated level of activity with age, term of office, sex, occupation, education, and party membership, and provide comparative data against which Tiraspol may be judged.[24] Similar considerations may also apply to gorkom members, among whom confidence might also develop as they become more familiar with the work of the party organ. It should be remembered, though, that the gorkom contains far fewer individuals with 'weak' characteristics; at least, all were party members, which should imply a certain positiveness of character and a measure of self-confidence.

Members' participation was also affected by a final feature of Soviet political life, characteristic of the Khrushchev era, but continuing after his departure: the custom of opening plenums and sessions to non-members, who were allowed both to attend and to speak. Presumably these outsiders were not allowed to vote; nevertheless, their presence, if not strictly controlled, might seriously affect the role of legitimate members: when meetings are so infrequent, time is a precious commodity. The effect on members is strikingly described by Kunaev in the article referred to earlier. Writing of party committee plenums, he stated that 'members of the elected organ became as it were dissolved in a mass of invited guests, and their role diminished. A business-like review of the questions which had been put forward for discussion in the plenums often gave way to showiness and noisy ballyhoo.'[25]

## PARTICIPATION

These patterns in participation have been observed elsewhere in the USSR, and the explanations that I outlined have been put forward by other writers. I now turn to Tiraspol, in order to answer the following questions: how far did the gorkom and soviet serve as forums for the expression of members' views? did any members tend to dominate the meetings? were any members conspicuously left out, and if so, what groups? In short, who were the *active* members of the elite? I shall concentrate on the period 1964–67, and for the soviet specifically the term of office that lasted from 14 March 1965 to 12 March 1967.

### The soviet

During this term, the soviet met thirteen times; extensive press reports covered eleven of these sessions, and my analysis is based on those. The newspaper accounts referred to seventeen reports (*doklady*) or co-reports (*sodoklady*) and eighty-two discussion speeches (*vystupleniya v preniyakh*), naming those who spoke. On two occasions the press named some participants, and added that 'others' also spoke; their numbers were probably small, and I shall ignore them in my discussion. We can already see that a minority of deputies played an active part in the sessions. A fairly generous estimate would permit a dozen contributions at a session; the highest number of speeches recorded at a single session in seven years (1950, 1955, 1960 and 1964–67) was fifteen (on 26 January 1966); most had ten or fewer. In fact, during the 1965–67 term, a mere forty-eight deputies are known to have spoken; even allowing for incomplete press reports, the number can scarcely have exceeded sixty or seventy – a quarter of the soviet.

Non-deputies seriously intruded on the time available for deputies to speak: they made twenty-six reported contributions, including thirteen by republican officials. On 25 September 1965 (reported in *Dnestrovskaya pravda* six days later), out of six speeches on development plans for the town, only one was by a deputy; the others were by planning and construction engineers from outside Tiraspol, brought in to brief deputies. Judging by the account, the representatives of the people were given little chance to make their own observations.

A second influence on the general level of participation was the habit of repeatedly selecting some deputies to speak: thirty-two deputies spoke at one session, whereas nine spoke at two, four at three, two at four, and one individual at seven sessions. This coincides with the research findings of Pavlov, Kazimirchuk and their associates: in their sample of over 4000 deputies at all levels, 1387 spoke not once in a year, and the 720 deputies who spoke five or more times contributed as much as all the remaining deputies together; these writers too criticise the practice of allowing invited guests to speak at the expense of deputies, adding the reminder that the session is above all a deputies' forum.[26]

Next we find that the debates tended to be dominated by 'strong' deputies. 'Weak' deputies did speak, but in far fewer numbers than their strength on the soviet would warrant. For example, 85.4 per cent of speakers were male; most were party members (89.6 per cent); the largest group fell into the 40–49 age group (39.6 per cent), while almost two-thirds (thirty persons, or 62.5 per cent of speakers) were aged forty or over in 1965. There was a similar relationship between occupation and participation: the deputies engaged in the more prestigious positions spoke more often than the rest. This applies especially to the report readers, who all tended to be in such positions: officers of the gorispolkom and its departments, a factory manager, the pro-rector of the pedagogical institute. Furthermore, the deputies in high-status occupations not only tended to dominate by reading the reports; they also participated in the discussion in greater strength than their humbler colleagues. Thus, over a quarter of industrial managers, over a third of party officials, and over two-thirds of the state officials spoke;

yet industrial workers spoke only in the ratio of one in sixteen. Here again, Tiraspol was not untypical: an article on Kitoiskii settlement soviet, Irkutsk oblast, says that there, too, most speakers were leading figures, whereas 'rarely was the voice of worker deputies heard, or of rank and file workers in general'. The author reports that this was improved following far better preparation of the sessions,[27] indicating the importance of adequate briefing for those deputies who are not in regular contact with state and party documentation and information.

As one would expect, the identity of contributors varied according to the topic under discussion. Thus, workers in education tended to speak on that topic, while a debate on trade and service facilities gave several deputies connected with that sector a chance to present their views. The invited guests were also chosen (reasonably enough) for their special expertise: in that same debate, the deputy chief artist of the town's artistic council spoke in his professional capacity, criticising the tasteless and colourless posters in the streets – an apt comment in practically any Soviet town.

One can say that in general the more senior (in the sense of more prestigious) members of the soviet regularly performed the role of spokesmen, and in this the situation in Tiraspol was not unlike that in local government elsewhere in the USSR and even abroad. Bezuglov's characterisation of deputies as 'active' and 'passive' is thus borne out, and it coincides with my own identification of 'strong' and 'weak'. However, there is one finding that my data do not corroborate: some Soviet studies have found first-term deputies more active, but this was not so in Tiraspol, at least with respect to speaking in debates. Precisely half the speakers (twenty-four) were in their first term, whereas about three-quarters of the deputies were serving for the first time; nine speakers were serving their second term, three their third, five their fourth, one his fifth, two their sixth, and four their seventh. Nor was participation very influential in securing re-election in 1967: 60.4 per cent of the speakers were re-elected, compared with 36.9 per cent for the soviet as a whole; but since the speakers tended to be in prestigious occupations, it seems likely that an individual's position at the end of his term of office was more important than his record of participation in the sessions. In some cases a deputy might indeed be promoted to a leading position following a successful participant career on the soviet, but it would be the new position that directly influenced his or her re-election. Many of the guest speakers did not secure membership at the next election.

To sum up my discussion of the 1965–67 term. I noted that considerable numbers of outsiders were invited to speak, and the deputies who spoke were mainly drawn from the more prestigious, the 'strong'; these practices reduced the impact of the more humble deputies. The same trend can be observed in earlier years, even going back to 1955, when two contrary tendencies affected the length of time available for deputy participation: first, meetings were more frequent – about one a month; secondly, sessions began at 3, 4, 6 or 7 p.m., rather than 10 a.m. as was usual later –hence meetings were shorter, and the number of speeches or their duration (or both) would have to be curtailed. The press reports of that time indicated that there were fewer discussion speeches – an average of six – and they too appear to have been made by the 'strong' deputies. In this situation, one might conclude that if ordinary deputies have a positive role, it lies less in the sessions of the soviet than in their other activities.

*The gorkom*

During 1964–67, twelve plenums are known to have discussed major topics; the debates included sixteen reports and 102 discussion speeches, delivered by eighty-two individuals. Eight persons delivered the sixteen reports, including eight by Petrik, gorkom first secretary from October 1964; his predecessor also read a report during her short tenure of the office. This prominence – greater than that of the gorispolkom chairman in soviet sessions – is widespread in party committees, as work on the Moldavian central committee and the Stalingrad obkom shows.[28] Yet in Tiraspol at least, it was a departure from tradition: in 1960, when four plenums were held, the first secretary reported to only one; in 1955 the first secretary read no report, but three were read by his deputy; in 1950 the first secretary reported to one of the five plenums, his deputy to the remaining four. The other rapporteurs were all in prestigious positions: the popular control committee chairman, the gorispolkom chairman, the Komsomol gorkom first secretary, and so forth.

Seventy-eight speakers spoke in the discussions, including four who also read reports. Most (sixty-one, 78.2 per cent) spoke only once during the four years; thirteen (16.7 per cent) spoke twice, two (2.6 per cent) three times, and one each on four and five occasions. This period covered two full terms of office, the xxvi and xxvii committees, involving 165 individual members; 135 of these did not speak at a plenum during the period. Yet twenty-seven speeches came from non-members, although a small number were past members, or later joined the committee. A few figures help us to identify the speakers: in the three debates of the xxvi committee, thirteen of the twenty-one discussion speeches were by full members, eight by non-members, and none by candidates; in the following committee, twenty-five of the fifty-two speeches came from full members, four from candidates, and twenty-three from non-members. Thus, the intrusion of non-members in the debates affected both full and candidate members, particularly the latter, whose participation was at a minimal level. Since they, like the guests, have no vote, their position appears anomalous.

What were the distinguishing features of those thirty members who were called on to speak? Twenty-seven (90.0 per cent) were male, two were female, and one was of unidentified sex; moreover, 24.5 per cent of males spoke, compared with only 6.7 per cent of females and 4.5 per cent of members whose sex was not identified. Males were clearly dominant, but whether this is a sign of bias against women as such is doubtful – the whole system appears to operate against them. Men were in a majority among the outside speakers too.

The very young and the old members also suffered: those in their forties stood a better chance of being called on to speak than those in other age groups (one-third, compared with less than a quarter in other groups). This probably reflects the fact that the kind of post that qualifies individuals to speak at plenums is usually held by persons of that age.

The occupation of members seems to be the most relevant factor, and this corresponds with the situation identified in the soviet, in higher party committees, and elsewhere. Among the thirty participants, administrators in the political apparatus or industry dominate. Representatives of these groups accounted for 93.3 per cent of the speakers, including twelve party officials, one state official, three trade union or Komsomol officials, and ten industrial managerial staff. Among committee members, industrial workers, medical workers, representatives of the press and other groups failed to speak in these plenums; yet these occupations *were* represented, by outside guests. Even in some groups showing a comparatively high level of participation there was 'competition' from outsiders, who included eleven party officials, ten industrial managers, three trade unionists. These figures bring me back to the nature and significance of gorkom membership, especially candidate membership: if debates are opened to usurpation of the members' role by outsiders, how does membership confer political influence on individual party members?

Further analysis distinguishes two broad groups of speakers: first, officials whose status qualifies them to speak as authoritative specialists; secondly, officials in key party posts, who speak on a variety of topics, not necessarily as experts on the topic, but as responsible apparatus officials. The example of the March 1964 plenum illustrates this. There, two of the speeches were made by party officials among the committee members, and one by an invited party official, the deputy secretary of the Tiraspol agricultural party committee, since this plenum was discussing ways of helping to develop agriculture. There were two further noted guest speakers, both collective farm chairmen from the district; the final two speakers were trade union officials. In this instance, the presence of agricultural representatives was sensible, as the press account (*Leninskoe znamya*, 4 April 1964) recognised:

> The attendance at the gorkom plenum of representatives from collective farms was useful in that the leaders of the town's enterprises and organisations heard from their mouths about the needs of the *kolkhozy*, and therefore will be able to plan their work in such a way as to seek out internal reserves for rendering assistance to the countryside in the intensification of agricultural production.

Nevertheless, this practice was not repeated in subsequent debates on that topic.

The only group represented among speakers at all plenums were, in fact, the party officials, and someone of at least PPO secretary status (the lowest full-time position in the apparatus) spoke in each debate. Their presence was particularly strong in debates on 'political' issues, while industrial managers were more prominent in debates on industrial topics. Thus, although in Tiraspol gorkom, as in Stalingrad obkom,[29] the plenums were effectively dominated by party officials, it can nevertheless be claimed with some justification, first, that the selection of speakers gave the voting members present a chance to hear a range of views from presumably competent speakers, and, secondly, that the party itself was more active in debates on more politically orientated topics. This suggests a development in the direction of rationality in these debates, with the party willing to take expert advice where appropriate; in the absence of details of what the individual speakers said, however, it is impossible to make a clear assessment.

Nevertheless, what can be said with certainty is that the gorkom, like the soviet, did not serve effectively as a forum that permitted a complete exchange of views and opinions. Even over a whole term of office, only a very small minority of members was able to speak in a debate. That minority consisted largely of members with characteristics that I have defined as 'strong'. Their dominance reflected to the disadvantage of 'ordinary' members from the weaker social groups, whose level of active participation was further reduced by the practice of inviting outside speakers.

### ORGANISATIONAL EXPERIMENTS

As I noted, Soviet commentators have themselves referred to the uneven pattern of participation in meetings of party and state institutions. In addition to exhortation, in the mid-sixties a number of experiments were conducted to try and extend the value of these meetings by involving more individuals in the debates. Two examples of such experiments were recorded in Tiraspol, one in the soviet and one in the gorkom, and they are of value in showing how the local political elite approached the task of raising the level of these debates.

The first experiment took place on 17 August 1966, and was reported in *Dnestrovskaya pravda* on August 24th, under the heading 'A New-Style Session' (*'Sessiya proshla po-novomu'*):

> Even the agenda itself sounded new. This time, there were brought forward for discussion by the session not simply questions of economic and cultural construction. The discussion dealt with further raising the role of deputies and the soviet aktiv in deciding these questions.

After a report by N. G. Deleu, gorispolkom deputy chairman, which referred specifically to the work of the permanent commissions, the session split up into the various commissions, which retired to separate rooms for an hour to discuss the matter. This device permitted eighty-three deputies to comment, and rapporteurs spoke on their behalf when the full session resumed. Moreover, the draft resolution had been circulated a fortnight in advance of the meeting, enabling deputies to prepare their ground. According to the press account, 'this is why this time the decision of the session was to a rare degree short and business-like. This is why the deputies with one voice declared: The new way of conducting sessions deserves approval.'

A similar positive and enthusiastic appraisal was carried in the press account of the gorkom's organisational experiment in September 1967 (reported in *Dnestrovskaya pravda*, 5 September). The range of those present was wide, including gorkom members and candidates, members of the auditing commission, PPO secretaries, leaders of industrial enterprises and other institutions, propagandists and other workers on the ideological front; they were gathered to discuss the question of training communist workers. No report was read. Instead, after a short introductory speech by the first secretary, Petrik, the debate began immediately. The point was that the substance of the report had been circulated to PPOs in advance of the plenum, thereby enabling over 4000 communists to familiarise themselves with the material; over 350 speakers had taken part in debates in 126 PPOs, so that by the time the plenum was held, the six individuals who spoke in the debate should have been much better informed of grass-roots party opinion than they otherwise might have been. This type of meeting, with reports circulated in advance rather than delivered at the session itself, has also occasionally been tried in the local soviets, and the practice goes back at least as far as 1960.[30] I do not know whether the experiment in Tiraspol gorkom was judged sufficiently successful for a repetition: no further plenum took place before the end of 1967.

There are one or two further considerations with regard to these formal experiments. First, the unusual soviet session was not arranged on a local initiative: it had been tried elsewhere and reported in the press. The most publicised example was in the Daugavpils town soviet (Latvia), first reported in the journal *Sovety deputatov trudyashchikhsya* in the summer of 1966, and referred to by several writers.[31] Another debate based on permanent commissions took place in the Kungur town soviet, in the Russian republic, probably in 1966 or 1967.[32] Thus, Tiraspol was simply following the general trend in various parts of the USSR to stimulate the activity of the deputies in the sessions. However, this seems to have been the only occasion when this form of meeting was tried, and subsequent sessions appear to have followed the conventional pattern.

In any case, merely experimenting with the conduct of the sessions would scarcely be sufficient to resuscitate the moribund state apparatus and to fire the deputies with initiative and enthusiasm, if this were the intention of the political leadership. There were, as we have seen, more fundamental factors operating in the contrary direction, especially the fact that the sessions tended to be dominated by advantaged individuals, whose repeated re-election gave them further advantage.

Experience elsewhere also suggests that the debates in the sessions concentrate on essentially trivial aspects of the topics under discussion; policy as such is not open to discussion; speeches tend to be stereotyped, and concerned simply with deficiencies in a specific locality or area of administration and suggestions for detailed improvement only.[33] In many cases the deputies – and even the soviet itself – are powerless to remedy insufficiencies, since they depend on central authorities for the allocation of materials to carry out their decisions, as the Kalarash gorispolkom chairman forcefully pointed out in an article in the newspaper *Sovetskaya Moldaviya* (12 November 1971). Even lamp bulbs for street lighting were in short supply, he states, and there was nothing the deputies could do about the situation; the writer says drily, 'In this we need help on the part of the planning organs'. All these negative features – most of which have been acknowledged in one form or another in the Soviet press – demonstrate the vulnerability of the local soviets, and seriously undermine the extravagant descriptions of the role of soviets as representative organs of state power, with which many Soviet writings still abound.

As for the gorkom plenum experiment, the newspaper account was instructive on several grounds. First, it showed that the fundamental principle of control by the buro was not infringed: the buro took the initiative, prepared and circulated the documentation, quite in keeping with normal procedures. Secondly, the normal situation was revealed: the plenum debates an issue, and only after a decision has been reached is the mass party membership informed of the issue. Thirdly, it seems to be a clear admission that the plenum normally does not act as a forum for a full exchange of views, since few members can speak, and they are not properly informed of grass-roots opinion. In this situation the buro controls simply by its possession of information. The ordinary committee members are assigned a subsidiary role: explaining to their party organisations the contents of decisions and resolutions over which they had little influence.

## THE PERMANENT COMMISSIONS

If full sessions of the soviet are of small political relevance in the system of supposedly representative government, the deputy's more valuable role may lie in the permanent commissions, which played such a crucial part in the organisational experiment described above, and which were, indeed, the subject of the debate. This was not the first time that the role of the deputies and the commissions had been discussed in public in Tiraspol. In an article in 1960, for example, the role of women in the permanent commissions had been commented on (*Dnestrovskaya pravda*, 9 March 1960). In October 1955, gorkom secretary L. G. Smirnova read a report on the work of the commissions, and indicated how successful they had been in performing their functions (the speech was reported in *Dnestrovskaya pravda*, 30 October 1955). At the first session, eight months previously, eight commissions had been formed, taking in 125 deputies of the 165 elected. They had subsequently brought forward over ninety proposals from electors for examination by the soviet or the gorispolkom. Turning to the work of three of the commissions, Smirnova identified strengths and weaknesses. Some deputies failed to participate in the commissions' work and to maintain contact with their electors: eighteen such deputies were named. Then, apart from the laxity on the part of individuals, some of the commissions failed to sit regularly, and failed to discuss 'the burning questions of economic and cultural development, the development of trade and the welfare of the people' – a reference to the inadequate service provided by shops, cafes and restaurants. Other deputies corroborated this testimony, and criticised the gorispolkom and its departments for failing to maintain sufficiently close links with the commissions and the individual deputies, and for not drawing them into the executive committee's work.

In other words, the ordinary deputies – inside and outside their commissions – were not being given the information and support needed to carry out their functions adequately. The session adopted a resolution aimed at rectifying the situation. Yet nine years later, on 26 June 1964, the soviet was still discussing the work of the commissions in rather similar terms; the experimental session of August 1966 was the first of its kind recorded in the town, and as I noted it was not adopted as the normal form for sessions.

Given their wide powers of inspection, and the fact that their meetings are smaller and need not take the form of set debates, the potential significance of these commissions is considerable. Indeed, the main advantages of the committee system in, for example, British local government, as expressed by R. M. Punnett, have equal validity in the Soviet context:

> As well as the general principle that the smaller the decision-making body the more effective it will be, the chief merit of the committee

system is that it brings individual members of the council into closer contact with the details of administration than would otherwise be possible.[34]

Yet unless the commissions are given the appropriate administrative support and – perhaps more important – encouragement to perform their duties in a more than perfunctory fashion, they cannot be expected alone to inject new significance into Soviet local government. Moreover, since they consist in the main of ordinary deputies, most of whom, as we saw, serve for only a single term of office, it seems unlikely that each commission could develop a body of expertise needed for playing a positive role. When the expertise is confined to one or two members re-elected from the previous term, or to professionals who have recently been brought into the soviet, lack of continuity and experience within the commissions must cast serious doubts on their value in keeping a check on the administrative departments. These considerations may be one reason behind the spate of books, pamphlets and articles that have appeared in recent years, explaining to commission members what they are required to do, and how to set about it. Time will tell how successfully they can be transformed.

### CONCLUSION

In this chapter I have been concerned with the participation of the elite members in the work of their respective bodies. The formal meetings (sessions of the soviet and plenums of the gorkom) took place, I noted, comparatively infrequently. They tended to concentrate on specific kinds of questions, but occasionally opened the area of debate to examine matters of less pressing importance. Certain questions regularly appeared on the agenda of both organs, and particularly organisational matters, in which case the deputies or gorkom members appeared to act largely as a formalising body. The balance of subjects for general debate reflected, I suggested, the broad division of functions between the two structures, with the gorkom mainly (but not exclusively) dealing with political questions, and the soviet concerning itself with the more practical aspects of administration.

However, as we saw, some topics were discussed repeatedly over the years, sometimes several times in quick succession, which indicates how ineffectual the soviet's debates and decisions can be. The deputies simply do not possess the genuine power and authority to take decisions and introduce measures that will radically improve the situation and eliminate particular shortcomings once and for all. They are too dependent on higher authorities, whose direct interest in finding permanent solutions to the problems facing the citizens of Tiraspol and elsewhere may be negligible. So problems remain to be talked about, year after year, by deputies in the sessions, and sometimes also in the gorkom plenums.

In both institutions the infrequency of meetings and their short duration made full participation in the debates by a wide range of members impossible; meetings tended to be dominated by the 'strong' – the more prestigious – at the expense of the 'weaker' members. The position of the latter in both institutions was further eroded by the presence and participation of non-members. These could speak in a professional capacity on technical matters (this being the positive aspect of their contribution); yet in most cases their expertise could be matched among the formal members, whose position thus became anomalous. Finally, I discussed examples of experiments aimed at improving this situation, but suggested that mere experimentation with the form of meetings would be unlikely to restore to these institutions the authority that some Soviet writers seem anxious to convey.

# CHAPTER 6

# Party and State:
# The Town's Political Elite

So far I have been concerned with analysing the membership of Tiraspol town soviet and party committee separately, with only a few comparisons between the two institutions. Quite clearly, however, as has been remarked more than once, this is a somewhat artificial division: these two bodies form part of one overall political structure, and in this chapter I deal more directly with the question of the relation between party and state at this level of administration.

## FORMAL ASPECTS

The position of the communist party vis-à-vis the state apparatus is one of the most complex features of Soviet political life, and it is as much a problem for western students to disentangle as it is for Soviet politicians to regulate. Fainsod's work on the Smolensk archive reveals a consciously designed system of 'overlapping, duplication, and parallel functions', so that clear distinctions between the two are impossible to make.[1] Institutional analysis, when applied within a legal–constitutional framework, appears singularly inadequate to account for political relationships realistically. Much Soviet writing is of that kind, and what A. H. Brown has referred to as 'an almost sublime example of formalistic work', namely the Webbs' book *Soviet Communism – A New Civilisation?*, remains perhaps the most notorious western example of the school.[2] My own analysis shifts the emphasis from the formal rules governing these institutions, and from the functions that may be ascribed to them, and examines their inter-relationship in terms of the individuals who participated in their work.

I shall begin, however, with a very brief outline of various means at the party's disposal in playing what is frequently referred to as its 'leading and guiding' role in Soviet society. The party is seen as 'a superior type of social organisation, which serves as the leading nucleus in all other workers' organisations, including those of the state',[3] and there are several ways in which it can and does exercise its control or guidance over the work of the soviets.

First, the party exercises control over the initial selection of deputies through the nomination and screening procedures, and can thus ensure that all deputies are party members or at least strong supporters of the party line; in this sense, *all* deputies are endorsed by the party.[4] In Tiraspol, as we saw in chapter 3, party members were always in a majority, and Komsomol members added further to the strength of the formally committed deputies.

Once elected, the party members among the deputies form a *party group*, which meets regularly to discuss the work of the soviet. The members are subordinated to the gorkom, and are obliged to strive for the implementation of its decisions; moreover, these groups themselves also prepare draft resolutions on questions for debate in the soviet, and agree on their position in advance of the sessions.[5] Similar party groups and ppos are attached to the executive committee and its various departments, which further permit the party to control the business of the state apparatus.[6] Here we see a parallel with, for example, British local government, where meetings of Labour groups perform similar functions and operate in a like fashion: indeed, one writer on British government has stated that 'In most local authorities . . . the work of the Council (and its committees) is dominated by party political organisations, with council decisions really being controlled by party group meetings'.[7] In the Soviet context, with only one party represented, this practice places its members in a strong position: they would normally have no difficulty in ensuring that the full soviet accepted the party group's own agreed viewpoint, since they formed a majority in any case.

A further important means of party control is the nomenklatura system, which effectively allots the prerogative of selection of officers and officials to the local or a superior party committee. The details of how the principle operates remain obscure, despite the work of a number of western scholars in trying to establish its nature.[8] Whatever the precise details, the fundamental point is that all appointees to such positions of responsibility are, at the time of their appointment, regarded by the party authorities as reliable and competent, even if they are not themselves party members; continued tenure of office depends less on maintaining the confidence of the body of deputies as a whole than on continued acceptability to the party bodies.

Already then, we see how powerful can be the party's control over the work of any local soviet, including that of Tiraspol, by influencing the selection of personnel in the state organ and its apparatus, and by the political behaviour in decision-making situations of its own members in strategic posts. To this list of devices at the party's disposal can be added a further measure of influence brought about by the phenomenon of overlapping or interlocking membership between the party committee and the soviet. A certain proportion of individuals are members of both bodies, and this enhances the power of the party in having its policies implemented by the state apparatus. The reasons for this are several: first, the gorkom members possess considerable prestige and authority, which gives them an influential role in debates within the soviet. Secondly, as members of a body that has the ultimate responsibility for policy decisions at a particular level, they are even more firmly bound by decisions that they helped to reach. Thirdly, their participation in gorkom debates gives them a degree of familiarity with official policy and its interpretation, which might enable to them to explain and promote the party line more effectively in the soviet. To the extent that the party committee deals with policy issues of relevance to the soviet, the phenomenon of overlapping membership is a further powerful means of control enjoyed by the party over the state.

My discussion to this point has been essentially one-sided, and with reason: this is how the relationship between party and state is frequently presented in the West. John Armstrong, for instance, in the recent third edition of his introductory textbook on Soviet government, repeats his statement that 'The Soviet state is . . . a façade behind which the real power of Communist control is exercised'.[9] Thomas Remeikis, in a chapter on government in Lithuania, writes that 'the federalist framework is dominated by a unitarily organized Communist Party that is centrally controlled from Moscow'.[10] The frequent use of such words as 'domination' and 'control' indicates a particular view of a relationship that I believe is more subtle and complex. In presenting my own interpretation, I accept Churchward's judgement that the party is the directing force of Soviet government, but that the precise relationship between party and state is not constant, either in time or across different levels of administration.[11] It is certainly true that the measure of influence that the party enjoys through its links with the state machine does restrict the degree of independence and initiative of the local soviets; hence the continual stress in party literature on not replacing or supplanting the state organs. Brezhnev's exhortation to the

XXIII CPSU Congress in 1966 is but one of many statements on this subject:

> Party bodies must completely eliminate their petty tutelage of the government bodies and the practice of replacing them, which begets irresponsibility and inertia on the part of the officials.[12]

However, the relationship can be viewed differently, and the overlapping membership may serve a positive purpose in the decision-making process. The existing situation is not simply one in which a party committee makes policy decisions in isolation, and then hands them over to a quite distinct structure for implementation. On the contrary, the presence of a number of deputies on the gorkom (and its buro) could, and indeed ought to, lead to more effective decision-making. Soviet deputies should be able to bring to the deliberations of the gorkom information on the feelings of constituents; state officials on the gorkom are aware of the practical situation and of problems of implementation with which the gorkom members as such might not be concerned. In calculating the implications for the local community of a broad policy decision, handed down from a higher party authority, the gorkom should be able to take advantage of the political and professional expertise of the members of the state body and its organs. Thus, the Rostov-on-Don gorispolkom chairman and the gorkom secretary report with approval that 'Reports of individual communist deputies have been presented to the buros of party raikomy'.[13] Secondly, the presence of deputies at the meetings and debates of the gorkom ensures that they can fully understand the intentions of any decisions that might affect their work as deputies. Finally, their participation in the work of the soviet, perhaps including a spell as an officer of the state body, should give to party officials and gorkom officers a degree of administrative experience and awareness that office in a party organisation alone cannot give. Participation in the work of the state apparatus can thus be seen as an important element in the party official's political training, and the relationship between party and state has several functions and operates in two directions.

## THE STRUCTURE OF THE ELITE

The success with which the various functions outlined above can be performed depends, in part, on the degree of overlap in personnel between the two structures; this also has strong implications for the nature of the town's political elite, and I now turn to consider this question in detail. This study concentrates on the two main institutions (soviet and gorkom) together with their executive bodies (gorispolkom and gorkom buro), which are formed from among the membership of the two organs. There are clearly several degrees of elite stratification that can be identified when these two structures are combined (see Fig. 6.1):

A. Membership of the town soviet;
B. Membership of the gorkom;
C. Membership of the soviet and the gorkom;
D. Membership of the soviet and the gorispolkom;
E. Membership of the gorkom and its buro;
F. Membership of the soviet, the gorispolkom, and the gorkom;
G. Membership of the gorkom, its buro, and the soviet;
H. Membership of the soviet, the gorispolkom, the gorkom, and the gorkom buro.

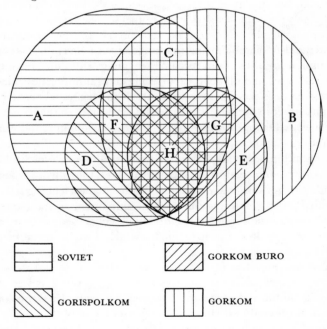

Figure 6.1 Structure of the elite

This scheme is a simplified model, which omits the variables of gorkom candidate membership and membership of the party auditing commission, a separate category which could be combined with membership of the soviet and the gorispolkom (but not the gorkom). The degree of elitism of these categories cannot be accurately rank-ordered on a purely intuitive basis (indeed, the whole idea of a strict hierarchy may be merely notional). But obviously the individual with membership of the soviet alone is in a far less powerful position than one who combines membership of the gorispolkom with a seat on the gorkom buro. Equally clearly, few would doubt that the party secretary who is not a gorispolkom member (i.e. is in Group E) would be more powerful than, say, a gorispolkom deputy chairman who is also on the gorkom (i.e. is in Group F). Bearing in mind that individual cases might well challenge the structure, one would guess that the hierarchy might be as follows:

$$H > G > E > F > C > D > B > A$$

### The significance of elite membership

I pointed out in chapter 1 that my usage of the concept of elite was a combination of Fleron's approach (defining elite membership in positional terms) and that of Keller (seeing elites as minorities 'set apart from the rest of society'). The analytical scheme suggested here permits me to go further in defining the features that distinguish the members of the elite from the population at large, and the various gradations in the elite from one another.

The most fundamental division is between those whose elite status derives from membership of the soviet, and those whose position depends on gorkom membership. While acknowledging the impossibility of demonstrating that membership of either of these bodies confers genuine power on the individuals concerned, certain other values or benefits do accrue to members, which, I would argue, confer a special status.

Taking membership of the town soviet first, it is clear that the deputies enjoy considerable prestige and, as Soviet writers frequently express it, 'authority' (*avtoritet*). Vasenin, for example, writes of the 'difficult but honourable duties of a representative of the people';[14] a deputy of the Moldavian supreme soviet has written that 'there is nothing more important or more honourable for a deputy than fulfilling the mandates of electors';[15] and a writer in the journal *Partiinaya zhizn'* opens his article with the words, 'To be a deputy is a great honour', and he continues:

> I became convinced of this through my own experience. The day will always remain in my memory when at the pre-election meeting for nominating candidates for deputy to the Ukrainian ssr Supreme Soviet my name was called. To be quite frank, at the beginning I thought I had misheard. But the speaker ... was speaking about none other than me.[16]

The official view implied here – which is equally applicable at the local level – confers honour and prestige on deputies in the soviets that is not available to outsiders. Deputies are officially regarded as 'the best', and their very election is a sign of special approval by the authorities.

Election to a soviet confers a number of rights and privileges, including time off from regular employment without loss of pay when attending to state business, occasional trips on official business to the republican capital or Moscow and perhaps other cities, immunity from arrest except with the sanction of the soviet,[17] and normally free public transport within the town.[18] The deputy also enjoys an enhanced social life, with his name and photograph occasionally appearing in the newspapers, and membership of other public bodies, which may add further to his prestige. The following captions, from a booklet published for a western readership, give some indication of the social activity of deputies and their position as celebrities: 'The deputy opens a new palace of culture ... The deputy is the first to congratulate the newly-weds ... To serve the people, to bring happiness to people – such is the duty of the deputy.'[19] Furthermore, since the introduction of the law defining the deputy's status, every deputy is distinguished from non-deputies by a lapel badge signifying his position, in addition to his normal deputy's identity card.[20]

The above features do not, of course, confer special *political* status on deputies; rather they are forms of social differentiation. Yet the deputy does enjoy certain rights that place him in a politically superior position to non-deputies, and that, in my view, permit us to rank him as in some sense a member of an elite. First, he has direct access, through personal acquaintance, to officers and officials at the local level, and occasional opportunities for access to representatives of higher authorities. Not only is this a source of prestige, it also gives a possible chance of influence; moreover, association with leading politicians may well lead to identification with them in the eyes of outsiders. Secondly, through the receipt of documentation and by his participation in meetings of the soviet, the deputy has access to a wider range of information than does the ordinary citizen, and this places him in a privileged position. Thirdly, through his membership of the soviet, he can become acquainted with legal procedures, and learn of informal channels through which to 'get things done'; to this general *savoir faire* may be added a degree of self-confidence that participation in the work of a major public body gives him. Most importantly, all these factors are combined through membership of a permanent commission: there the deputy meets political and industrial leaders and, as the work of the commission requires it, he has access to information about a range of problems in a number of institutions; his familiarity with the law is also enhanced; and he can possibly establish contacts to use for the benefit of his constituents or himself. These features place the deputy in a special position, separate from those citizens who are not deputies.

Membership of the gorispolkom adds further to these advantages: its numbers are severely restricted, which alone adds to the exclusiveness of membership; it brings access to leading politicians of the town and the republic more regularly than does ordinary soviet membership; its members confer more often, and have access to a wider range of information; they have some control over administration, and considerable authority and influence over the work of the ordinary members in the sessions and outside. The majority of ispolkom members are state employees, whose contact with political life is constant; for those members drawn from ordinary life, the special benefits of selection to this body distinguish them from ordinary deputies and the general public.

Membership of the gorkom is also likely to confer similar benefits, although the law does not provide for the special privileges of free transport, immunity from arrest, and the badge of office; nor does the party committee member enjoy the special status conferred by the title 'representative of the people'. Yet in other respects the gorkom member is distinguished from non-members: in *practice* party membership does convey a measure of immunity, which we can presume to be enhanced in the case of committee members, and their position is further enhanced by contacts with local and higher-level politicians and other leaders, access to confidential information, a limited chance to raise issues in a deliberative forum, and – like the members of the permanent commissions of the soviet – an opportunity to visit enterprises and institutions as propagandists and inspectors, armed with the authority of the party rather than the law. Thus, an article in *Dnestrovskaya pravda* (19 May 1960), entitled 'The Party Gorkom Member', described how, on the initiative of a particular gorkom member, a check was made on the fulfilment of a party directive by the town glassworks. The party investigation revealed a number of features for criticism, including the work of the factory's trade union committee, and the matter was further raised by the gorkom buro. The article praised that gorkom member as a propagandist. Another writer has stated that since 'gorkom members are always in the midst of the masses and know the situation in working collectives and the people's mood', the gorkom buro 'listens attentively to their comments and suggestions'. He also writes of gorkom members often reading reports to meetings of ppos – a situation in which the authority of his position becomes apparent.[21] The measure of prestige that the gorkom member has in common with the soviet deputy can be increased by successful work in stimulating greater industrial output; this can lead to much personal publicity for the individual concerned. Thus, one writer speaks of a particular gorkom member as enjoying 'great authority, not only in his own enterprise, but also throughout the town', after setting an example of outstanding work that was emulated by other workers.[22] It is in this sphere that the gorkom member enjoys the greatest possibility of making his mark, and his party committee membership without doubt adds weight to his example. The gorkom member is thus distinguished from ordinary party members and the general public by greater authority and prestige, through membership of an important institution at the local level. His access to information and contact with leaders give him considerable potential influence.[23]

Beyond that, membership of the buro adds to these advantages in the same way as gorispolkom membership enhances the position of the deputy: membership of a smaller body is, by definition, more exclusive; contacts with leading politicians are closer, more regular; the range of information to which members have access is greater; the possibilities for influencing decisions are thereby increased.

After these two basic elements in the town's political elite come those grades combining membership of both, and it will be seen that the prestige, authority, signs of success, privileges, access to information, contacts with leaders, experience of political and administrative life gained through even more regular political participation, all add to the elite status and potential for influencing decisions of those individuals who combine membership of the gorkom with membership of the soviet. Even further is the position of an executive body member enhanced when this is combined with membership of the other institution, so that the greatest prestige and the greatest possibilities for influencing decisions at various levels would be encountered among those who enjoy membership of the gorispolkom and the gorkom buro, a status normally reserved – as we shall see – to full-time career appointees in the party or state apparatus.

### The distribution of the elite

I now turn to discuss the structure of the elite, in order to identify the distribution of the various elite grades, and the social characteristics of their members. There are two major sets of questions associated with this analytical scheme: one relates to the picture at any given time; the other to the patterns through time. These may be briefly stated as follows: what is the 'typical' structure at any one time – how many individuals fall into each category; what is the degree of structural differentiation among the elite; how big is the overlap? Secondly, has the 'typical' distribution tended to change over time – has the degree of differentiation altered over the period covered by this study? Finally, how does the distribution relate to the social characteristics of the various groups identified and to the patterns of participation that were analysed earlier in this study?

In chapter 4 we saw that the 1728 places on the soviet and 1331 places on the gorkom were occupied by 1013 and 600 individuals respectively. Yet, owing to the overlapping membership between the two bodies, the total number of persons identified as participating in the combined elite during the period was 1310,[24] distributed as follows according to the elite grade or status that they attained:

|  | \ | \ | \ | \ | Elite group | \ | \ | \ |
|---|---|---|---|---|---|---|---|---|
|  | A | B | C | D | E | F | G | H |
| No. | 698 | 290 | 231 | 12 | 7 | 22 | 37 | 13 |
| % | 53.3 | 22.1 | 17.6 | 0.9 | 0.5 | 1.7 | 2.8 | 1.0 |

These figures indicate the overall structure of the elite, bearing in mind that among those who combined membership of a party with a state body, not all held membership of both simultaneously. There are a number of striking elements here. The first is that over half (710) never joined the gorkom, in many cases because lack of party membership disqualified them (Groups A and D). Secondly, it can be deduced that a party committee member was more likely to join the soviet than a soviet deputy was to join the gorkom: the overlap of 303 individuals (Groups C, F, G and H) accounts for 50.5 per cent of the 600 who joined the gorkom (Groups B, C, E, F, G and H), but only 29.9 per cent of the 1013 who became deputies (Groups A, C, D, F, G and H). The situation among the executive members is also interesting. There, the likelihood of any individual achieving executive committee status without at least ordinary membership of the other major body is not high: out of forty-seven persons who served on the gorispolkom (Groups D, F and H), only 25.5 per cent failed to serve on the gorkom (i.e. those in Group D); out of fifty-seven who served on the gorkom buro (Groups E, G and H), a mere 12.3 per cent did not also serve as deputies (i.e. those in Group E). However, out of all identified elite members, only 1.0 per cent became members of both the executive bodies (i.e. joined Group H), while the proportion who served *simultaneously* in both capacities was only 0.8 per cent: I shall examine the identity of these outstanding local politicians below. We can learn more about this overall structure by looking at the changes over time, as old members left and new members came in. Allowing for missing data, the available evidence gives us the elite structure at twenty-two points in time, that is, following each election to either the soviet or the gorkom.[25] We find that over the years ordinary deputies (Group A) consistently formed over half the elite, with a mean of 59.2 per cent, or about three-fifths. Ordinary gorkom members (Group B) – a much smaller body, as we have noted – accounted for an average of 17.8 per cent, but in one case (following the soviet election in February 1955) as little as 7.3 per cent. The strength of joint membership (Group C) fluctuated between 24.2 per cent (February 1955) and 6.6 per cent (January 1965), with an average of 15.8. In the executive bodies we see fairly steady numbers, with an average strength of 2.0 per cent for Group D (gorispolkom), 0.4 per cent for Group E (gorkom buro), 1.6 for Group F (gorispolkom and gorkom), 2.8 for Group G (gorkom buro and soviet), and 0.7 for Group H (gorispolkom and gorkom buro); as the size of the total elite increased, the proportion of members in these executive grades declined.

The most interesting long-term feature is a sudden fall in the level of overlapping membership in the early sixties, accompanied by a reduction in the overlap among executive committee members. A few figures will illustrate this: up to and including the soviet election in

March 1961, the strength of Group A among all deputies was about two-thirds; in 1963 it rose sharply, to 82.6 per cent, and remained high in subsequent elections; Group C fell from about a quarter to 11.7 per cent, and remained low in 1965; the number of members in the overlapping executive grades (F, G, H) fell from a dozen or more in earlier years to eight in 1963 (although the former strength was restored subsequently). When we focus on the situation following gorkom elections, we similarly find that in December 1962 the proportion of Group B members (gorkom membership only) shot up from usually less than one-half to 71.2 per cent, and the overlap in ordinary membership (Group C) fell from over one-third to 18.3 per cent. More simply expressed, the number of deputies serving on the gorkom almost halved between 1961 and 1963, and proportionately more than halved, as did the proportion of gorkom members on the soviet between September 1961 and December 1962. This is an important trend, and merits comment.

It can first of all be seen as a reflection of a policy identified by Schapiro, whereby 'Khrushchev . . . has been making steady efforts to keep the boundaries between party and state more distinct than at any time before in Soviet history'.[26] Schapiro wrote that in 1961, but in Tiraspol, the policy as applied to membership of local political bodies was only just beginning to take effect, and the greatest degree of separation of the party and state organs was to come in the last three or four years of Khrushchev's rule. I have no evidence on which to establish whether this was a general phenomenon, or one specific to Tiraspol. If the latter, it might 'be a reflection of a maturing party organisation in the town, so that the party authorities no longer felt they needed to rely on gorkom members to provide a nucleus among the deputies, but 'ordinary' party members could fulfil this role adequately. It should be noted, however, that interlocking membership did not disappear, and always the majority of buro members were deputies, thus maintaining a measure of overlap among the more influential sectors of the elite. By reducing gorkom strength among the deputies, the soviet could be used as a vehicle for giving a wider range of party members and others the experience of public service.

However, several western scholars have pointed out that this period (1960–64) witnessed a significant reduction in the role of the soviets[27] – a period that coincides with this reduction in the level of overlap. Here seems to be the more likely explanation of the trend, pointing to a different interpretation. The reduction in the level of overlap from 37.6 per cent of ordinary gorkom membership in September 1961 to 18.3 per cent in December 1962 implies that the soviet was in a weakened position to influence the debates in the gorkom on issues relevant to its own role as the town's legally responsible administrative body. Furthermore, overlap among the executive members also fell at this time, so that following the election of the xxiv gorkom in December 1962 there was not one individual who spanned membership of the gorispolkom and the gorkom buro. Given the influence of party committee buros in political administration, this was obviously not a strong position for the state body to be in; even the membership of Group F (gorispolkom plus gorkom) fell, to as few as two persons in March 1963. Here I stress again that overlapping membership is a two-way process: not only do gorkom members on the soviet help to ensure that party policies are effectively carried out by the administration; in the reverse direction, deputies on the gorkom can contribute the administrators' and constituents' viewpoint to the party organ's debates. Thus, the greater the overlap, the greater might be the chances of the soviet, as an institution, influencing decisions affecting the town's administration. By contrast, the argument may be advanced that when the degree of overlap is small, this is a sign that the party authorities do not regard the soviet as of sufficient importance to place their most influential members on it as deputies.

There is no obvious way of checking the validity of these interpretations. However, it seems significant that the policy of trying to revive the position of the soviets, undertaken by the post-Khrushchev leadership, was accompanied by a return to a high level of overlap, amounting to 47.3 per cent of ordinary gorkom membership (58.9 per cent of the total committee membership, including the buro) by December 1967. This might reflect a positive recognition on the part of the authorities, first, that the soviet was now important enough to make proper party control worthwhile and necessary (and in this connection it will be recalled that the elections to the 1967 soviet restored the former high level of full party membership among the deputies, as we saw in chapter 3), and secondly, perhaps that the soviet had a distinct contribution to make in the debates and discussions of the gorkom.

If this argument is correct, we thus arrive at the seemingly paradoxical conclusion that a greater measure of overlapping

membership between gorkom and soviet is a sign *not* that the position
of the soviet in the local political system, and especially vis-à-vis the
party committee, is weakened, but rather that it is enhanced.

### THE COMPOSITION OF THE ELITE

Having examined the structure of the town's political elite and how it
changed over time, I now consider the identity of the individuals in
the various categories. For this purpose, I return to the overall
structure defined earlier in this chapter, embracing all 1310
individuals who ever served on the gorkom or on the soviet. We shall
see that the clustering of variables identified in the earlier part of this
study affects the distribution of individuals among the different grades
of elite membership.

#### Sex

Table 6.1 gives figures for the distribution of the sexes in the elite
membership. These figures can be approached from two directions.
First, we can see that males are far more strongly represented than
females in groups that involve overlapping membership of state and
party bodies: in Groups A, B, D and E (non-overlapping), 414 out of
903 (45.8 per cent) were women; in the overlapping groups (C, F, G,
H), they form a mere 45 out of 303 (14.9 per cent).[28] Secondly, the
trend is still clearer when the relative penetration of the various
sectors of the elite by the two sexes is compared: 80.4 per cent of
women rose no higher than ordinary deputy status, compared with
44.0 per cent of men; in the 'executive' grades, D–H, we find fifteen
women (3.3 per cent of known women) and seventy-six men (10.2 per

TABLE 6.1   *Sex distribution among elite groups*

| Sex | A | B | C | D, E | F, G, H | Total |
|-----|---|---|---|------|---------|-------|
| | | | *Elite groups* | | | |
| Male | 329 | 149 | 193 | 11 | 65 | 747 |
| Female | 369 | 37 | 38 | 8 | 7 | 459 |
| Not available | 0 | 104 | 0 | 0 | 0 | 104 |

cent of a much larger number); in the category of ordinary membership of soviet and gorkom (Group C) we have identified 25.8 per cent of the men and only 8.3 per cent of the women. From this I conclude that men are much more likely than women to reach those grades of elite membership that are *prima facie* more influential; and even though the likelihood is low for any individual, of either sex, to achieve executive body status, the chances are higher for a man than for a woman.

### Age

We see a similar distinction when we consider careers according to the age at which the individual first entered the elite, and this concords with the differential turnover rates among the various groups of elite members identified earlier. Those results lead one to expect that younger elite entrants will largely be restricted to the status of ordinary deputy (i.e. Group A), while individuals entering at a more mature age are likely to attain membership of the more important sectors, embracing state and party organs. Despite the absence of data, on Group B in particular, the general pattern is clear from an examination of other groups, as we see from the figures in Table 6.2. The majority in most age groups attained only membership of the soviet, but the proportion is much higher among the younger members, many of whom were Komsomol members and hence not eligible for membership of most of the other sectors: 88.4 per cent of those under 30 served in Group A, compared with an average of 54.6 per cent for the other four age groups; in the 'executive' grades (D–H), we find five who first entered aged under

TABLE 6.2   *Age distribution among elite groups*

| Age Group | Elite groups A | B | C | D, E | F, G, H | Total |
|---|---|---|---|---|---|---|
| Under 30 | 213 | 1 | 22 | 1 | 4 | 241 |
| 30–39 | 218 | 0 | 84 | 6 | 29 | 337 |
| 40–49 | 151 | 0 | 81 | 5 | 30 | 267 |
| Over 50 | 34 | 1 | 20 | 1 | 5 | 61 |
| Not available | 82 | 288 | 24 | 6 | 4 | 404 |

30, compared with seventy-six in the other age groups taken together. A general interpretation of these figures would be that for most young persons, membership of the town's political elite is likely to be restricted to a short term, as a deputy in the soviet; generally they do not remain in the elite until such time as they might qualify for membership of other elite groups. The greatest opportunities for penetration of the 'inner' elite seem to be for those who enter the elite in their thirties – seven of the thirteen in Group H did so. This is partly because a number of these are appointed at that age to key posts from outside the town, rather than rising within the town's own institutions: careers begun elsewhere are advanced in Tiraspol; Tiraspol's own rising politicians tend to be moved on. This question will be further examined in chapters 7 and 8.

*Party membership*

Because full party membership is a requirement for election to the gorkom and its buro, the possibility of an individual *entering* the elite without this qualification can apply only to Groups A and D. However, it is also possible that someone who entered the elite as a non-party deputy could have joined the party later and then progressed to membership of other sections of the elite. Figures in Table 6.3 describe the distribution of the variable of party membership among the elite members. It is clear from the figures that the person who enters the elite without the benefit of communist party membership is not likely to progress very far in local politics: eight out of 328 non-party entrants reached one of the 'overlapping' grades (2.4 per cent), as did five out of 101 Komsomol entrants (about 5.0 per cent); by contrast, 282 out of 773 party full members

TABLE 6.3   *Party membership distribution among elite groups*

| Party membership | Elite groups | | | | | |
|---|---|---|---|---|---|---|
| | A | B | C | D, E | F, G, H | Total |
| Full | 187 | 290 | 213 | 14 | 69 | 773 |
| Candidate and Komsomol | 117 | 0 | 9 | 2 | 2 | 130 |
| Non-party | 317 | 0 | 7 | 3 | 1 | 328 |
| Not available | 77 | 0 | 2 | 0 | 0 | 79 |

(36.5 per cent), and six out of 29 (20.7 per cent) candidate member entrants, did so. Thus, very few of those who entered as non-members went on to achieve full membership of the party and later induction into the executive grades of elite membership, or even gorkom membership. There are some notable exceptions to this general rule, but by and large an individual's political career in the town is determined – perhaps indirectly – by his or her party status when first selected for elite membership.

## Occupation

Here too we find that the elite member's career is governed by the position held on entry into the elite, and that the overlapping and executive grades are largely the preserve of the high-status occupations. However, a clear difference exists between the level of elite membership attained by industrial managerial staff and that reached by individuals in the more directly 'political' positions, as the figures in Table 6.4 demonstrate. This is a key variable, and I shall discuss it at length.

Taking first the elite members who occupied 'weak' positions in industry, education, trade and medicine, we find that the majority

TABLE 6.4   *Occupational distribution among elite groups*

| | Elite groups | | | | | |
| Occupation | A | B | C | D, E | F, G, H | Total |
|---|---|---|---|---|---|---|
| Industrial production | 421 | 3 | 44 | 1 | 5 | 474 |
| Industrial management | 46 | 14 | 69 | 0 | 12 | 141 |
| Party officials | 11 | 55 | 19 | 2 | 15 | 102 |
| State officials | 26 | 1 | 12 | 6 | 13 | 58 |
| T.U., Komsomol officials | 2 | 4 | 8 | 0 | 7 | 21 |
| Law | 2 | 0 | 7 | 1 | 0 | 10 |
| Security | 14 | 0 | 11 | 1 | 9 | 35 |
| Trade | 25 | 0 | 4 | 0 | 0 | 29 |
| Education | 68 | 2 | 28 | 4 | 2 | 104 |
| Medicine | 30 | 0 | 4 | 1 | 0 | 35 |
| Communications | 13 | 1 | 3 | 0 | 4 | 21 |
| Others | 8 | 1 | 2 | 0 | 1 | 12 |
| Not available | 32 | 209 | 20 | 3 | 4 | 268 |

never rose higher than ordinary deputy status: an average of 81.5 per cent in those occupations remained in Group A; their average strength in Groups D–H stood at 2.5 per cent, and in Group C at 15.4 per cent. An interesting feature of this distribution (as revealed in the figures) is the stronger representation of education in the inner grades: 1.9 per cent in Group G, 3.8 per cent in Group D, and 26.9 per cent in Group C. In this, however, they did not rival the more prestigious occupations. Taking together industrial management, party officials, state, trade union and Komsomol officials, an average of 24.3 per cent never rose higher than Group A (deputy status alone), with a figure of 44.8 per cent for state officials – substantially lower than the 65.4 per cent for educationalists. An average of 22.4 per cent of representatives of these occupational groups achieved membership of Groups D–H, in many cases directly, without prior ordinary membership of the soviet or gorkom, alone or jointly. Among industrial managers we find a relatively high level of representation in Group C (48.9 per cent), as we do also with lawyers (77.8 per cent).

One or two further points stand out: the largest number of workers in communications and the mass media (a category that includes both postal workers and newspaper editors) became simple deputies; identified security officials were mainly found among the ordinary deputies, although a substantial proportion of them – over a quarter – were found in the inner executive grades F and G. Finally, there is an interesting contrast between the distribution of state and party officials in the inner grades F, G and H: although numerically party officials reaching these grades outnumbered state officials, the percentage figures of 14.7 for party and 22.4 for state officials show that it was more likely that a state official would reach those grades. Moreover, 10.3 per cent of state officials reached Group D (gorispolkom membership), against no party officials; while only two party officials (2.0 per cent) reached Group E (gorkom buro membership alone), against no state officials. These figures reflect the comparatively larger number of party officials identified (102, compared with only 58 state employees), and this in turn probably relates to a high rate of turnover among PPO secretaries, many of whom did not rise very high in the elite. In fact, when we focus on Group B, we find that 53.9 per cent of party officials became only gorkom members, perhaps during a temporary tenure of office in a primary organisation, but did not endure long enough to merit election to the soviet, or to the gorkom buro.

It seems certain that a number of positions within the town carry automatic membership of gorkom *and* soviet. Apart from leading posts in the executive bodies of each institution, and the directorship of the '1st May' works, which I discussed earlier, other posts that can be identified include the first secretaryship of the Komsomol gorkom, the post of town procurator, the editorship of the local newspaper, and the directorship of the 'Kirov', perhaps the 'Tkachenko', and possibly other industrial works; perhaps also one of the governing positions in the pedagogical institute, and one or two others – frequent reorganisations make it impossible to trace directorships in some cases.

## THE ELITE STRUCTURE AND PARTICIPATION

The above discussion shows that a further dimension must be added to the analysis of the town's political elite presented in earlier chapters. Not only can two distinct sets of individuals be distinguished in each institution, whom I have called 'weak' and 'strong', but these distinctions are reflected in the overall structure of the elite. I would argue that the sectors of the elite that possess the greatest political significance are those that combine gorkom membership with membership of the soviet, and that an individual's political influence, potential if not necessarily actual, is further enhanced by membership of one or both of the executive bodies. My analysis reveals that those individuals who already exhibit a clustering of 'weak' characteristics tend to achieve only the status of soviet deputy. Most of these, it will be recalled, tend also to serve for only short periods in that capacity, and so are not elite members long enough to take advantage of any change in their personal status; in only a few cases did individuals entering the soviet with weak characteristics proceed to other grades in the elite. By contrast, individuals with a combination of 'strong' characteristics normally entered the elite at a higher grade, combining membership of the soviet and of the gorkom, that is, joining one body and shortly afterwards being selected for member-ship of the other. Moreover, as we saw, their membership of the elite tended to be somewhat prolonged, and this would add further to their self-confidence and prestige, and hence, I would argue, to the likelihood of their playing a more positive political role. In this section, I shall examine this question in some detail, by looking again at participants in the public debates of the gorkom and the soviet in terms of their elite grade membership. As before, the analysis will concentrate on the years 1964–67.

## The soviet

During this four-year period, a total of 155 contributions to sessions of the soviet were made by individuals who at one time or another belonged to the elite as I have defined it; 143 were made by persons in the elite at the time they spoke. This contrast between the status of speakers at the time of their contribution and the elite status that they attained suggests that there may be a link between participation in the debates and progress in the elite: the speakers tended to have been past members of the more influential elite grades, or subsequently entered those grades. For instance, of these 155 contributions, seventy (45.2 per cent) were made by persons who were ordinary deputies at the time; but only thirty-four of them (21.9 per cent) came from persons who never rose higher in the elite; *current* members of Group C (gorkom and soviet ordinary membership) accounted for thirty-four speeches, yet fifty-nine speeches (38.1 per cent) came from persons who at some stage achieved Group C membership; thirty-eight speeches (24.5 per cent) came from current members of Groups D–H, but sixty-one (39.4 per cent) were made by individuals who eventually reached one of those grades. It is impossible to determine cause and effect here. I concluded in chapter 5 that participation in the debates had a negligible effect on a deputy's re-election chances. However, the possibility cannot be ruled out that a deputy who made his mark in the sessions of the soviet might then be selected for membership of the party committee: seventeen individuals who were members of the soviet or gorkom alone at the time of their contribution, and five who were members of neither, did serve eventually as ordinary members of both. However, a further plausible interpretation would involve the concept of a group of 'activists' in local politics – a select number of individuals of some political standing in the community, who tend to speak in the sessions; these are the 'duty orators' referred to by Safarov in his criticism of the lack of spontaneity in the sessions:

> Unfortunately, cases are still met with where sessions follow a scenario prepared in advance. Even before the opening of the

session, lists are compiled of deputies who will speak. Sometimes one and the same 'duty orators' speak [at session after session].[29]

These 'duty orators' may in many cases be detailed by the party authorities to speak, as a form of party assignment. They are known by the party authorities to be respected individuals, who can be trusted to deliver the appropriate criticisms of recognised shortcomings, and have already proved themselves by membership of the party body. A further group of speakers may also be prompted by the party or other authorities: persons whose political reliability is on trial, for whom successful participation in the debates of the soviet may be a recommendation for appointment as, for example, PPO secretary, followed by election to the gorkom at a subsequent party conference. In cases such as these, speaking in a session is, in a sense, 'hack' work – a response to external pressures in the light of political self-interest, and largely unconnected with constituents' pressures. A factory party organisation might thus detail one of its members to speak in a debate, as a party assignment, telling him more or less what to say, after which he is rewarded with further political promotion. I cannot say how far this characterisation of speakers is an accurate reflection of soviet political reality; but certainly the notion is compatible with the career patterns that I have identified, and with the comments of Soviet writers on the stylised debates.

A final point concerns the very high level of participation among the executive groups: we find that 24.5 per cent of *speeches* were made by current members of Groups D–H; 39.3 per cent were made by persons who attained membership of those groups; and 22.3 per cent of the *speakers* reached those elite grades. These figures reflect the fact that the *readers of reports* were mainly drawn from these groups. The total number of 'speeches' includes the reports, of which there was at least one at every session, sometimes more; these were usually read by members of those groups, whose steady level of contribution to the sessions was maintained by this means. Of the thirty-four reports, twenty-seven (almost two-fifths) were delivered by persons who attained those elite grades. Again, this adds to the point that the more active individuals are those whose membership is not restricted to ordinary membership of the soviet. However, here too one cannot conclude that the rapporteurs are acting independently; indeed, even more than the discussion speeches, the keynote reports are likely to have been carefully vetted by the authorities, even discussed by the gorkom and its departments, before being given to the appropriate gorispolkom official for delivery. The state body may have had some influence at the drafting stage; but the picture of effective party control over the content of reports perhaps more accurately portrays the balance between the two institutions. It also supports my contention that the greater the overlap between state and party bodies, especially at the executive committee level, the greater the chances that the soviet will have influence over its own affairs.


*The gorkom*

In the gorkom, I could not identify the current status of contributors during 1964 because no membership list of the xxv gorkom, in office during that year, was published: the remarks that follow are therefore based on the three-year period 1965–67. During that time, seventy-six contributions were made by identified elite members, including fourteen by persons not then in the elite, but who were past or subsequent members: thirty-six speeches – almost half – came from members of Group C, while eleven contributions were made by persons who attained only party committee membership (Group B); twenty-four speeches came from executive body members, including sixteen from Group G (gorkom buro members who also served on the soviet). As with the soviet, the figures are somewhat distorted by the inclusion of major reports, all thirteen of which were made by executive body members, including eight by Petrik, gorkom first secretary, in Group G, and three by the gorispolkom chairman, in Group H.

Here again, it seems as though membership of the other main political body (the soviet, in this case) adds to the political authority of gorkom members, while membership of one of the executive bodies adds further to an individual's political stature, and leads to greater public participation for him. But once more, it is perhaps reasonable to suggest that the speeches are far from spontaneous in most cases. The reports, often dealing with matters of national concern, were probably drafted by the republican party authorities, and read by the gorkom first secretary or other influential figures in order to give the appropriate sense of authority. The speeches from ordinary members, often indicating precise ways in which their own party organisation can help to carry out the policy under discussion, might constitute the more meaningful part of the debate, if they have been properly briefed by the PPO to speak in a particular sense.

## The activists

In the section above on the soviet, I put forward the idea of a group of 'activists' who tended to speak in sessions. This notion is given some support by the existence of overlap among the speakers to the soviet sessions and the gorkom plenums. In the years 1964–67, seventy-six elite members spoke at sessions of the soviet and fifty-seven at gorkom plenums. Yet the total number of individual elite members involved was 113, indicating an overlap of twenty persons who spoke at meetings of both bodies: this represents 35.1 per cent of speakers at the plenums and 26.3 per cent of those who addressed soviet sessions. Of these twenty persons, one was in Group A (although since she held the position of head of the gorispolkom's education otdel when elected in 1967, she might later have been recruited to gorkom membership and thus moved to Group C, as did her predecessors); among the remainder, eleven were in Group C, five were in Group G, and three in Group H.

### POLICY INFLUENCES

This discussion of the levels of participation among elite members puts into greater perspective the analysis in chapter 5, where it became clear that very few members of either body had a chance to speak at meetings. The chances seem to have been higher for a set of individuals whose personal position caused them to merit membership of both major political organs, coupled frequently with membership of one or both executive bodies. In my discussion above I suggested that there is probably a controlling link between the party authorities and the work of the soviet. I conclude this chapter with a brief examination of this question: what form of link can be identified, if any? For example, does the chronology of the topics debated enable us to identify any direct policy influence? Do personnel changes in one institution presage changes in the other?

In fact, during the period 1964–67 (and in earlier years) there is no identifiable thematic link between the topics discussed in the formal sessions of the soviet and the gorkom plenums. Indeed, as we saw in chapter 5, there seems to be a broad division of functions between gorkom and soviet, with the party committee debating general political problems and wider national issues, and the soviet concerning itself with more practical aspects of administration in the town. The chronology of these formal sessions shows that not once was an issue debated in one body and then again in the other. Thus, the gorkom as such does not decide on issues, and then transfer its membership to the soviet to give legal status to that decision.

On two occasions, however, links can be identified. The first concerns personnel changes, which were of such significance that they required a plenum and a session within three days of each other, both restricted exclusively to these organisational questions. The gorispolkom chairman, V. I. Yulin, had left Tiraspol, and was to be replaced; the post went to V. I. Telenkov, then second secretary to the gorkom, who was relieved of that position 'in connection with his transfer to other work' (*Dnestrovskaya pravda*, 21 February 1967). Telenkov's secretaryship went to V. I. Timukhin, who was relieved (by the gorkom plenum) of the chairmanship of the town committee of the popular control, a post that went to V. V. Nikolaev. Other minor changes were also made among gorkom personnel. Only Yulin and Telenkov were *directly* involved in the changes in the state apparatus, but the change of gorispolkom chairman was accompanied by other cadre changes, at the very time when the town was preparing for fresh elections. Presumably in the run-up to the election a gorispolkom deputy chairman could competently have held the fort until new officers were appointed by the incoming soviet: the fact that such a shake-up occurred at the time it did shows how important these changes must have been.

The second occasion when direct party–state links can be seen was in September 1966, when a joint party–soviet aktiv met to present awards to the outstanding vigilantes[30] in the town and to discuss the campaign to combat delinquency and hooliganism. Although no doubt many soviet deputies and gorkom members took part in this meeting, it was not a formal session of either body.

The conclusion that must be drawn from this discussion is that the links between the gorkom and the town soviet tend to be informal. There can be no doubt that the executive bodies are in constant contact – they are, after all, situated in the same building – and the party authorities keep a close watch over the work of the soviet, the gorispolkom and its departments, and probably keep the state bodies informed of current developments. No information is published on the meetings of the gorkom buro or the gorispolkom;[31] however, overlapping membership between the executive bodies would ensure that the party authorities were always aware of the current situation in the work of the soviet and its executive, and hence in a position to intervene with instructions at any time if necessary. Similarly, there were gorispolkom representatives on the gorkom, and the practice of inviting responsible outsiders to attend plenums could ensure that all were present who needed to be informed or to make a contribution to party deliberations: during my visit to Tiraspol, the gorispolkom secretary, I. D. Roshkovan, not a gorkom member, had to put off an interview 'because of a plenum'. Nevertheless, the plenums themselves are not of key importance. The more vital business of the town is conducted behind the closed – and thickly padded – doors of the offices of the two executive bodies, to which neither the press nor the public has free access.

Ultimately, the power to intervene in sorting out problems, getting things done, rests with the *party* authorities, as references in the Soviet press and my own experience in Tiraspol indicate. Thus, a deputy to a raion soviet in Estonia explained in an article in *Sovety deputatov trudyashchikhsya* how he succeeded in getting footpaths repaired by calling on the raikom secretary, after a series of state and industrial officials had failed to respond to his requests for assistance. He adds, 'after this, the repair work went significantly better'.[32] I experienced a similar party intervention in October 1967: arriving with a Soviet colleague to attend a conference in Tiraspol, the town's 'Friendship' (*Prietenya*) hotel – directly opposite the House of Soviets – turned out to be officially full; however, a telephone call from a gorkom official prompted the quick finding of a room. The presence of guests sleeping on the hotel landing outside our room seemed to add credence to the manifestation of power displayed by the party official with his telephone across the street.

CONCLUSION

My discussion of Tiraspol tends to confirm the generally held interpretation of party–state relations. It is clear that it is the party, represented by the gorkom, that holds ultimate responsibility, as Soviet discussions of the question lead one to believe. However, I have also identified a tendency to maintain distinctions between the two bodies, and the number and nature of personnel links varied substantially over time. My analysis also suggests that the relationship is not a simple one, whereby the party in some way controls the soviet. I argue from my data that it is a two-way relationship, and that overlapping membership is vital and beneficial so long as the division of functions between party and state institutions is maintained. In other words, so long as the party retains its current position of holding final responsibility for the country, the soviet – as representative of the views of electors and administrators – needs a substantial measure of overlapping membership as a means of influencing the broader political discussions in the direction of greater responsiveness and rationality.

I present these arguments and conclusions fully conscious of the nature and limitations of my data sources; however, only the archival material on meetings of the executive bodies and the soviet and gorkom themselves would permit the kind of exhaustive check needed to confirm my interpretation. Such sources are unlikely to be available in the foreseeable future.

# CHAPTER 7

# Relations With Other Bodies

I now turn my attention to relations between the gorkom and soviet members and other political bodies, inside and outside the town. This will place the political institutions of Tiraspol in the broader context of Soviet political life, and show how the members of the town's political elite participate in the work of other bodies.

## THE TOWN KOMSOMOL ORGANISATION

When I examined trends in the social composition of the town soviet in chapter 3, I discovered that Komsomol members played an increasingly important role as deputies, a feature that Tiraspol shared with other soviets all over the USSR. By definition, they were mainly younger; they were very often females; and the majority were in low-status occupations. This combination of characteristics, it was clear, was usually accompanied by only a short spell of soviet membership – usually one term of office – after which most of these young politicians returned, presumably, to 'ordinary life'. Indeed, in very few cases did former Komsomol member deputies return to give further service in the town's main political organs.

An important exception, however, are the officers of the Komsomol gorkom, who were already communist party full members by the time they reached that position. Ten of these were identified as members of the soviet or gorkom, hence members of the town's political elite as I have defined it, and seven went on to achieve membership of one or both executive committees. On this basis one might suggest that a secretaryship in the town's Komsomol committee is a valuable entry-point into the political elite. These individuals must have already been singled out for appointment to the Komsomol position, and success in that post led to further promotion. The first secretary was always, *ex officio* as it were, a member of the gorkom buro; other secretaries were also members of the gorkom and soviet.

Career developments after relinquishing their Komsomol post varied, but the variations are interesting. In three cases the person concerned disappeared from view, and no further trace has come to light. Two former secretaries – both women – later headed the gorispolkom's culture department. One of these, L. M. Bozhu, had meanwhile served as chairman of the town's Red Cross society and later as director of the town theatre (an example, incidentally, of how even such institutions are directed by persons who are essentially politicians). She served on the soviet from 1959 and the gorkom from September 1961, and attended the Moldavian party congress in 1966. Born in 1934, she was only 25 when she first rose to prominence in the soviet as secretary of the Komsomol organisation in the 'Tkachenko' works. When interviewed by me in 1968, she appeared to be a very lively woman, full of enthusiasm in her task of bringing cultural life to the town's rather drab existence.

This example and the next one, that of V. I. Timukhin, confirm the political significance of industrial enterprises, specifically the 'Tkachenko' works. Bozhu became Komsomol gorkom secretary after a period as Komsomol primary organisation secretary in the works, at a time when Timukhin was Komsomol gorkom first secretary; he later went to the works as secretary of the works party buro, before moving on to the chairmanship of the party–state control committee, and later second secretary of the party gorkom. His successor as Komsomol gorkom first secretary, V. V. Nikolaev, also later became chairman of the control committee, having served in the intervening period as secretary of the party committee in the 'Elektromash' factory. Clearly a period in industrial party organisation administration can be seen as an important training stage in a political career.

Timukhin can be identified as perhaps the most successful of that generation of politicians who rose during our period, and whose career began effectively within the town, with the Komsomol gorkom first secretaryship as his first major posting. In 1967 he had before him the prospect of a career to match that of a predecessor, S. A. Morozov, who served as Komsomol gorkom first secretary in 1950. Morozov's example also suggests, however, that Timukhin could probably not advance much further without a move away from Tiraspol, perhaps involving special training at a party school. By March 1963, Morozov was identified as first secretary of the Kagul gorkom (*Sovetskaya Moldaviya*, 7 March 1963), a member of the

Moldavian supreme soviet and central committee; in July 1964 he was transferred to head a council of ministers department (identified in *Sovetskaya Moldaviya*, 3 July and 10 October 1964).

The prospects for a Komsomol gorkom *first* secretary to, play a prominent role in the town's political life (and later in that of the republic) seem considerable. However, the same prospects do not necessarily extend beyond the first secretaryship: V. I. Naumenko, elected second secretary in 1954 (one of the few instances where details of Komsomol office-holders were published) did not enter either the soviet or the gorkom at any time, nor did his successor, S. V. Shevchenko; other secretaries too have been identified who played no part in the town's political elite, as defined here. The post of first secretary alone is sufficiently important for the political authorities to select the incumbents with great care and bring them into the political elite proper. In other words, the post probably goes to individuals who have already demonstrated their potential; they are already chosen for a political career before that honour and responsibility are bestowed on them. While in the post they can gain further administrative experience, which then assists their further rise in the political elite.

There is a further element that ties the Komsomol into the overall political structure: participation by politicians in its work. The occasional press reports of Komsomol meetings reveal that a number of Komsomol-member deputies spoke in the plenums of the Komsomol gorkom and at town Komsomol conferences, as did officials of the gorispolkom. Thus, to cite one example, the speakers at the xxii town Komsomol conference, held in January 1965 (reported in *Dnestrovskaya pravda*, 28 January 1965) included V. V. Tkachenko, Komsomol gorkom first secretary, a deputy (and gorkom buro member), who read a report, D. Dimitrova, a soviet deputy, from the 'Fortieth anniversary of the Komsomol' factory, I. T. Voloshin, head of the town's militia department, and T. S. Ovcharek, head of the education department. Party gorkom officials also occasionally took part in the work of the Komsomol organisation: Petrik (gorkom first secretary) attended the xxiv Komsomol conference in December 1967; A. P. Skvortsov, gorkom secretary, attended and addressed a Komsomol gorkom plenum in August 1960; and in October 1950 a meeting of the Komsomol aktiv was attended by A. I. Gutsalo, party gorkom second secretary.

The links between the Komsomol and, especially, the party

organisation are sufficient to indicate the importance with which the political authorities regard it. Indeed, for A. M. Korolëv, the Komsomol is 'one of the most important transmission belts from the party to the masses'.[1] We can see clearly that the leading position in the Komsomol committee is one of the vital political offices in the town; moreover, the measure of overlap in membership of party, state and Komsomol organs for which evidence has come to light means that the elite model I put forward in chapter 6 could be further extended to include Komsomol gorkom membership overlapping with soviet and party gorkom. In the case of Tiraspol, information on the Komsomol gorkom is too scant to permit a proper study; it might be possible, however, to attempt such a complete analysis at a higher level, say the republic.

## TRADE UNIONS

The press contains scarcely any information about the formal activities of trade unions. Their ordinary membership is well represented in both soviet and gorkom, since virtually all employees in the country are union members. Yet the available evidence suggests that the trade unions are not an effective base from which to enter political life. Of all the elite members during our period, a mere thirteen individuals have been identified as holding a trade union office, and not all of those held it simultaneously with political elite membership. One was identified in 1953 as chairman of the town committee of the educational workers' union, a position he still held in 1965 when he was director of the town's House of the Teacher – the union office, with recreational, library and other facilities for use by the town's teaching fraternity. By that time, however, he had lost his membership of both the soviet and the gorkom, which had been intermittent in each case.

In three of the remaining cases, the position of trade union branch chairman is known to have been followed later by a PPO secretary-ship. This may indicate that a union branch committee chairman-ship is one of the lowest rungs on the political ladder, below the position of PPO secretary. However, several individuals were identified in such a union position after serving on the gorkom, and in at least two cases *after* a term as PPO secretary.

My general conclusion is that tenure of a trade union office is of relatively little political significance. It may help an individual to gain a foothold, by bringing him into contact with party and soviet officials; on the other hand, it might also be a sign in some cases that an individual has lost some of the prestige that he had possessed by virtue of elite membership. In any case, given that the tenure of a union position was revealed in so few instances, it seems reliable to conclude that the trade union structure is only marginally involved with the main political structures at the town level. This is in contrast to higher levels: at the level of the republic, the trade union council chairman is always a central committee member and normally at least a candidate member of the republican politburo (in fact, that post in Moldavia was taken in 1972 by Petrik, first secretary of Tiraspol gorkom); and at the central level, the all-Union central trade union council chairmanship is normally taken by a central committee politburo member; at both levels, the chairman is usually deputy to the appropriate supreme soviet.

When reports of trade union activity did appear in the press, participation by elite members was in evidence. In March 1955, for example, a meeting of the town's trade union aktiv was addressed by gorkom secretary Gutsalo, on the theme of the recent CPSU central committee plenum and its implications for the town's trade union organisations (*Stalinskii put'*, 20 March 1955); he spoke at a further aktiv later in the year (*Stalinskii put'*, 23 November 1955). Once again, however, the fact that few other names were mentioned in these sparse accounts suggests that the political importance of these discussions was not high. The presence of a gorkom secretary adds a little dignity to the occasion, and ensures that the exclusively party and political interest is firmly represented. But the trade union organisation seems not to be the place where a politician might make his mark: the gorkom secretary's speech appears to be more of a ritual than a politically significant event in his career.

## Control Organisations

A similar conclusion must be drawn about the control organisations, the party–state control and the popular control which replaced it in 1965. As we saw above, the chairmanship of the town's control organisation was entrusted to individuals of some standing – in at least two cases to persons with a Komsomol background.

Occasionally the press carried reports of meetings of the town's party–state control aktiv. One held on 15 July 1965 (reported in *Dnestrovskaya pravda*, 20 July 1965) had 'almost four hundred' control activists present, and a report on measures to improve efficiency and quality in production was read by gorkom first secretary Petrik. Four discussants were named in the press account, and none was a current member of the elite, although one was a former gorkom candidate member and one later became a full member. At a similar meeting in March 1964 (reported in *Leninskoe znamya*, 14 March 1964), a report had been read by a gorkom secretary; none of the other three speakers has been identified as a soviet or gorkom member at any time. In general, despite these occasional links, the references to the organisation and its officers in the pages of the local press were so rare that one must conclude that its political – as opposed, perhaps, to its economic – significance is slight.

## OTHER FORUMS ATTACHED TO THE MAJOR ORGANS

Apart from taking part in the meetings of other institutions, elite members also had a chance to take part in conferences and assemblies arranged under the auspices of one or both of the major political organs. The most important of these are the town party conference, at which the gorkom was elected, and meetings of the town party aktiv and other, specialised aktivs.

### The town party conference

Technically the highest organ of the town party organisation, the conference met periodically throughout the time covered in this study, although not always as prescribed by party rules: annually under the 1952 rules, biennially after 1961. Some conferences were held ahead of schedule, others were delayed. The maximum period between them was twenty-three months (between the xxvii and xxviii conferences); the minimum possibly as little as three months (between the xiv and xv). The somewhat unpredictable pattern may mean that these events take place at the discretion of political leaders – either in the town itself or at the republican level – rather than out of respect for the demands of the rule book. This practice has been legitimised by an amendment adopted by the xxiv cpsu Congress

(1971): these conferences should now be held at least twice in any five-year period, that is every two to three years.[2]

Apart from the election of a new committee, the conference convenes in order to consider a report on the work of the gorkom and the whole organisation during the period since the previous conference. Two reports formed the bulk of the agenda: one by the first secretary, on the work of the gorkom, and one by the chairman of the auditing commission, on that commission's work. The debate that followed permitted up to twenty or more party members to speak; a representative of the Moldavian central party apparatus also usually made a speech.

The press accounts generally revealed little of the tenor of contributions from the floor, although a lengthy list of participants was normally published. At the xxvii conference, in January 1966, for example, twenty-one conference delegates were reported as having spoken, apart from the main speakers (*Dnestrovskaya pravda*, 18 January 1966); a year earlier, seventeen discussants' names appeared in the report of the xxvi conference (*Dnestrovskaya pravda*, 19 January 1965). Most of these speakers were well-known politicians, already established in the town's political elite as deputies, gorkom members and executive body members. In 1966, all but four of the speakers were elected by the conference to membership of the new gorkom, and one of those, the raikom secretary, was unlikely to be elected to the town organ. Among the individuals who spoke in the debate were the party–state control committee chairman, the Komsomol gorkom first secretary, the town procurator, the director of the Moldavian power station (situated on territory that fell under the jurisdiction of the Tiraspol soviet) and of several other industrial enterprises, and the secretaries of nine ppos in the town. Without details of what was said, this brief list indicates the nature of these conferences: this was a forum at which established politicians could gain personal publicity and perhaps impress their superiors in the republican capital, rather than one where rising politicians could make their mark on the town's political life; even less where representatives of the party grass roots could express the views of those whom they in some sense represented.

A similar interpretation is suggested by the reports of earlier conferences. In 1955, the xvii conference was held, and given fairly extensive press coverage (*Stalinskii put'*, 23 and 26 October 1955). The first secretary's report reflected problems that have remained with the Soviet economy for a long time: he spoke of 'serious shortcomings which cannot fail to evoke disquiet', in particular low productivity in industry, failure to fulfil plans, high incidence of manual processes (i.e. under-capitalisation), and party organisations' lack of attention to the quality of goods. The workers of the gorkom's industrial otdel were roundly criticised by the speakers for being 'rare visitors' to industrial enterprises. This was strong criticism, and much of it came from responsible party and industrial officials. Presumably they spoke with the sanction, if not directly at the prompting, of central party authorities. The irony of the situation is, of course, that they were the very officials who were in a position to do something to alleviate the situation, by pleading with higher authorities for resource allocations. Those who discussed the speech – industrial managers, ppo secretaries, a trade union branch chairman, the town's military commissioner – could really only agree with the points made. These leading local figures were discussing in the open matters that must have been well known to them all in a town the size of Tiraspol. This being the case, the role of the conference is seen in a special light: it is a vehicle for giving publicity to problems that are well known to those who speak about them, but that are raised before the general public according to the current priorities of central authorities.

There seems to be a significant distinction between the conference here and at higher levels. For Stewart, the oblast party conference 'seems to serve primarily as a school or training session for lower level Party and state officials'.[3] This conference, at which hundreds of party organisations in scores of towns and rural districts are represented, can indeed, as Stewart suggests, serve as a forum at which local representatives can 'acquire some of the attitudes and values necessary for making decisions in their own area of competence' through their formal and informal contacts with colleagues from other districts and with responsible officials who are themselves only one tier below the very summit of political life, and who are very often members of the cpsu central committee.[4] The same might also apply to conferences in major cities with very large party organisations (Moscow, Leningrad, Kiev, and the like). It seems significant too that the oblast conference discussed major economic questions,[5] whereas the business agenda of Tiraspol town party conference was normally restricted to the reports of the work of the organisation and its committees. In short, the scale of the conference is much more modest in a small city, where party and local government officials are known to each other and to the mass membership. In the context of a republic as small as Moldavia, the republican party congress is the nearest equivalent to the oblast party conference, and fulfils an educative role comparable with that of the oblast gathering. The regular conference of a town or rural district is much more in the nature of a political rally, at which well-known local political leaders affirm the appropriate line, taking their cue from the gorkom first secretary, under the watchful eyes of a representative of higher authority.

## *The aktiv*

A further forum attached to the party organisation is the party aktiv, which may be called to discuss both edicts of central party bodies and questions of local significance. Over the years, and increasingly in the 1960s, the work of gorkom plenums was supplemented – perhaps even supplanted – by sessions of the aktiv, which appeared to function very much like plenums. This was particularly true when the plenums themselves were thrown open to a wide circle of committee non-members, and in this Tiraspol party organisation was emulating practices identified elsewhere.[6] Whereas during the 1950s there were usually merely one or two aktiv meetings, there were three in 1964, two in 1965, three in 1966, and four in 1967, including two within days of each other in January. These include more specialist aktivs (party–state, party–economic), but the trend, and the coverage given in the press, show the extent to which this ill-defined body developed in importance during the sixties, accompanied by a similar rise in the frequency of gorkom plenary sessions: a sign perhaps of revitalisation in the party organisation.

The range of participants in meetings of the aktiv is indicated by the following list, from a report of a meeting to discuss the theme, 'Communist aesthetics in production and everyday living':

...members and candidate members of the party gorkom, secretaries of party organisations, leaders of industrial enterprises, construction, transport, communal and trade organisations and institutions, chairmen of trade union committees, secretaries of Komsomol organisations, heads of construction bureaux, managers of clubs, libraries and agitpunkty [political education centres], school directors, and leaders of amateur artistic groups.[7]

The range of topics discussed by the Tiraspol aktiv ranged from broad

general issues such as the above, to the CPSU's struggle for the
solidarity of the world communist movement (January 1967), party
leadership of trade union organisations (May 1967), education
(March 1965), and measures to develop industry (June 1955); the
party–state aktiv of September 1965 discussed problems of delinquency in the town. The agenda was often prompted by a recent
CPSU central plenum's resolution and occasionally the main report
was read by a leading politician from the republican central
committee. Normally, however, it was delivered by one of the gorkom
secretaries, and the speakers in the discussion were largely drawn
from present or past members of the elite, or in some cases persons
who later became soviet or gorkom members.

Many of the speakers held responsible party, managerial or other
leading positions in the town, but the range of professional interests
represented seemed somewhat broader than that of the plenums.
Take 1967, for example, when thirty-three different individuals spoke
in the four meetings of the aktiv. They included ten PPO secretaries
and one gorkom secretary, two Komsomol gorkom secretaries, three
industrial managers and a foreman, the gorispolkom chairman, the
town procurator, the head of the town's public catering organisation,
two who were at the time chairman of the 'Znanie' public
enlightenment society, the rector of the education institute, and two
employees of DOSAAF.[8]

If we look at speakers in terms of their membership of the political
elite, we find some interesting results: seventeen were elite members at
the time of their contribution; there was also a measure of overlap
among speakers at the aktiv, the plenums and the soviet sessions.
Quite apart from the leading officials who delivered reports, in the
four years 1964–67 we find that twenty-one discussants spoke in a
plenum and at a meeting of the aktiv, and the same number at a
session and an aktiv meeting. Furthermore, if the rapporteurs are
included, eight persons spoke on one or more occasions at all three
forums. This measure of overlap backs up the notion I put forward in
the previous chapter of a limited circle of activists who tended to
speak at political meetings in the town, and not all of them were
members of the elite as I have defined it. It is clear then that elite
members were severely restricted in their chances of speaking at the
limited number of public meetings of the major political organs; and
beyond that, the level of their participation was further reduced by
the existence of a restricted circle of activists who tended to dominate

the public activity of the political institutions. One might speculate about how attentively these 'duty orators' (Safarov's concept can be extended to apply to all public political activity in the town) were listened to. They were certainly given all due press coverage and publicity; presumably, too, they were given their full quota of 'stormy, prolonged applause'. Yet one cannot help wondering whether the ordinary newspaper reader, the ordinary deputy, gorkom member, delegate to a conference, or member of an aktiv meeting, might have reacted with more than a quiet groan at the sight of the same individuals parading to the rostrum on one occasion after another.

In this situation, with party, soviet, trade union and Komsomol representatives participating in the business of all kinds of public meeting, the distinctions between the different assemblies become blurred. This applies particularly to the two party forums, which look to the outsider as essentially the same, even in terms of who was present. However, there is some suggestion in the topics discussed at plenums and aktiv meetings towards the end of our period of an attempt to separate the functions of the two. Not all plenums were reported in the press, and some seemed to be restricted to dealing with 'organisational questions'. In those cases, the meetings were presumably not open to outsiders, except representatives of the central republican apparatus. In these circumstances, the gorkom members might be seen to play their genuine party-constitutional role, assuming the provision of adequate discussion and meaningful votes. By retaining for the committee the politically vital prerogative of staffing and appointment, the intended significance of gorkom membership – eroded in the extended plenums – was restored.

Whether this tendency represents a definite development is unclear to the end of 1967. For most of our period, the main feature distinguishing plenums from aktivs, it seems, was a purely legal one, relating to the competence of each forum to take decisions of a particular validity and authority: the aktiv may adopt resolutions of exhortation to all the communists in the town's party organisation; the gorkom plenum takes decisions on matters that require specific implementation by party organisations; the soviet passes resolutions that have legal force within the town. The aktiv also has a major educative purpose, rather than political decision-making, and joint party–state aktivs give widespread publicity to specific problems.[9]

Thus we arrive at a rough functional division between the various institutions in which the town's political elite members were actively involved. In the remaining sections of this chapter I consider relations with bodies outside the town, beginning with the Tiraspol rural district.

### RELATIONS WITH THE RAION

The administrative offices of Tiraspol rural district – those of the raikom, the raiispolkom and their various departments – were housed in the same building as those of the town, and the two administrative areas shared the same newspaper throughout much of our period; yet links between the two appear to have been minimal. In an interview with gorispolkom officers, it was stressed to me that they were not competent to speak on behalf of the raion authorities (although they could arrange introductions). Only very occasionally did raion affairs intrude into the work of the town authorities.

Some of these occasions have already been mentioned. Gorkom plenums several times discussed agricultural matters, when the debate centred largely on the practical assistance that enterprises and institutions in the town could give to the farms of the raion. In at least one of these debates, raion representatives were present and made useful contributions (the plenum of 31 March 1964). Two of the three raion speakers were deputies of the raion soviet, and all three are believed to have been members or candidate members of the raikom, including its deputy secretary. The raikom first secretary occasionally participated in the work of the town party organisation, as did the gorkom first secretary in the raion organisation's work – for instance, bearing the fraternal greetings of their respective committees to the town or raion party conference.

There were, too, occasional joint functions, such as a 'jubilee session' of the town and raion soviets, held in September 1950 to celebrate the tenth anniversary of the formation of the Moldavian SSR, opened by Pechërkin, gorkom secretary, and addressed by Bronnikov, gorispolkom deputy chairman.[10] Training sessions for party workers arranged by the town's party authorities were sometimes also open to workers from the raion, as the following announcement (from *Dnestrovskaya pravda*, 18 September 1965) indicates:

On September 20 at 10 a.m. in the political education room of the gorkom begins a six-day seminar (with release from regular work) for propagandists of basic political schools.

Party Gorkom.<br>Party Raikom.

The direct links were thus sparse; yet an article in the newspaper *Znamya pobedy* for 25 March 1955 informed readers that 'From month to month, links between the workers of Tiraspol and the collective farmers and mechanised workers of our raion are growing stronger', and party meetings throughout the town had discussed ways of improving their role in the rural area. The gorkom itself had recently sent out nineteen propagandist groups, consisting of 'the most highly qualified lecturers and rapporteurs', who were touring the agricultural undertakings giving lectures on party and governmental decisions on agriculture, the international situation, and 'the struggle of the workers for peace'.

The town party organisation was clearly required to play a politically educative role in rural areas, a role that seems to have continued. Thus, a gorkom plenum of April 1965 (reported in *Dnestrovskaya pravda*, 24 April 1965) debated the agricultural question and what the town could do to help solve the mounting problems revealed in the March CPSU central committee plenum. The plenum's resolution criticised in particular methods of farm management, recruitment policies, and the general lack of responsibility in the countryside.[11] Public institutions, including the soviets, were instructed to help extend the democratic principle inside collective farms, as a means of improving agricultural administration. In view of the general weakness of the party in rural areas, and the suspicion of the rural population towards science as revealed in the central committee's resolution, much of the educative burden naturally fell on urban party workers and institutions, not only to explain policy requirements to the peasantry, but also to produce equipment for the farms, and carefully and patiently.demonstrate its use and value.

There was a further problem, which these measures helped to overcome: the peculiarities of the economic institutional structure. The town's factories are responsible for their production and for deliveries of their output to the ministries that control them. They have no direct responsibility to the ultimate customer – the collective farms – because of the complex intervening state trading organisation. Producer–customer relations are therefore normally remote, and from time to time the *political* institutions become involved, to help solve politically relevant economic problems, by supplementing and circumventing the normal economic and commercial channels, and bringing producers and customers into direct contact.

Apart from these functional and business links between town and raion, there were also occasional links in personnel. Twenty-eight members of the town elite are believed to have been members of the raion elite, similarly defined; one member of the auditing commission also served as a raikom candidate member; and a former employee of the raiispolkom apparatus later became a town soviet deputy and head of one of the gorispolkom departments, a gorkom candidate member, and, towards the end of our period, secretary of the gorispolkom PPO. In some cases, individuals held simultaneous membership of raion and town elites: I. A. Bragin, military commissioner, served on the gorkom between 1958 and 1967 and on the town soviet from 1959 onwards, and also on the raion soviet in 1963–65 and on the raikom during 1965. M. M. Lesovaya, raikom secretary during the 1950s, interrupted her raion soviet membership to serve on the town soviet for the term 1957–59. More frequently, however, elite membership in one area (town or raion) preceded membership in the other. A. S. Kosorukov, raikom secretary (later first secretary) between 1951 and 1962 and a raion soviet deputy from the 1953–55 to the 1961–63 term, had by July 1964 been appointed deputy director of the town's '1st May' fruit bottling works, and by the end of August 1967 director of the number six bread combine; in this capacity he was elected to the gorkom in December that year. Similarly, A. V. Levitskaya, a school headmistress in Slobodzeya village who served intermittently on the raion soviet and raikom between 1951 and 1961, transferred in about 1960 to become director of a school in the town, entered the town soviet in 1961, and added gorkom membership in January 1966.

Among other town and raion elite members, about whom little further information is available, it seems likely that an occasional token representative served on one of the political organs in the other area, to symbolise the links and interests that existed between the two. However, in no sense could the top leadership of town and raion be classified as a single 'inner elite', such as Cattell identified among the leaders of Leningrad city and oblast.[12] There is no information at all about whatever informal links may have existed between the town and raion workers in the Tiraspol House of Soviets. Contacts must surely take place daily; yet for most purposes, judging by the published record, the two administrations remained entirely distinct, formally linked only by occasional joint meetings and rare individual participation by members of one elite in the affairs of the other.

## RELATIONS WITH HIGHER BODIES

I have more than once said that the town's administration is part of a wider system of government, and that the elite is not an independent and distinct unit. I now explore further the relationship between that elite and the Moldavian republican authorities, particularly the supreme soviet and the party central committee.

The two principles of 'democratic centralism' and administrative subordination imply that local political bodies in party, state and other institutions are 'guided' in their work by higher organs. The town soviet is subordinated to the Moldavian supreme soviet, the gorispolkom to the council of ministers and its departments to the appropriate ministries, and the gorkom to the republican party central committee. Published information does not indicate how far higher bodies do direct the work of the town's political organs; once again, we should need access to archives to look at that question in detail. However, there are a number of pointers to indicate the position.

First, we have seen that the party committee in particular often used a higher committee's resolution as a basis for debate – took its cue, in other words, from the work of central authorities.

Secondly, these meetings were attended by representatives of higher authorities; this applies not only to the party conference, but also to gorkom plenums, soviet sessions, and meetings of various aktivs. The visiting speakers in the period 1964–67 included I. I. Bodyul, first secretary of the republican central committee (July 1967), the minister of culture (May 1964 and August 1965) and other ministers, and other leading Moldavian public figures. The presence of these distinguished visitors on the one hand enhanced the dignity of the occasion and gave the local elite members a chance to rub shoulders with the influential, and on the other hand gave the republican authorities a chance to observe the behaviour of the town's politicians, and most likely make an inspection tour of the town.

Thirdly, the key practice of nomenklatura effectively gives the higher committees the power to select the occupants of particular positions in the town's political and administrative organs. This applies especially to party committee secretaries, gorispolkom officers, doubtless the Komsomol first secretary and so on; but general supervision also extends to run-of-the-mill administrative appointments, in housing offices for example, as an article in _Sovetskaya Moldaviya_ of 23 November 1973 made clear. After stating that 'leaders of housing and communal enterprises are normally appointed by the ministry on the recommendation of the local soviet and party organs' (which alone points to some limitation on the powers of local bodies), the article went on to complain that local soviets were firing such officials without the ministry's consent. In other words, nomenklatura or a similar principle gave the ministry the final say, but local soviets were infringing that prerogative. The article was an attempt to re-establish the principle. This principle obviously restricts the local politicians, and its application to the town's leading positions is supervised by the presence of central committee representatives at the town party conferences and at the first plenum of the newly elected committee, and similar attendance at post-election sessions of the soviet.

A final link between local and republican levels of administration is the presence of the town's representatives in the republican institutions, particularly the supreme soviet and the CPM central committee, and here we see some personnel overlap with the town's political elite.[13] I shall conclude this chapter by considering this question.

### The Moldavian supreme soviet

Twenty-nine Tiraspol elite members became deputies of the republican supreme soviet. As might be expected, they tended to be drawn from the more prestigeful sectors of the elite, indicating that the higher one's status within the town elite, the greater the chances of selection for deputy service at a higher level:

|  | Group | | | | | | | |
|---|---|---|---|---|---|---|---|---|
|  | A | B | C | D | E | F | G | H |
| No. | 8 | 5 | 8 | 0 | 0 | 1 | 2 | 5 |
| % _of group_ | 1.1 | 1.7 | 3.5 | 0.0 | 0.0 | 4.5 | 5.4 | 38.5 |

This reflects, in part, a selection system for supreme soviet membership similar to the one I identified at the town soviet level: a number
of individuals are, as it were, the town's *ex officio* representatives in the
republican legislature. The gorispolkom chairman and frequently the
gorkom first secretary represented Tiraspol, together with a number
of other leading figures in the town, and one or two ordinary workers.
This finding echoes Perttsik's study, where over 8 per cent of
respondents were deputies of several soviets; some, he reported, 'are
still elected simply on the basis of occupation', despite the cpsu
central committee resolution of April 1957 condemning this practice.[14]

One interesting question on which my study sheds some light is the
possible effect of supreme soviet membership on an individual's career
within the town elite and beyond. The example of B. M. Mazuryan is
a case in point. He entered the town soviet in 1959, a Komsomol
member aged 21, and employed as a building worker; two years later
his social status had not changed, and he was re-elected to the soviet;
in 1963 he was elected to the supreme soviet, by which time he had
qualified as a mason; he became a full member of Tiraspol gorkom in
January 1965, and served two terms before being dropped in
December 1967. I would suggest that his supreme soviet membership
was of some influence in securing his election to the gorkom. A more
impressive record is that of N. D. Polyakov: he entered the gorkom as
a candidate member in December 1962 and joined the town soviet in
the following March, when he was identified as chief engineer of a
building administration. By August 1964 and again in January and
May 1965, however (*Sovetskaya Moldaviya*, 16 and 25 August 1964, 26
January and 14 May 1965) someone with the same name was
identified in the position of deputy head of 'Mezhkolkhozstroi', a
rural building concern; in March 1967, he entered the supreme soviet
as representative of a constituency in Dondyushany raion, and was
appointed chairman of the council of ministers state committee for
construction affairs (*Sovetskaya Moldaviya*, 16 March 1967). One of the
most outstanding examples of a politician whose career began in
Tiraspol and extended beyond, taking in supreme soviet membership,
is that of I. S. Shkorupeev, town soviet and gorkom member in 1950,
when he was chief engineer in the 'Kirov' works and head of a
political school attached to the factory's party organisation. He left
the town in the early 1950s, and graduated from the Leningrad
industrial institute in 1956, according to biographical details

published in *Dnestrovskaya pravda* (11 March 1957). He came into the supreme soviet in 1963, was re-elected in 1967, served as deputy chairman of the Moldavian supreme economic council (*sovnarkhoz*) from 1963 to 1965, was promoted chairman in February 1965, and appointed minister for the food industry in October 1965, a post that he still held in 1967. His connection with the Tiraspol area was not entirely severed, however; when elected in 1967, he represented a constituency in Tiraspol raion.

A further aspect of supreme soviet relations with the town is the whole question of representation. Examination of lists of newly elected deputies suggests that of the limited number of seats available (five in 1951, six in 1959, nine in 1967) only a very small number are available to residents in the town, since several were regularly allocated to leading politicians at the republican level – Shkorupeev's representation of Tiraspol raion in 1967 is a case in point. In 1951, for example, one place was reserved for Mikoyan, member of Stalin's politburo, and another for N. A. Shchëlokov, a government official from Kishinev, who later became Brezhnev's minister for internal affairs. Of the remaining three places, one went to Pasikovskii, gorispolkom chairman, and two to workers in the '1st May' works, one of whom was a member of both soviet and gorkom, the other at that stage only of the town soviet. In 1955, Mikoyan was again reserved a place, as was Shchëlokov, then deputy prime minister in Moldavia; Bronnikov, gorispolkom chairman, took another place, one went to S. I. Babin, sovkhoz director in Tiraspol raion, and two to ordinary workers in the town. By 1959, the practice of electing politburo members had ceased, and Shchëlokov, two workers and the gorispolkom chairman were joined by a research institute director and a factory manager. In 1963, the gorispolkom chairman was not elected, but the gorkom first secretary was, along with a factory director, the chairman of the Moldavian central trade union council and a host of workers. A similar situation obtained in 1967.

Tiraspol was thus 'represented' in the republic's legislature by, first, one or more outsiders with probably little direct interest in the town's welfare; the chairman of the gorispolkom or the gorkom first secretary, for whom connections with the town, and hence identification with its interests and problems, might also be only a temporary phenomenon; and a number of non-career politicians, only one of whom normally had the prestige and status of an important managerial position. Some of the remainder were not members of the

town soviet or gorkom at the time of their supreme soviet membership, possibly implying lack of familiarity with current political
problems in the town, and hence a further reduction in the impact
they might have in the republic's political life. In short, not only at
the town level, but also with respect to the supreme soviet, the
selection and representation system seems to be biased in favour of the
strong, whose institutional position gives them both prestige and
confidence so that they can dominate the system.

### The Moldavian central committee

The situation identified among Tiraspol's supreme soviet deputies is
duplicated among those who served on the republican central
committee. Twenty-seven elite members served as full or candidate
members during the period under review; five more served on the
auditing commission. Of the twenty-seven, six were drawn from
Group A (0.9 per cent of that group); 3 from Group B (1.0 per cent);
6 from Group C (2.6 per cent); 2 from Group E (28.6 per cent); 1
from Group F (4.8 per cent); 4 from Group G (10.8 per cent); and 5
from Group H (38.5 per cent). Thirteen of these also served as
supreme soviet deputies, including gorispolkom chairmen and
gorkom first secretaries, emphasising once again the interlocking
nature of political elites in the Soviet system. None of those who
served on the central committee was an ordinary worker: all held
responsible administrative posts in one or other branch of political or
industrial administration; only two identified workers in the town's
elite served on the central party organs – as members of the auditing
commission.

As with the supreme soviet, I can confidently say that a number of
places on the central committee are in effect reserved for the
occupants of specific posts in the town, principally the gorkom first
secretaryship. This confirms from a different angle my conclusion, in
a detailed study of the Moldavian central committee in the early
1960s, that central committee membership is linked with the tenure of
specific posts in the administrative machine.[15] However, it should not
be forgotten that the party central committee is not intended to be a
representative organ in the same sense as the supreme soviet, so that
members are not identified as 'representing' particular geographical
areas. Election to the committee seems to depend much more on an
individual's personal standing, which also influences what posts he is

given. Thus, the gorispolkom chairman was not always a member of the committee (or even of the supreme soviet, as we saw above): A. P. Skvortsov, chairman from 1963 onwards, following a spell as gorkom secretary and earlier industrial management service, merely served one term on the auditing commission.

## CONCLUSION

The full relationship between an individual's personal standing, the posts he occupies, and various political bodies of which he is a member is clearly a complex phenomenon, which goes beyond the scope of this study. In some cases, membership of the central committee or supreme soviet is a reward for services rendered to the party, which gives temporary high status to a small number of individual workers.[16] For perhaps the majority such membership is a perquisite of the position the individual holds in the town. In all cases, however, there can be little doubt that central committee membership, in particular, adds to the personal prestige and authority of individuals in the town's elite, and may signify a measure of career success. This success is also indicated by the degree to which political elite members participate in the work of other institutions, and the findings of this chapter confirm the existence of an active sector within the total elite, and one that is concentrated – but not exclusively – in the overlapping and executive grades. It is also clear that my initial assumption that it is appropriate to think in terms of a unified political structure is substantially accurate, and in the next chapter I shall examine this question further in a short discussion of a number of political careers.

# CHAPTER 8

# The Elite Illustrated

My concern in chapters 3 to 7 has been to identify trends and organisational factors in the composition of the elite, the members of the town's two main political organs; I attempted thereby to provide a basis for assessing the nature of the elite and the role in political life played by the two institutions. Much of the discussion involved generalising from correlations among a number of variables relevant to an analysis of the composition and functioning of the elite. In this chapter, some of these generalisations will be illustrated by recounting the careers of a number of individuals who served in various capacities within the elite.

It may be helpful in categorising my examples to introduce a further concept, and speak of a 'broad' and 'narrow' elite, much as Petrov speaks of the 'broad' and 'narrow' party aktiv.[1] 'The party aktiv', he writes, 'is a very broad category', comprising elected members of party organs and workers in the apparatus, and 'a huge army of ideological workers – propagandists and agitators, party committee lecturers, workers in the press, party member activists of the "Znanie" society and other political enlightenment organisations.' He continues: 'In our article we shall be speaking of the party aktiv in a more narrow sense, namely party group organisers and PPO secretaries, communists elected to party organs, from the workshop party buro to the raikom and gorkom inclusive, and partly the supernumerary aktiv of the party committees.' In other words, the 'narrow' aktiv consists of a more restricted number of individuals, most of whom hold some official position that adds to their status and responsibility in the party organisation; the 'broad' aktiv contains many more party members – indeed, about 50 per cent of the total party organisation. If we apply this kind of approach to the elite, we might define the 'narrow' elite in terms of those individuals who achieved membership of one or both executive bodies, combined with membership of the other organ: that is, Groups F, G and H, as I defined them in chapter 6. The 'broad' elite would include *all* Groups

A–H, but for purposes of descriptive analysis of careers will be restricted to Groups A–C; Groups D and E may also be regarded as a somewhat separate category – executive membership of just one institution, and examples of individuals from those groups will be considered independently.

## THE BROAD ELITE

I pointed out in an earlier chapter that the overwhelming majority of individuals who became involved in the work of the town soviet and the gorkom enjoyed ordinary membership of one or the other body for relatively short periods. I also established that a clustering of social characteristics permitted a rough analytical division into what I called 'weak' and 'strong' elite members. The richness of the data in the case of the soviet deputies brought out this phenomenon particularly clearly in that body, and a few examples demonstrate the point. Among the 'weak' we find the following:

Tamara Zhovtnyak, a female unskilled worker in the chemical works, a Komsomol member, born in 1937, hence 28 years old when elected to the soviet in 1965; she served only that one term of office.

Yevgenii Stel'mashenko, male, aged 27 when elected, also a Komsomol member, and a pneumatic drill operator in a building concern; also served a single term, 1963–65.

Yekaterina Gazya was already 43 years old when elected in 1959; but her maturity did not outweigh her female sex, her lack of party membership, and her relatively modest occupation of plasterer in a building firm: she too served only one term.

Klavdiya Apostolova, female, Komsomol member, aged 22 in 1965, a sterilizer in a fruit-processing works – served one term.

Anna Bondarenko, Komsomol member, 24 years old, a cook in the 'Dnestr' restaurant, elected in 1965 – served one term.

At the other end of the scale, we find the clustering of 'strong' characteristics:

Dmitrii Dubkov, one of the few deputies whose service spanned the whole eighteen-year period (possibly extending beyond 1950 and after 1967). Born in 1910, hence 40 years old when elected in 1950, he was already a party member, and in fact held office as head of a gorkom department. By 1959 he had transferred to industry, as director of the bread combine, a post that he retained right until the end of the period covered in this study. His soviet membership was continuous, apart from the 1963–65 term, and in 1961, 1965 and 1967 he was made chairman of a permanent commission; he also enjoyed prolonged gorkom membership.

Zinaida Polishchuk was the outstanding woman whose sex seems not to have been a handicap: she was born in 1918 and first entered the soviet in 1955, probably nominated from outside the town to the post of head of the gorispolkom finance department; she immediately joined the gorispolkom; at the same time she was elected to the party auditing commission, and rose to be its chairman in later years. She served on the soviet until the end of our period, retaining her post as head of the same department and her place on the executive committee; by 1967, therefore, her prestigious position was carrying her into her seventh term of office, and outweighing the disadvantage commonly experienced by members of her sex.

These examples not only illustrate the general pattern in deputies' personal characteristics, but also identify individual exceptions to the rule – such as Polishchuk. There are one or two other noteworthy exceptions, whose example proves that the rule is by no means rigid:

Pëtr Yadzhuk, a male party member, first elected in 1961, at the age of 35, when he was a departmental head in the gorkom apparatus. This combination of 'strong' characteristics might have indicated a long period of service as a deputy; yet after serving two terms, he was not re-elected in 1965 or 1967 – possibly indicating that he was a casualty (or beneficiary, if he had been promoted to a post outside Tiraspol) of Khrushchev's dismissal in 1964.

Aleksandr Yakovlev, another prominent party official (head of the gorkom ideological department), aged in his forties, served only one term from 1965 to 1967 before disappearing from the political scene.

Nevertheless, despite these examples that challenge the rule, the fundamental generalisation about patterns in social composition and re-election that I enunciated in chapter 4 still obtains.

Among the ordinary gorkom members, there is a great deal of missing data, so that little is known of those ordinary gorkom members who did not serve also on the town soviet. In general, this means that a gorkom member who served for only one or two terms of office could not be further identified. There are, however, exceptions to this, where individuals' names appeared in the press during their term of office, yet who never attained membership of the soviet:

N. I. Kasprevich, candidate member of the xii gorkom, was in 1950 and still in 1965 chief engineer of the wine and cognac factory.[2]

R. S. Zelikova, a woman, member of the xxvi gorkom, was in 1963 a metal worker in the 'Kirov' works.[3]

V. D. Yastrebov, candidate member of the xxviii gorkom after one term on the auditing commission, was identified in May 1967 as secretary of the spinning mill ppo.[4]

A. I. Kharitonovich, full member of the xxi and xxii committees, was in 1960 secretary of the ppo attached to the town's department of trade.[5]

These pieces of information are sparse, and far from complete. It seems probable, for instance, that a number of individuals identified as workers had, in fact, recently been promoted to a post in a ppo, and it was this that qualified them for gorkom membership. The case of Konstantin Shkrabov (or Shkryabov) illustrates this: when elected to the town soviet, in March 1965, he was identified as a metal worker in the electrical apparatus works; by August that year he had been elected secretary of the factory's party buro, a nomenklatura post that he still held in November and the following January;[6] his election as a full member of the xxvii gorkom came in January 1966.

In some cases advancement in the elite paralleled advancement in the individual's non-political career. R. D. Titova, a Komsomol member who worked as a forewoman in the clothing factory, was elected to the 1959 soviet at the age of 23. She later joined the party and was elected to the gorkom in December 1962; three months later, when elected to the 1963 soviet, she had been promoted to be a deputy section head in the factory. It is difficult to establish on the basis of the available information whether professional advancement had a bearing on political advancement, or the reverse; it is conceivable that her election to the gorkom followed appointment as a party group organiser in the factory, and that experience gained there had a bearing on her promotion. Be that as it may, it seems clear that those individuals who attained membership of both soviet and gorkom were generally endowed with what I defined as 'strong' characteristics, and in particular they reached a position of some responsibility in their employment.

## THE EXECUTIVE BODIES

There were, as was seen, very few individuals who served on the executive bodies without at least ordinary membership of the other body. Of those who have been identified on the gorkom buro without membership of the soviet, all served there for only one term, two of them at the very end of the period covered in this study. In some cases, buro membership appears to have been during a very temporary tenure of office in Tiraspol (N. Z. Gagarin – elected first secretary in February 1951 – seems to have been removed from the town almost immediately; S. I. Polozov, head of the Tiraspol *okrug* department of the ministry of state security, was only indirectly connected with the town[7]). It was thus very unusual for an individual's political career in the town to reach this level of prominence in the party without a measure of participation in the work of the soviet.

However, the reverse is not necessarily true, and the gorispolkom did contain individuals of some prominence who were never elected to the gorkom. Foremost among these are three persons whose lack of party membership disqualified them from party office, led by I. I. Antosyak, whose career is particularly striking. Despite his lack of party membership, he served eight terms on the soviet, served as chairman of a permanent commission for six of those terms, and was a gorispolkom member in 1950, at the age of 34. In his case, perhaps a combination of personal merit and a prestigeful position helped to overcome his handicap: in 1950 he was director of the pedagogical institute; by 1955 he had evidently been demoted to a schoolmaster's position, but two years later had become deputy director for academic and scientific work in the pedagogical institute, a post he retained until the end of our period. Moreover, Antosyak was one of the most active deputies in the 1960s, and spoke at sessions more often than even most of the current gorispolkom officers.

This is an example of a somewhat outstanding individual, however, and it seems significant that all three non-party deputies served on the executive committee for only a single term of office, including one woman (M. Ya. Doba, a teacher) as deputy chairman, in 1953–55. In other cases, administrative positions in the state apparatus – chairmanship of the planning commission, secretaryship of the gorispolkom and others – did not bring gorkom membership to particular incumbents, although their predecessors or successors were elected to the committee. Here, and in one or two cases where gorispolkom membership was an obvious reward to ordinary workers, the personal qualities of the individuals concerned were probably a significant factor in determining their elite status.

## THE INFLUENCE OF NATIONAL POLITICS

I suggested in my discussion of turnover levels (chapter 3) that membership patterns, particularly in the gorkom, are influenced by national political considerations. In particular, I referred to the major political crisis of 1961, and my interpretation of trends in turnover showed clearly that the town was not unaffected by the national upheaval. Assuming that interpretation to be correct, I can now look more closely at these all-USSR political tendencies, and see how they affected the careers of individual politicians at the local level, as manifest in Tiraspol. An examination of a number of careers illustrates how the ordinary elite member, as well as those in exposed positions, might be affected.

In some cases, a person who had not secured his position by the time of the political change was removed from the elite for good. M. M. Gladunov, identified in September 1960 as secretary of the PPO in the number one housing office,[8] entered the gorkom in November 1959, was re-elected in January 1961, but was reduced to the status of auditing commission member in September that year, and left the party organs completely after that. Longer-serving members also suffered. Aleksandr Goncharov, director of a clothing factory, served on the gorkom from at least October 1953, but suddenly disappeared during 1961; a plausible explanation is that he was a victim of the leadership crisis of that year. Konstantin Maika, whose membership of the soviet had been intermittent between 1950 and 1959, and who served as a gorispolkom otdel head and gorispolkom first deputy chairman, was made a member of the gorkom in November 1959 and January 1961, but likewise disappeared from public view after that.

In some cases, however, demotion was only temporary. Dubkov, former gorkom otdel head and buro member and industrial manager of some standing, whom I discussed in an earlier section, was demoted after the XXII term of office to auditing commission membership, after unbroken gorkom membership since at least 1950; he disappeared from even that commission after the xxiii term, but returned to the gorkom as full member in January 1965; his career as a deputy showed a similar gap. Vasilii Nikolaev, former head of the gorkom's agitprop department and editor of the local newspaper, also disappeared in 1961 after long membership, but returned in January 1965. Mikhail Yasinskii, another former head of agitprop, was also demoted at the same time, and returned to the soviet (but not the gorkom) in 1965, as director of the town's number seven trade school. These examples indicate the fate of some fallen local politicians. A noteworthy example, drawn from 'ordinary' ppo officers, is that of Pëtr Kovalëv, a train driver. He came into the gorkom in November 1954 as a candidate member, aged 33, when he was ppo secretary at the railway station; he had already served four years on the soviet, and remained a deputy until and including the 1961 soviet; he was promoted to gorkom full membership eleven months after joining the committee, and retained that status for six terms. He was dropped in September 1961, and subsequently lost his place on the soviet. In 1965, however, he reappeared as a deputy; in January 1966 when he spoke at the xxvii town party conference, he was again referred to as secretary of the railway station ppo, and in that capacity was re-elected to the gorkom, after five terms' absence.

I would suggest that the most likely explanation of these interrupted political careers, given the timing of the interruptions, is that they were influenced by the national political crises of leadership, which went right to the roots of the political system. There are also examples of individuals who benefited from such crises, perhaps the most striking being that of Nikolai Yemelin, head of the town's militia department, who served on the gorkom until 1961; he disappeared from the scene in Tiraspol at that time, only to turn up in June 1964 as deputy minister of public order in Moldavia, and head of the ministry's militia administration (*Sovetskaya Moldaviya*, 18 and 25 June 1964). He was identified in this post as late as November 1965 (*Sovetskaya Moldaviya*, 11 November 1965), but appears subsequently to have disappeared from political life. He can thus be seen as a beneficiary of the Khrushchevite victory in 1961, and his political allegiances later led to his undoing after the new regime had consolidated itself.

Finally in this section, I will note that there were some local elite members whose careers appear to have escaped such modification in response to changes elsewhere. The most illustrious example of political longevity is that of Aleksei Tsarëv, born in 1883, and a participant in the battleship Potëmkin mutiny of 1905. This fact gave him something of the quality of a political relic, an object to be treasured and displayed on all suitable occasions. In 1950 he was a member of the auditing commission, and served as party buro secretary in the wine and cognac works. By the time of the xxiv conference (October 1953) he had been elected a gorkom full member and served constantly until the end of our period (assuming membership of the xv and xxv committees). His membership of the soviet also spanned eighteen years, although he did not serve in the 1963 and 1965 soviets. He was never given gorkom office, or even membership of the buro, during this period, but as a revolutionary trophy of the town's party organisation he was hardly an object to be discarded in a purge. His temporary withdrawal from the soviet may have been occasioned by old age or ill-health, and his return to active work as a deputy in 1967, at the age of 84, was perhaps a poignant occasion for all deputies, as they witnessed the tradition whereby the oldest deputy opens the first session of a new soviet.

These cases – and others – show the effects of political leadership crises on the lower ranks of leading party workers: some suffered dramatically; some were apparently unaffected; others evidently benefited. Whatever the case, it seems clear that the leadership crises reached right to the bottom of the political ladder, and affected some of the longest-serving (and presumably most respected) party members in the town. The effects were restricted neither to the newest recruits into party office, nor to the politically exposed officers and officials of the apparatus, but affected the middle ranks just as much. These examples show that the soviet elite did not escape either.

## THE NARROW ELITE

This term is used to denote the bulk of executive body members, who also achieved membership of the alternative body, normally concurrently, and in some cases the other executive. It is here that individuals possess ostensibly the greatest opportunities for influencing political life in the town, and in these grades are encountered people with responsibility for administering the party, the state and industry. It is among these administrative posts that the principle of nomenklatura seems to be most firmly applicable, and there is considerable movement between these posts. This suggests the existence of, as it were, an 'elite within the elite'. It consists of individuals frequently recruited from outside Tiraspol, who move directly into these 'inner' grades, and maintain their position in them even when transferred from one administrative post to another, until they are perhaps transferred elsewhere or demoted. Relations within this sector of the elite, with other sectors and with political life outside the town, can be illustrated by observing the careers of individuals and their tenancy of a number of specific positions in the town.

The most important position, it seems clear, is the gorkom first secretaryship. Thus, for Scott, 'The post of first secretary is probably the most powerful single office at any level throughout the Soviet state',[9] while Stewart says of the obkom first secretary, 'On him more than anyone else depends the degree of influence that any other bureau member, or for that matter any official within the oblast, will have on the formation of policy within the obkom'.[10] Incumbents are selected with care and, it would appear, normally brought in from outside the town. Generally speaking, only when no suitable candidate for permanent appointment has been available has a local politician been placed in that responsible position, and then only as a temporary measure. Moreover, they are (as one would expect) vulnerable to the winds of political change. These conclusions are reached through a study of the history of the appointment in Tiraspol.

During the period of my study, six individuals served as first secretary. The first, I. P. Pechërkin, aged 57 in 1950, probably served in the 1940s, but he did not survive politically long into the new decade. By February 1951 he had been replaced, most probably in consequence of the CPSU central committee resolution of June 1950 criticising the work of the Moldavian central committee, to which I referred in chapter 3. Pechërkin read a report on this resolution, in which he condemned the work of the gorkom, particularly with respect to the selection of leading cadres.[11] That was in July 1950, and Pechërkin was not heard of again. Reports at subsequent plenums were read by his deputy, A. I. Gutsalo, and a new first secretary was elected following the next party conference, in February 1951.

This was N. Z. Gagarin, and his appointment bears all the signs of having been imposed from above. He was drafted in from the Orgeev raikom first secretaryship (a post that he held when elected to the Moldavian supreme soviet in 1951: *Sovetskaya Moldaviya*, 21 January

1951), and served only one term in his new post. He was a full member of the republican central committees elected in April 1951, September 1952 and February 1954, and was identified at the time of the 1955 supreme soviet elections as head of the central committee department of party organs (*Sovetskaya Moldaviya*, 29 January 1955). He subsequently disappeared from Moldavian public life. His appointment to the Tiraspol gorkom first secretaryship was thus a very temporary affair; we can conclude that he was sent by the central republican apparatus to sort out the mess that Pechërkin had described at the fourth gorkom plenum, and for which Pechërkin himself had been largely responsible.

This example can be interpreted in the light of the work of Stewart and his associates on career analysis among Soviet politicians. They write, 'Transfers are made not only for training but for troubleshooting. The "trouble-shooter" would probably be a more experienced secretary from a more developed region to strengthen the leadership of a less developed region that may be in serious trouble economically.'[12] In the case of Tiraspol, 'a more developed' region could refer to the central apparatus, and the 'trouble', in the early 1950s, was as likely to be political as economic: note Brezhnev's appointment at this time from the CPSU central apparatus to the Moldavian first secretaryship – a temporary move that parallels Gagarin's move to Tiraspol. Gagarin's career does not appear to have been adversely affected by the critical events of May 1953, when the town party organisation was again roundly criticised for incompetence, this time specifically in industrial matters (see p. 90 above).

Gagarin's successor was V. G. Lykhvar', then aged 42, and a candidate member of the Moldavian central committee, subsequently promoted to full membership. He served ten terms as first secretary, until September 1961; at the XXIII town party conference, held that month, he retained his place on the committee, but was replaced as first secretary. His political career went into a decline: he was not elected to the XXIV gorkom or to the town soviet of 1963. However, he made something of a come-back in 1965, when he returned to the soviet, and in January 1966 he returned to the gorkom as a full member; by then he had left the direct political arena, and was a school director. This change in Lykhvar''s fortunes seems attributable to the leadership crises of 1961 and 1964: he can be seen as a victim of the 1961 purge by the Khrushchev faction, and after Khrushchev had been removed in October 1964 Lykhvar' was rehabilitated and brought back into the town's political elite. Meanwhile, the first secretaryship had changed hands twice. Lykhvar' himself had been replaced by A. V. Nechaenko, then aged 47, who was director of the 'Kirov' machine works, and had been a deputy of the soviet since 1953 and a gorkom member since 1951; he had three times previously been a buro member. His promotion also brought membership of the republican supreme soviet of 1963; he had already been a central committee member since January 1960. However, his appointment to the first secretaryship lasted only a couple of years. At the end of 1963 he was transferred to Kishinev, to work in the central committee apparatus as head of the industry and transport department, and in October 1965 was made minister of local industry.[13]

It seems possible that had he not received this elevation Nechaenko might have survived as gorkom first secretary, and there seems to have been some difficulty in filling the post. It went initially to Valentina S. Solov'ëva, a remarkably successful woman, born in Tiraspol in 1918 into an employee's family, according to biographical notes in *Dnestrovskaya pravda* for 7 March 1967. She spent six years as a teacher before joining the number two clothing factory in 1948. There she learnt trade and management techniques, rose to head a section, graduated from a light industry college, and was appointed chief engineer in 1952. Five years later she came to political prominence when elected to the soviet and, still without party membership, the gorispolkom. By 1959 she was a probationary member of the party, and was shortly admitted to full membership. She was also appointed director of the factory, now amalgamated with two more clothing factories and renamed in honour of the fortieth anniversary of the Komsomol, and became a gorkom member for the first time in November 1959, entering the buro in January 1961; in January 1960 she had been made candidate member of the Moldavian central committee, and was advanced to full membership in September 1961. Her appointment to the Tiraspol gorkom first secretaryship on 29 December 1963 was thus the culmination of a very rapid rise to political prominence. When I visited the factory in the spring of 1968, I was received by Solov'ëva, a most charming woman, efficient, and (one would imagine) a pleasant enough boss. The factory, one of the most modern in the republic, has often been cited as an outstanding example of how an industrial enterprise should be run. Thus, a half-page feature article in *Sovetskaya*

*Moldaviya*, 8 March 1974, analyses Solov'ëva's achievements and ascribes the success of the factory to her personality and her teaching and managerial experience. One is inclined to agree with this estimate, but would add that her extensive political contacts have probably not been entirely immaterial.[14] The appointment of both Nechaenko and Solov'ëva followed a pattern that was a particular feature of the Khrushchev era: the recruitment of gorkom first secretaries directly from industrial management positions, in order to ensure that party officials were technically competent.[15] The practice was abandoned by the post-Khrushchev collective leadership however,[16] as the subsequent history of the post in Tiraspol testifies. Solov'ëva's appointment proved only temporary, for in October 1964 she was replaced by an outside appointee, a Ukrainian by nationality, P. P. Petrik, until then head of the ideological department for the direction of agriculture, attached to the Moldavian central committee. His biography, published in *Dnestrovskaya pravda*, 7 March 1967, shows that this new post was a complete change for Petrik, aged 40 when first selected for the post. His previous positions had all been in rural areas, as raikom first secretary. In the late 1950s he left Moldavia for training in the CPSU central committee higher party school, graduating in 1959 (having graduated from the republican party school in 1952), and again worked in rural Moldavia, before being promoted to the central apparatus in Kishinev, again in an agriculturally orientated post. He survived as gorkom first secretary until the end of our period, and indeed until 1972, when he was again brought to Kishinev, to head the Moldavian council of trade unions.

This discussion points to an apparent break in the career structure of party secretaries, between second (and other) secretaryships and first secretaryship. In only one case (Pechërkin) was a first secretary replaced by his deputy (Gutsalo), and then merely temporarily. In subsequent changes other secretaries were not even appointed on a temporary basis; either a permanent appointee was drafted in from elsewhere (thus placing the Tiraspol gorkom post in the republic's political career structure), or 'non-politicians' drawn from industrial management were seconded to the position. In Nechaenko's case, tenure of the post can be construed as an important step in a career that brought further advancement; Solov'ëva returned to her former position as factory manager with no loss of prestige – indeed, she has remained prominent in the republic's political bodies, being elected to the supreme soviet and central committee in subsequent years. There is apparently no direct step from second to first secretary of a party gorkom. As a general rule, promotion to a gorkom first secretaryship is a career stage that involves (as Petrik's case shows) special training at a party school and experience elsewhere in the apparatus. That experience may well be in areas of administration that, on the face of it, would prepare the individual poorly for leadership of an industrial town, and one might surmise that a newly appointed first secretary with, say, Petrik's background, might have to rely heavily on the advice and support of his colleagues in the gorkom buro, and specifically the gorispolkom chairman.

When we consider the history of the latter post in Tiraspol in the 1950s and 1960s, we find both similarities and differences with the pattern seen in the first secretaryship. Again, six individuals occupied the post, beginning with A. I. Pasikovskii, the incumbent at the opening of the period, then aged 39. Little is known of his background, and in any case he did not remain long in the post after 1950, before being promoted: he was identified in January 1955, when re-elected to the supreme soviet, as chairman of the Kaushany raiispolkom; by March 1966 he was a sector head in the Moldavian central committee apparatus (identified in *Sovetskaya Moldaviya*, 4 March 1966), and a year later head of the central committee's general department, when again nominated for supreme soviet election; his career also involved intermittent central committee candidate membership, and he was reappointed to the general department headship in February 1971 (*Sovetskaya Moldaviya*, 27 February 1971).

After his departure from Tiraspol, his place was taken in 1953 by V. N. Bronnikov, previously deputy chairman. He was reappointed in 1955, and also elected to the supreme soviet, but subsequently disappeared from view, without explanation. In 1957 he was dropped from the soviet, and his position as gorispolkom chairman went to an outsider, A. I. Matsnev, who had been identified in the election campaign as gorkom secretary in neighbouring Bendery (*Dnestrovskaya pravda*, 15 February 1957). His career details, as published in the local newspaper (*Dnestrovskaya pravda*, 8 March 1957), reveal that he began work on the railways in 1933, aged 27, but continued his studies at the Leningrad railway institute; after army service (where he was four times decorated) he went to Moldavia in 1944 as party buro secretary at the Beltsy railway depot, and later rose to a secretaryship of the Beltsy gorkom. Then came training at the higher party school, from which he graduated in 1954, and posting to Bendery on his first major assignment. His selection for the Tiraspol gorispolkom chairmanship shows the nomenklatura system in operation: he campaigned for election while still Bendery gorkom secretary, yet was immediately elected to the gorispolkom post. Membership of the gorkom and its buro followed in November 1957, election to the supreme soviet in 1959, and membership of the Moldavian central auditing commission in 1960, followed by candidate and then full membership of the central committee. For Matsnev, tenure of the Tiraspol post was thus an important stage in his political career, and it lasted until 1963: he was last elected to the gorkom in December 1962, and by March 1963 had transferred back to Bendery to the post of gorkom first secretary, a position that he still held in April 1973 (*Sovetskaya Moldaviya*, 7 March 1963 and 8 April 1973).

In 1963 the chairmanship went to A. P. Skvortsov, who transferred from the post of Tiraspol gorkom secretary – a precedent that was to be followed later. Skvortsov had risen to prominence through industrial management, having in 1957 (when first elected as a deputy) served as director of the town's industrial combine; he was already a gorkom member (elected in December 1956), and his sudden prominent appearance indicates that he had probably been drafted in from outside the town. By 1959 he was director of the number two clothing factory (when Solov'ëva was chief engineer), and became a member of the gorispolkom. In November 1959 he was elected gorkom secretary at the xxi party conference; the factory was merged to form the 'Fortieth anniversary of the Komsomol' clothing factory, and the directorship went to Solov'ëva. The fact that two managers of this factory were so closely involved in the town's political management suggests that the directorship is of considerable political significance.

Skvortsov held the chairmanship between 1963 and 1965; he conducted his election campaign as chairman (*Drapelul Leninist*, 6 March 1965), but was not re-elected to the post after the elections to the soviet. Instead, the post went to V. I. Yulin, who had suddenly appeared in the town in November 1964, and was elected gorispolkom deputy chairman at a soviet session on the twenty-fifth of the month (*Leninskoe znamya*, 28 November 1964), a somewhat irregular occurrence as he was not even a deputy, and hence ineligible for appointment.[17] He was elected to the gorkom in January 1965, and to its buro a year later; Skvortsov meanwhile returned to industry, remained on the gorkom, and when re-elected to the soviet in 1967 was director of the woodworking combine.

Even Yulin did not stay long in the post of chief executive in Tiraspol. He served only one term on the soviet, and was replaced as chairman in 1967 by V. I. Telenkov, then aged 37. He had been drafted in from outside Tiraspol, but had already gained considerable experience inside the town before attaining the chairmanship. Telenkov first came to Tiraspol in the early sixties, and was appointed to head the 'Kirov' works in replacement of Nechaenko on the latter's elevation to the gorkom first secretaryship. Telenkov entered the soviet in 1963 and immediately chaired a permanent commission; he had joined the gorkom in December 1962, and in January 1965, following the xxvi conference, he was made gorkom second secretary, a post that brought gorispolkom membership in 1965. His factory directorship, interestingly enough, went to A. I. Bol'shakov, until then director of the woodworking combine, and as we have just seen, this post now went to Skvortsov on his retirement as gorispolkom chairman. Telenkov was still chairman of the gorispolkom at the close of 1967.

## RECRUITMENT IN THE NARROW ELITE

This discussion of relatively few key positions and individual careers gives a clearer impression of elite recruitment patterns at this level, which appears to distinguish them from the rank and file broad elite members. We can see much shifting from one position to another, with a small number of individuals following each other from one factory directorship to another, into the political organs via the party committee, then perhaps across into the soviet structure, then sometimes back into industry, into positions vacated by persons recruited into political posts. Occasionally, long-standing elite members are creamed off to a higher level, or they die, or are removed from office and demoted, and this may give younger men their opportunity for advancement. However, the recruitment pattern here, particularly recently, suggests that the chances for advancement within the town alone are very limited.[18] At least some of the more important industrial positions are themselves highly politicised, and appointment to them is often from outside the town, in common with the more directly political posts. This extends to secondary positions such as gorispolkom deputy chairman and gorkom secretary, to which few were appointed after serving as lesser officials in the town.

Exceptions mentioned in chapter 7 may be individuals who rose to prominence through the Komsomol, who might then receive special training followed by tenure of a post elsewhere in the apparatus. This discussion also strongly suggests that, at the level of the small city, *the elite is not strongly differentiated*: individuals seem to have moved with relative ease among the three main sectors – industry, party, and state. Thus, Skvortsov moved from industry to party, to state, and back to industry; Solov'ëva moved from industry to party, and back to industry; Nechaenko moved from industry to party, remained in the party apparatus on his promotion out of Tiraspol, but eventually switched to the state as an industrial minister; Telenkov began in industry, moved to the party, then to the state; Matsnev came from the party apparatus outside Tiraspol into the town's state machinery, and eventually returned to the party in Bendery; Pasikovskii, after his state position in Tiraspol, is known to have moved through posts in the state apparatus before ending up in the Moldavian communist party central apparatus. All, of course, simultaneously or intermittently held membership positions in both party and state organs.

Other careers showed a similar tendency to move from one structure to another, after those involved had left Tiraspol. Morozov, a Komsomol gorkom secretary, was identified in a party post in 1963 and 1964, but is known to have later switched to the state apparatus (see chapter 7); two former Komsomol secretaries held responsible posts in the control organisation; another, after a spell in industry, held a party post outside Tiraspol, but later returned to the town in an industrial–educational position.

Among these individuals who switched from one sector of administration to another, presumably acquiring a wide range of experience of different kinds of problem, there also worked a number of politicians whose careers showed greater specialisation. One example is N. G. Yemelin, appointed head of the town's militia department between 1957 and 1961, and later identified as deputy minister of public order (*Sovetskaya Moldaviya*, 25 June 1964 and 11 November 1965). The careers of the more permanent first secretaries also exhibit a greater degree of specialisation. It seems very likely that

Lykhvar''s previous career was mainly in the party; Petrik's career was exclusively so, once he had established himself through Komsomol work (although, as we have seen, on leaving Tiraspol in 1972 he switched to the trade union apparatus). The Komsomol and party may thus form a single, specialised career structure, but there is in any case considerable switching to other sectors of the administrative apparatus.

Taking the period as a whole and bearing in mind that the sample is very small, it is possible to say that the level of interchange among various positions permits application of the concept of a unified leadership pool. In this way, the example of Tiraspol would support the view of, for instance, Armstrong and Laird, against that of, for example, Fleron and Gehlen. The question is whether the Soviet political leadership does constitute a single body of individuals, who may be recruited to responsible positions in any branch of the apparatus; or whether, on the other hand, there is specialisation within the various structures. Armstrong's study of the Ukrainian apparatus led him to conclude that '. . . there is such a high degree of interchange between the middle levels of the state and Party bureaucracies that it is impossible to look upon these organisations as separate elite segments', and 'The Party–state grouping already appears to extend to some degree to the industrial manager group'.[19] For Laird, the Soviet system is marked by 'the domination by a single political elite':[20]

> Thus, for example, an official that one day is a key Party secretary in a regional office may be promoted the next day to an important state post at the republic level, since there is completely free movement between Party and state agencies.[21]

In this connection, Stewart *et al.* write of 'a conscious effort by the Brezhnev–Kosygin leadership to develop economically competent generalists' and 'the desire to provide officials with experience in varied types of work'.[22]

Fleron, by contrast, distinguishes between recruited officials, who 'entered the political elite at very early stages in their careers and who thus had little opportunity to form close ties with a professional–vocational group', and co-opted officials, who 'entered the political elite in mid or late career and who had probably established very close professional–vocational ties outside the political elite'.[23] Gehlen remarks (and data from Tiraspol tend to support him) that 'it is quite possible and even likely that Komsomol functionaries continue to be drawn into regular Party work', but he suggests that they are increasingly disadvantaged when compared with individuals with professional training, as a tendency develops 'to allow individuals to work their way up within a single hierarchy rather than to transfer them back and forth between various hierarchies'.[24] This view is further supported by Frolic, who writes that 'Crossover between Party and non-Party posts has decreased, and officials are becoming now more committed to long-term careers which require extra specialisation and early career orientations'.[25]

It should be pointed out that Gehlen, in particular, is referring specifically to the high-echelon *apparatchiki* (officials) and he makes no claim for the applicability of his conclusions to the more local level. My example suggests nevertheless that it would be premature to dismiss the notion of a 'common leadership pool', a concept put forward by Rigby in 1954.[26] However, I am acutely aware that my conclusion is based on a very small number of political careers, and further research would be required in order to reach confirmation. Quite obviously this precise question has an important bearing on our understanding of the nature of the town's political elite, and this question – what kind of elite exists in the town? – will be discussed in my concluding chapter.

# CHAPTER 9

# Conclusions

This study has been concerned with the political sociology of a fairly typical Soviet small city. I have directed my attention towards the subject from two major angles: first, the composition and functioning of the town's main political organs – separately, complementarily, and in relation to other bodies inside and outside the town; and secondly, the social identity and public activity of the individuals who formed the body of participants, which I identified as the town's political elite. This final chapter is concerned with summarising the main conclusions of the study, and evaluating the role of the political institutions in which the elite was active, in the light of the foregoing analysis. I shall also consider briefly some of the concepts and approaches of political science that I believe are helpful in understanding the processes I have analysed.

## MAIN CONCLUSIONS

I began my study by examining trends in the composition of soviet and gorkom. A major finding, confirmed by my analysis of the social characteristics of the individuals involved, was that there is a clustering among such characteristics, which permitted me to distinguish two fundamental types of elite member: the 'weak' and the 'strong'. The 'weak', it will be recalled, were generally younger, not party members, in low-status occupations, and very often female; the 'strong' were generally male, older, party members, and holding prestigious jobs. This line of analysis was pursued, and the distinction was found to be reflected in selection patterns and turnover rates among the soviet deputies and party committee members, in their level of participation in the public business of the gorkom and the soviet, in membership of other political organs and participation in their affairs, and in the elite status attained by individuals in the town.

A further line of enquiry concerned the relationship between the political life of the town and the broader context in which it existed. Variations in trends were noted between Tiraspol and elsewhere, suggesting limits on the degree to which the system is centralised, and pointing to a measure of discretion and apparent independence for local authorities, at least in their selection policies. I remarked, however, that levels of turnover among elite members, and specifically among the occupants of certain important administrative positions, could be confidently related to major political upheavals at the summit of Soviet political life; this showed that the effects of these crises reach to the bottom of the Soviet political structure.

This was one aspect of relations between the centre and the periphery that revealed the degree to which politics in the localities depend on some form of political stimulation from above. There were others for which evidence appeared, notably the principle of nomenklatura. Here, the evidence was circumstantial rather than direct, but it seemed clear that a number of important positions in the town's political administration, and also apparently in the field of industrial management, were staffed by persons nominated by higher authorities and frequently drafted in from outside Tiraspol. In this my work corroborated that of other scholars who have examined the nomenklatura system. This practice also affected the possibilities for career advancement within the town, which appeared to be limited: an individual would normally have to acquire training and experience outside Tiraspol before being appointed to one of the key leading positions. For other individuals, however, a spell in such a post in Tiraspol might be an important career stage, which would continue with promotion to a position elsewhere in the republic.

In other ways, too, politics at higher levels of administration had their effect on the town's political life. As we saw, resolutions adopted by superior bodies frequently served as the basis for debates in the town's institutions, so that the town party committee in particular reflected current policies and problems faced by the Soviet government. There appeared to be a rough division of functions, however, between the party committee and the soviet, with the former tending to discuss broader policy questions, while the soviet dealt with largely administrative matters.

Finally, I noted ways in which political practices common at the higher levels served as a precedent for the level of the town, so that inexplicit regulations were elaborated by borrowing practices from central institutions. Thus, I remarked on the practice – common under Khrushchev and continued under his successors – of extending meetings of both party and state organs to a wide circle of non-members, who not only attended, but also participated, to the apparent detriment of the members. I identified too the custom – sanctioned for the CPSU central committee but not specifically for lower levels – of replenishing the ranks of party committee full members by promoting candidate members. Similarly, in common with other party committees all over the USSR, Tiraspol followed the precedent of the CPSU central committee in holding party conferences and electing new committees at irregular intervals, presumably in order to accommodate certain political requirements, possibly prompted by a higher level.

The division of elite members into 'weak' and 'strong' is a phenomenon that has also been identified at the summit in the Soviet state system, suggesting that here too Tiraspol was simply following a widespread custom and implementing nationally endorsed selection policies. It was a point, I noted, that has been made by Soviet researchers into the social composition of deputies in local soviets. This division – which takes on a structural quality through the differential turnover rates – has implications for both an assessment of the nature of the elite and of its usefulness as a concept in this context, and an evaluation of the role of the institutions. These are questions to which I now turn in summing up this study.

There are, it would appear, at least two ways in which the elite can be differentiated for analytical purposes. The first is the one I used when first introducing the concept: in terms of the elite members' institutional or 'positional' situation. According to this criterion, I was able in chapter 6 to distinguish various degrees of elitism, depending on an individual's membership of the town soviet, the gorkom, or both, perhaps combined with membership of an executive body. The various grades each confer on their members a greater or lesser range of social and political values that distinguish them from non-members of the elite, and from elite members in other grades. Using the concept in this relative way, a rough hierarchy could be identified.

A second factor, however, was the distribution of social characteristics among the elite members, and the division into 'weak' and 'strong' provides a further means of differentiation, which may conceivably reflect more accurately differences in the potential

influence and power between them. I would argue that a combination of 'strong' characteristics, including especially the tenure of a
responsible position in the political apparatus or industrial management, or in other branches of administration, gives the individual an
immediate advantage over those who are not so endowed. I would
further argue that to some extent the disadvantages of a combination
of 'weak' characteristics could be overcome through the individual's
gaining experience of political processes and establishing contacts
with responsible officials, such as might be obtained by a lengthy
period of participation in the work of political institutions. However,
I found that the differential turnover rates among 'weak' and 'strong'
effectively deprive the 'weak' of the opportunity for gaining that
experience, so that they have little chance of acquiring the political
skills that might qualify them for advancement into the ranks of the
more permanent elite members. Accordingly, the majority of elite
members enjoy only temporary office in the soviet or gorkom, and are
offered few chances to work their way to a leading position within the
town's political elite.

When I combined the two means of differentiating between elite
members, I found a particular pattern in the distribution of 'weak'
and 'strong' characteristics among the various institutionally defined
sectors of the elite. The weak tended to be restricted to ordinary
membership of the soviet, while the strong tended to combine
membership of both party and state bodies, and in a considerable
number of cases also of one or both executive organs. If the social and
political advantages of such institutional membership are added to
the already high status accorded by the individuals' personal
characteristics, it is not hard to see how the town might effectively be
dominated by these particular sectors of the elite, who might thus
constitute an 'inner elite', 'power elite', or 'elite within the elite'. By
such an approach it might be possible to identify an elite that is
distinguished by its possession of opportunities for power and
influence: such an elite would encompass basically those positions that
combine membership of the soviet with membership of the gorkom,
and the remainder would be seen as a 'broad' or 'outer' elite, whose
membership is a purely temporary phenomenon of perhaps little real
political significance.

Combined membership of the soviet and the gorkom thus becomes
an important variable by which to estimate an individual's influence,
and this gives us a possible means of identifying the influentials. Such

an approach differs from that of, for example, Seweryn Bialer, who uses as an indicator of elite membership 'occupancy of a high office in the hierarchy of authority, ... combined with participation in such symbolic institutions as the Supreme Soviet (or the Party Congress)'.[1] In a town the size of Tiraspol, one might plausibly assume that the holders of such positions are intimately acquainted with one another. They tend to be employed in the managerial–administrative structure, and hence come into professional contact; their membership of the soviet also brings them together on a regular basis, and they play a dominant role there; similarly, their contacts are enhanced by regular meetings of the party committee, and probably of various sub-committees in party and state. The chances of their establishing strong informal ties seem to be high, and this would add further to their dominant position. They are linked, moreover, by a common interest in maintaining the success – economic and otherwise – of the town. There also seems to be a common system of recruitment to these positions, with members apparently moving on a more or less random basis between positions in the party, the state apparatus, industry and perhaps other branches of administration. The view might thus be put forward of a town dominated by these 'strong' individuals, whose potential influence depends on a combination of personal characteristics (including the occupancy of a key post) and the tenure of membership positions in both of the two major political organs.

However, I would be reluctant to present such a picture of life in Tiraspol, for several reasons. First of all, by identifying the elite by membership of both soviet and gorkom we automatically exclude any non-party members who might nevertheless be likely influentials. In this case, the name of at least one individual springs to mind: I. I. Antosyak, whose career was outlined in chapter 8. A long-serving deputy who also served at least one term on the gorispolkom, he was the most frequent contributor to the sessions of the town soviet in the years I examined, and held important posts in the educational institute. It is hard to conceive that Antosyak could not legitimately be considered a member of the town's political elite. Other, similar cases could also be cited, which convince me that Frolic's perspective of the Soviet urban political elite, again confined to party members, is too restrictive.[2]

Secondly, and similarly, I have raised the notion of a number of posts carrying *intermittent* membership of one or both of these bodies after a period outside the elite, defined in terms of current membership of soviet or gorkom. The question that must be asked, however, is whether such individuals can necessarily be regarded as having departed from the ranks of the influentials during their period outside one or other institution? For example, was P. I. Dvornikov, director of the town's scientific research station, really not part of the town's political elite between December 1962 (when he left the gorkom) and March 1965 (when he returned to the soviet), especially since he was a Moldavian supreme soviet deputy between 1959 and 1963 and a central committee full member from January 1960 until his death in 1967? And if Dvornikov retained some form of elite status within the town during his absence from formal membership of the institutions, what of those whose temporary absence was due to political reasons? Did V. G. Lykhvar', the gorkom first secretary who lost his position in the 1961 purge but returned to favour after Khrushchev's dismissal, lose all association with the political decision-makers in the interim period?

Moreover, what was the general effect of temporary elite membership on the individual's position in the town? I pointed out that during his tenure of office a considerable degree of prestige and status accrues, possibly combined with greater opportunities for influencing decisions. After an individual has left the elite, institutionally defined, does he return to his former position as a virtual non-entity, or does some of the glory persist, so that a special status is maintained, at least temporarily? Is he able to retain his contacts with the decision-makers, and possibly turn them to advantage?

Obviously questions such as these cannot be answered on the basis of the information at my disposal on Tiraspol; nevertheless they have important implications for the use of the concept of 'elite' in the study of Soviet local politics, and conceivably Soviet politics as a whole.[3] It may be fair to assume that top leaders such as Khrushchev are 'unpersoned'[4] and banished from politics when removed from office, but Tiraspol at least raises questions as to the generality of such an assumption, and this is a question that would, in my view, merit further investigation.

There is one more crucial element in elite recruitment that makes me reluctant to accept the picture of the town as dominated by an elite of the strong: the fact that it is not a closed system. There is, as we saw, a high level of recruitment from outside the town to leading positions in all categories of administration. The fact that these local leaders are often brought in from elsewhere in the system – and are promoted to positions beyond the town – must have an important impeding effect on the maintenance of group cohesion among these sectors of the elite. It may indeed be a deliberate policy on the part of the central authorities to use nomenklatura precisely in order to prevent the development of a coterie basing its power on its effective control of the town. It seems significant that there appear to be few opportunities for individuals to reach the top via promotion from the ranks, so that the elite was far from self-perpetuating: it was higher authority that seemed to have the ultimate control over elite recruitment. Frolic draws a similar conclusion from his work on Soviet urban politics: 'urban autonomy has increased slightly in the 1960s, although Soviet municipalities still remain very much restricted by superior party and governmental authorities operating under the centralizing principles of Party dominance and dual subordination.'[5]

This and other features helped me to place Tiraspol in the framework of wider politics in the republic. Tenure of an office in the town was for a number of politicians simply one stage in a career that as often as not began elsewhere and would be pursued further elsewhere. This raises important issues about the degree of identity that such career administrators had with the town and its progress, apart from the fact that their own future depended on it. As Frolic has indicated, 'Unlike the majority of Western municipal community leaders, Soviet urban political leaders frequently have no pronounced loyalties to the city in which they hold a post'.[6] It seems reasonable to assume that they saw themselves more as representatives of the central authorities in the town, than as representatives of the town in their dealings with the central authorities. The fact that, say, Petrik was brought in from a career in rural areas, and was later transferred to the trade union council in Kishinev, raises interesting questions about the degree to which he might understand the specific problems of the small industrial city and present these to the central authorities, and how far he was indeed interested in doing so. Provided the town's economic and political life continued to satisfy the central authorities (meaning, essentially, high production and political peace), the first secretary could take the credit for success and enjoy the rewards of promotion. In this situation, the potential influence of locally based elite members, aware of the aims and problems of administration in the town, might be considerably enhanced: it is they, after all, who know how to run the town, and the first secretary might be very dependent on their loyal support.

The question of elite recruitment and career patterns has substantial implications for the nature of the entire political system, and it has been accorded much attention in recent years.[7] There are a number of issues involved, including whether it is appropriate to regard the leadership as a unified elite (a 'common leadership pool') or whether there is selectivity and specialisation in recruitment and training practices; whether current tenure of office implies identification with the interest of the structure or institution in which that office is held, or whether the socialisation and training experience of politicians is likely to be of greater influence in determining their attitudes towards political matters. The answers to questions such as these determine the appropriateness of concepts such as 'totalitarianism' and 'pluralism' in describing the Soviet political system, issues that are more fully explored in the sources referred to in note 7 above. I pointed out that in the case of Tiraspol there did appear to be a wide measure of switching from posts in one apparatus to posts in another, both during an individual's tenure of office within the town, and also among the individuals whose careers were traced beyond their sojourn in Tiraspol. Yet there also appeared to be some degree of specialisation, particularly within the party structure, among those individuals drafted in from outside to fill the post of first secretary and those who occupied the Komsomol gorkom first secretaryship; the security forces also seem to be distinguished by their functional specialisation in career development inside and outside the town.

However, too much must not be made of this example: case studies, as Harry Eckstein has pointed out, never 'prove' anything.[8] Tiraspol may be indicative of broader trends in early political and functional recruitment; but it should be borne in mind that this is a comparatively modest level in the Soviet power structure when set against the CPSU central committee, the USSR council of ministers, and the politburo. How far can officials in Tiraspol – some of them still fairly young – be said to be properly launched on their careers? Indeed, my data are compatible with a recruitment pattern that embraces membership of a 'common leadership pool' at the local level, where individuals can gain a wide range of experience in the earlier part of their career, after which they are selected for a more specialist orientation when promoted to positions of greater responsibility at the higher level. (It should be borne in mind that large republics such as the Ukraine or the RSFSR have further administrative tiers, notably the oblast, where individuals may advance their careers.) In my view, a much more extensive examination of political careers within the entire republic and beyond is required before firm conclusions can be drawn.[9]

### Scheme of Mobility within The Elite

Here I may perhaps explore briefly the question of mobility within the elite, and suggest a range of concepts that might help to clarify the processes involved. Implicit in my analysis in chapter 6, where I differentiated a number of elite groups, is the notion of gradation: a 'ladder', which individuals may climb, adding further social and political values at each step; or perhaps a building with a series of floors, linked by staircases, which individuals may use to progress from the ground floor (ordinary deputy status) to the attic, or rather luxury apartment on the top floor (membership of both executive bodies). However, I discovered in my empirical analysis that such social and political climbing from one grade or level to another was a relatively rare occurrence. Individual members came into the elite in one particular grade, and by and large remained at that level during their membership of the elite. The concept of a 'ladder' is clearly inappropriate – unless it be a ladder that may be stepped on to at many different levels. The notion of an elite building, with floors linked by stairs, lifts and escalators, may be a more appropriate image. Such a building, moreover, need not be entered at ground level – it has entry facilities on each floor, including the top (perhaps, in the 1960s and 1970s, a helipad, to facilitate the arrival of nomenklatura officials from Kishinev and elsewhere!). The building is not necessarily pyramid-shaped: the upper floors have to accommodate fewer persons but considerably more political values.

Here is a brief picture of how movement within this building may operate. The floors are stacked as in my tentative hierarchy on page 110, with A the ground floor. For those who enter at the ground floor, election to, say, a PPO secretaryship may serve as a lift that raises him to the fourth floor – retaining soviet membership and adding gorkom membership; a factory manager, perhaps already on floor four, transferred to a gorkom secretaryship may thereby acquire access to an escalator linking that floor with floor seven (gorkom buro and soviet), whence the staircase to the top floor may become available in due course. Movement is not, of course, only *up* the building: an individual who loses prestige or position might be swiftly carried down a lift, perhaps pausing at lower floors, and bundled out of the building; others may be pushed from a window (or down a garbage chute) following a political crisis or serious economic failure; in a few cases, a trapdoor may lower them into a basement, not part of the building proper, where they are kept out of harm's way, until such time as they are allowed to emerge and climb back into the building – perhaps following major changes in the national political climate. We have seen examples of these kinds of career movement within the elite. The building is also, of course, linked with other similar buildings at the upper floors: there are transfers into and out of leadership positions by leaders in other towns and districts. Anyone who reaches the top two or three floors may also be given a key that opens a corridor to the republican-level palace.

Such a simple image is not, of course, presented as a theoretical model; it may, however, help to clarify the range of movements that was identified in Tiraspol. Those who moved up or down within the building did not simply mount or descend a ladder or flight of steps: certain career developments served as keys that operated escalators or lifts (or helicopters taking them off elsewhere), as did some major political changes in Soviet society. A small number of individuals were kept, as it were, in the basement – or perhaps the back yard – after passing through the building (and sometimes being un-ceremoniously thrown out) and eventually allowed back inside. The majority who spent time in the building, however, were restricted to one floor: they entered the building at one level, walked to the other side, and left, their personal attributes or career developments failing to serve as keys to operate the devices connecting the floors.

## DEVELOPING COUNTRY MODEL

A further theoretical approach must also be considered before I assess the work of the two institutions that I have examined, and draw my final conclusions from this study. This is the appreciation that some of what I have said about the characteristics of the elite and the political implications for the role of the institutions and their officers can be understood if we bear in mind that Tiraspol is part of a developing country system. In other words, rather than looking at the town's political elite and its activity solely in terms of abstract concepts of representation, efficiency and so forth, we can see part of the explanation of political practices by looking at the social context and over-riding political objectives that form the setting. Indeed, I pointed out at the very beginning of this book that fundamental change and development has been a characteristic feature of the Soviet Union this century.

Other scholars specialising on the Soviet Union have pointed out that the 'development model', devised for the most part with reference to the so-called 'third world', ex-colonial countries, does have considerable explanatory power when applied to the Soviet Union and in fact most other communist-controlled states.[10] Certainly, when reading the literature on political development and modernisation, one repeatedly comes across features that are characteristic of the Soviet system. Indeed, in his leading study of modernisation, with its description of the 'mobilization system', David Apter refers to Leninism as 'an extreme form of the mobilization system',[11] the model moreover that developing countries have tended to imitate. The single party of solidarity, with its special directing role, the stress on economic growth as a (or *the*) major societal goal, the ideology that takes the form of a political religion: these and other features are characteristics that the Soviet Union and developing countries have in common with Apter's model.

The political system, perhaps especially at the local grass-roots level, has also been subordinated to this task. The aim of the Soviet regime (as of those in emergent countries) has been, in short, to mobilise the population: mobilisation (a word the Soviet leadership itself is inclined to use, as T. H. Rigby has pointed out[12]) thus becomes a distinguishing and characteristic feature. This concept is worth pursuing briefly for the light it sheds on processes in Tiraspol.

Apart from Apter, two scholars who have paid particular attention to the concept of mobilisation are Karl Deutsch and Peter Nettl.[13] For Deutsch, social mobilisation is 'an overall process of change', involving a whole variety of spheres: residence, occupation, social setting, institutions, roles, and others; the cumulative impact of these changes, which take place at a specific historical stage in a society's or country's existence, is a modification, even transformation, of political behaviour.[14] Nettl explored and developed the mobilisation concept with special reference to the political setting. Mobilisation becomes 'an induced attempt to raise the level of acculturation', hence political mobilisation is 'primarily a forced process of familiarization with politics'. Nettl goes on,

> In countries where mobilization is deliberate, where we have a commitment to compression of time and social distance, where one of the main functions of politics is the rapid involvement of peripheral members of society, it is easier to view mobilization as a deliberate process and to regard it as in large part aimed at culture formation.[15]

This clearly applies to the Soviet Union, as Nettl points out, referring to the party's role as one of 'stalactite mobilization' (i.e. mobilisation of grass-roots support from the top downwards), and identifying the economic development and planning system as a political symbol providing ideological control and 'a structure of commitment, information and communication' (p. 283). Nettl explicitly compares the Soviet planning model as a system of mobilisation with similar phenomena in developing countries (especially in his Chapter 8); he also suggests (p. 309) that the USSR will 'continue to supply a more suitable model' for developing countries than do the western democracies, although it will not necessarily be copied with complete accuracy.

Nettl's approach does seem helpful in explaining some of the features that I have identified, notably the important position in the elite occupied by administrators, whose role in plan fulfilment is crucial; it also explains the preoccupation of public meetings with economic issues, defined at the top, rather than demands arising among the populace. More generally, however, by viewing the overall political aim as one of rapid political culture formation, we see more clearly the point of bringing so many 'ordinary' citizens into the elite, if only for brief periods: they thereby become familiar with institutions, political processes and practices, policies and issues, and this changes (develops) the political culture.

This kind of approach has recently been further examined by Robert Tucker, with special reference to Soviet and communist societies.[16] In arguing for a cultural approach to studying communist societies, Tucker indicates that the overall aim of these regimes is, in effect, to replace one, pre-existing culture (including attitudes and behavioural norms) with another, which stems from the ideology. Hence the stress on creating the 'new Soviet man', whose whole outlook, hence attitudes and actions, in the political as well as other spheres, indeed whose overall personality is in line with the 'dominant political culture'.[17] Involving citizens in the work of carefully controlled institutions is to be regarded as an effective way of internalising the appropriate norms, through the influence of group behavioural psychology: the principle that 'an individual's membership groups have an important influence on the values and attitudes he holds'.[18] This, at least, seems to be the belief, in both the Soviet Union and developing countries: involving citizens in the work of political institutions will develop psychological and attitudinal supports for the system. Whether it *is* effective is perhaps open to question, and in my view it cannot be assumed that bringing in large numbers of ordinary citizens for a short spell as a deputy will in itself develop such supports. Indeed, I argued in chapter 4 that some of the frustrations encountered in office may have quite the opposite effect. As C. H. Dodd has noted, again with special reference to societies undergoing political development, 'The assumption (in the literature) seems to be that a government gains in power and authority as more people participate in the political system. But this rests on the assumption that participation equals support. This might occur in a very public-spirited democracy, but generally participation does not take so high-minded a form'.[19] One awaits reliable evidence that Soviet deputies and former deputies (and even present and past members of party organs) do possess such attitudes: one study reported that 26 per cent of deputies were dissatisfied with the help they were receiving from their executive committee.[20] We might conclude that they were less than wholehearted supporters of the local government system; moreover, their experience of the system from the inside' may have pinpointed weaknesses of which they were previously unaware.

In another way, too, the developing country model may help to illuminate a feature of Soviet local politics: this is the question of the fund of political skills available in the society. Lucian Pye has drawn attention to this question, pointing out that, just as a developing *economy* requires a rapid extension in the range of production and administrative skills in the population, so too a certain range of political skills and attitudes needs to be instilled in order to promote an aware and capable citizenry and leaders able to operate the *political* institutions competently.[21] As I have suggested, simply drawing people in may not necessarily achieve this, and the simplistic 'political education' available to the mass of the population does not adequately prepare them for the task; the stress in recent years on training for deputies reveals the need for giving them these special extra skills. The somewhat uncertain role of deputies, operating within ostensibly democratic representative structures, but in fact playing a part in the mobilisation system, is something that the Soviet Union further shares with developing countries.[22] The 'real' leaders are those in the higher elite groups: professional administrators in industry or the political apparatus, who are given special, more sophisticated training, often in party-run schools, and experience in managerial, Komsomol, party or state posts. They form a special segment of the elite, well-acculturated, although not politically neutral, and mobile within the republic and indeed the whole country.

This kind of approach does thus shed light on the situation in Tiraspol. Processes have more in common with the development system than with those in our familiar western system. Where the western system can help in understanding Soviet local (and national) politics is by providing a frame of reference by which to judge the efficacy of institutions. The soviets at least, and to a certain extent the cpsu, claim to be democratic and representative. These are concepts derived from western liberal political philosophy, and it is thus appropriate to use that theory as a yardstick against which to measure the performance of Soviet local government: how far does it achieve the aims that it sets out for itself? what are the present trends and future prospects? In this, I am following the example of Soviet researchers, who in recent years have been judging the role of the soviets in precisely these terms, as some of the sources quoted in this study show.

### ASSESSMENT OF THE WORK OF SOVIET AND GORKOM

I now turn therefore to an assessment of the work of the two institutions I have examined, and I return to a fundamental question with which this study opened: whether an examination of the sociological aspects of the town soviet and party committee tends to confirm or modify the traditional western view of those institutions and their relationship with one another.

The immediate answer is that in many ways such an analysis confirms the standard view, particularly of the soviet, and adds a further structural element that affects the role it might play. It is true that a high level of turnover helps to draw a wide circle of citizens into the process of local administration. This in itself is no doubt to be applauded, since the general level of civic awareness is thereby raised: that indeed is one aim of the policy, as I have pointed out. However, it seems far more doubtful that the citizenry can enjoy the kind of influence that such a situation might imply. Certainly the role of deputies within the soviet itself seemed to conform to the accepted view, and the division into 'weak' and 'strong' adds further confirmation of this perception. Quite apart from the constitutional restrictions on the role of the soviet – the limitations on their budgeting powers, the infrequency of their sessions, the need to spend considerable time in ratifying trivial regulations drafted by the executive committee, and (above all) the principles of democratic centralism and subordination to higher bodies – the sociological aspect adds further to the restraining factors. First, the sheer size of the soviet restricts the possibilities for active participation in the debates. Secondly, the division into 'weak' and 'strong' deputies led to domination over the sessions by the 'strong'. In this, the political behaviour of Tiraspol town soviet differed perhaps little from practices in other kinds of political system; but it did conflict with some of the expressed basic aims of the Soviet system of local government, and Soviet writers have expressed concern, as I pointed out.

Turning to the town party committee, we found that despite the regrettably high incidence of missing data similar principles seemed to apply, although the overall composition of this committee was apparently more 'elitist' (in the sense that membership seemed to be drawn from among those groups of citizens with 'strong' characteristics). Relatively few were identified as ordinary workers and employees in low-status occupations, whereas the political and managerial administrative fields were especially strongly represented. This in turn probably had its effect on the degree to which gorkom members were vulnerable to political changes outside the town: it was that body which, more than the soviet, manifested changes in membership that could be confidently associated with major national crises.

The public meetings of the gorkom, like those of the soviet, also tended to be dominated by a small circle of members, and I recorded the adoption of the widespread practice of virtually duplicating the plenums of the gorkom by meetings of the town party aktiv. This had its implications for the role of the gorkom itself, and for the position of its members, as did the custom of extending the plenums to a wide measure of participation by outsiders. It was hard to distinguish between these two forums on the basis of their content or form, and it was suggested that the difference was mainly in their legal status. An examination of the identity of the speakers at a number of party and other forums (including the soviet sessions) indicated that it is perhaps not inappropriate to speak of a fairly small circle of 'activists', who tended to be vocal on these occasions, again to the detriment of the ordinary members.

As regards party–state relations, apart from a functional distinction between soviet and party committee, some attempt also seemed to be made to keep the personnel distinct, although the extent of this varied over time, and the implications are not completely clear. Certainly the measure of overlapping membership was fairly sizeable, suggesting confirmation of the traditional view that the soviets are controlled by the party and its organs, in part through such features as interlocking membership. I argued, however, that the process is not simply one of domination by the party over the soviets, but is considerably more subtle than that. A substantial degree of deputy representation on the gorkom, I suggested, indicates that the soviet is in a stronger position to influence discussions in the party body, so that the latter would be more likely to produce more rational decisions in its interpretations for the town of directives and resolutions issuing from higher bodies. Moreover, the measure of overlap also appeared to serve as an indicator of the changing political status of soviets: a greater degree of dual membership reflected an enhancement of the soviet's position in the eyes of the party.

In any case, this underlines the view that the party intends to maintain effective influence over the soviets. The emphasis that has been placed since the mid-1960s on improving the role of the soviets does not imply that they are to be developed as independent organs of power to rival the party. Indeed, as an article in *Partiinaya zhizn'* put it in 1973,

> The local organs of power are called upon to carry out their functions more fully, to take upon themselves a significant share of the work of translating into fact the decisions of the party, to render

effective influence on the development of the economy and culture and raising the welfare of the people. *All these tasks can be successfully resolved only with constant attention and leadership of the soviets on the part of the party committees.*[23]

The extent to which the soviets are allowed to develop is clearly to be measured by the party authorities, who are likely to continue to think of the state bodies mainly as institutions through which party policies are implemented.

Even the attempts to strengthen the financial base of local soviets and their executive bodies, and to extend their role by transferring control of industrial enterprises from central ministries, are likely to have little real effect on party–state relations or on relations between the centre and the localities.[24] Indeed, mere modification of the local government structure would be quite inadequate to bring about the revitalisation that is presented as official policy; at the very least some of the sociological factors would need to be tackled as well. It is not without significance that Soviet social researchers, in examining the effectiveness of local government bodies, have concentrated on precisely the same kind of question as I have discussed in this study, and have put forward some radical proposals:[25] for example, that the permanent commissions should be made responsible for administration, in place of the otdely;[26] or that permanent commission chairmen be given one or two days off work each month in order to attend to their duties;[27] the need to balance the distribution of social characteristics in the soviets with those in the population has also been mentioned;[28] more radical still is the suggestion that the population should have a positive say in choosing those deputies who are to run for re-election, who would then have to run for the same constituency;[29] this could in turn lead to the development of a personal following for deputies among their constituents, which might substantially alter power relations at the local level by giving popular deputies a base of genuine electoral support. There has also been a recognition that effective representation requires not only the time to carry out representative functions, but also a measure of experience and the provision of proper facilities.[30]

It seems significant that in all the discussion of the role of local government by both politicians and social scientists, attention has been focused on the role of the individual deputies. It seems possible that the revitalisation of their work, through the permanent commissions and with their electors, which occurred towards the end of our study period (and has continued subsequently), might add considerably to the value of local soviets. Hough, for example, has suggested that the development of the permanent commissions of the USSR supreme soviet between 1965 and 1966 may be seen as heralding an important development in the role of the soviets.[31] The experimental session of Tiraspol town soviet in August 1965 pointed to a possible advancement in this direction, which was a considerable improvement on the position of a decade earlier, as I pointed out. However, the information published on these commissions at the local level was not enough to allow me to make a firm judgement on this question. Similarly, I had no evidence for Tiraspol on which to base an assessment of the deputies' activities outside the formal apparatus, so that I could not make a complete evaluation of their role. Soviet students of the deputies, to be sure, suggest that this is one of the most important aspects of their activity,[32] and even Fainsod, who emphasises the limits on the role of the constitutional apparatus, points out that 'Since deputies are sometimes influential persons in their own right, they may intercede with the ministries to obtain some redress of grievances for the localities they represent', while adding that there are limits to this activity.[33] This is clearly an area that could benefit from a different line of research, and the present study can merely raise hypotheses about the likely effects of certain identified sociological factors in the composition of the elite.

## An Assessment of Soviet Local Politics

As far as an overall assessment of Soviet local politics is concerned, judged against the standards of representative institutional theory, my study of Tiraspol causes me to make little modification to the widely accepted view of relationships among the various institutions. I have pointed to a number of functions that are performed – at least intermittently – by soviets and local party committees: serving as a forum at which initiatives on local issues may be made; performing a great deal of necessary administration; acting as communications channels between the localities and the centre; playing an important role in political socialisation and elite training. Yet so long as these institutions remain deprived of the effective right (as opposed to the legal right) to respond directly to needs and demands perceived and expressed by citizens, Soviet political life will remain largely divorced from the interest-based politics of the 'allocation of values' system that is familiar elsewhere, and Nettl's 'stalagmite' (conferring legitimacy by grass-roots action in the system) is unlikely to take over from the 'stalactite' (mobilisation of support from above). And for the foreseeable future this seems likely to be true. The notion of 'developing' the role of local government, which has been widely disseminated in the Soviet Union of late, is evidently not to be understood as implying a *change* in the traditional role, but rather strengthening the institutions so that they may play their former role more effectively. The development of the role of these bodies would require a fundamental political decision of the highest order, radically modifying the position of the communist party in society; for that very reason, such a development is scarcely to be anticipated. To that extent, at least, this study has vindicated the conclusions reached through the application of other approaches to the subject – legal, ideological, Kremlinological; indeed, I hardly expected otherwise.

Nevertheless, it does appear from my work that the whole question of Soviet local political life is substantially more subtle and complex than it might have seemed, and here I return to the perspective of Soviet politics with which this study opened. My investigation of the sociological factor has added a further important dimension to the study of the political process. When viewed from the summit of the system – the locus of power on which many observers concentrate their attention – the level with which I have been concerned appears extremely modest, not to say insignificant, and its participants appear for the most part to be perfectly ordinary citizens. The sociological analysis tends to confirm this view. Yet is it adequate as an interpretation of local political life? Does not the sociological analysis also serve as a reminder that the political process involves people at large, for whom *this is politics* – the only politics they have? The politburo and its so-called power struggles are, as I pointed out, so remote that they effectively lose their significance. It is in their local elite that ordinary Soviet citizens see the first tier of the country's power structure; it is to their local elite members – if to anyone – that they turn for assistance. It is at the level of his own locality that the ordinary citizen has the greatest opportunities for experiencing the social and political benefits of membership of a political elite. Thus, when viewed from the perspective of the lower end of the scale, local political life acquires a degree of importance that seems unwarranted when judged simply in terms of the total power distribution in the country.

The signs are that increasing emphasis is likely to be placed on those aspects of political life in the localities that have been dealt with in this study, with adjustments both to structures and to recruitment and training policies (perhaps along the lines I have occasionally suggested), in order to make the institutions more representative and effective in coping with the needs of an ever more complex society. Even if I do not foresee a short- or medium-term development towards pluralist or interest-based local politics, such modest developments as I have outlined are likely to lead to an increase in the significance of Soviet local political life.

# Notes and References

CHAPTER 1

1    Daniel Bell refers to the abundance of literature on Soviet affairs graphically in his article 'Ten Theories in Search of Reality: The Prediction of Soviet Behavior', in his *The End of Ideology: On the Exhaustion of Political Ideas in the Fifties*, revised edition (New York: The Free Press, 1962) pp. 315–53 (p. 315). It is scarcely necessary to record such works here; for a select bibliography, see P. H. Vigor (ed.) *Books on Communism and the Communist Countries* (London: Ampersand, 1971).

2    These phrases are taken from well-known writers on Soviet politics: see Michel Tatu, *Power in the Kremlin: From Khrushchev's Decline to Collective Leadership* (London: Collins, 1969) p. 15; Robert Conquest, *Power and Policy in the U.S.S.R.: The Study of Soviet Dynastics* (London: Macmillan, 1961) Part I, and his *Russia After Khrushchev* (New York: Praeger, 1965) p. vii; Sidney I. Ploss, *Conflict and Decision-Making in Soviet Russia: A Case Study of Agricultural Policy, 1953–1963* (Princeton: Princeton University Press, 1965) p. 278.

3    See Bell 'Ten Theories', p. 325. For further discussion of the Kremlinological method, see the contributions to *Survey*, no. 50 (January 1964).

4    The view that the Soviet political system is centralised is expressed forcefully by Roy D. Laird, who sees it as 'a unique paradigm of a successful centralized monohierarchical polity': see his *The Soviet Paradigm: An Experiment in Creating a Monohierarchical Polity* (New York: The Free Press, 1970) p. xviii. Compare David Lane's unequivocal statement, 'in practice, the government of the USSR is centralised': see David Lane, *Politics and Society in the USSR* (London: Weidenfeld & Nicolson, 1970) p. 164. Few would quarrel with this assessment.

5    See in particular Sidney and Beatrice Webb, *Soviet Communism – a New Civilisation?* (London: Longmans, Green, 1935–7); Bertram W. Maxwell, *The Soviet State* (London: Selwyn & Blount, 1935).

6    See, for example, Merle Fainsod, *How Russia is Ruled*, 2nd edition (Cambridge, Mass.: Harvard University Press, 1965) and Derek J. R. Scott, *Russian Political Institutions*, 4th edition (London: George Allen and Unwin, 1969), both of which concentrate on the central institutions; Frederick C. Barghoorn, in his *Politics in the USSR* (Boston and Toronto: Little, Brown, 1966) generally stresses the higher organs, as does Lane (*Politics and Society*).

7    Khrushchev's so called 'secret speech' was a now-notorious attack on Stalin's rule, delivered at the xx Party Congress in February 1956. An abridged text of this was released by the U.S. State Department later that year, and has been reproduced many times; for example, in Henry M. Christman (ed.) *Communism in Action: A Documentary History* (New York: Bantam Books, 1969) pp. 158–228. The Khrushchev 'memoirs' were published in the West in the autumn of 1970 under the title *Khrushchev Remembers* (London: Andre Deutsch); their authenticity has not been accepted by all scholars. A second volume, sub-titled *The Last Testament*, appeared in 1974.

8    Svetlana Alliluyeva, *Twenty Letters to a Friend* (London: Hutchinson, 1967);
     Milovan Djilas, *Conversations with Stalin* (London: Rupert Hart-Davis, 1962).

9    For an account of the restricted development of sociology in the USSR, see Zev
     Katz, 'Sociology in the Soviet Union', *Problems of Communism* [*PoC*] vol. xx, no. 3
     (1971) pp. 22–40; on the development of political science, see David E.
     Powell and Paul Shoup, 'The Emergence of Political Science in Communist Countries',
     *American Political Science Review* [*APSR*], vol. LXIV, no. 2 (1970) pp. 572–88,
     especially pp. 573–80; also Rolf H. W. Theen, 'Political Science in the USSR: "To
     Be, Or Not To Be?" . . .', *World Politics*, vol. XXIII, no. 4 (1971) pp. 684–703.

10   Robert Conquest, 'In Defence of Kremlinology', *Survey*, no. 50 (1964) pp. 163–73
     (p. 171); reference is to Conquest, *Power and Policy*.

11   See Borys Levytsky, *The Soviet Political Elite*, xeroxed manuscript distributed by the
     Hoover Institution on War, Revolution and Peace, Stanford University (Stanford,
     Calif., 1970).

12   For example, Robert E. Blackwell, Jr, 'Elite Recruitment and Functional Change:
     An Analysis of the Soviet Obkom Elite, 1950–1968', *Journal of Politics*, vol. 34, no.
     1 (1972) pp. 124–52; Peter Frank, 'The CPSU Obkom First Secretary: A Profile',
     *British Journal of Political Science* [*BJPolS*], vol. 1, no. 2 (1971) pp. 173–90; Sergei
     Vorontsyn, 'Oblast and Krai First Secretaries', *Studies on the Soviet Union*, vol. VIII,
     no. 4 (1968–9) pp. 32–5.

13   See Philip D. Stewart, *Political Power in the Soviet Union: A Study of Decision-Making
     in Stalingrad* (Indianapolis and New York: Bobbs-Merrill, 1968); and T. H. Rigby,
     *Communist Party Membership in the Soviet Union, 1917–1967* (Princeton, N.J.:
     Princeton University Press, 1968).

14   See Jerry Hough, *The Soviet Prefects: The Local Party Organs in Industrial Decision-
     Making* (Cambridge, Mass.: Harvard University Press, 1969); and Michael P.
     Gehlen, *The Communist Party of the Soviet Union: A Functional Analysis* (Bloomington
     and London: Indiana University Press, 1969).

15   See Merle Fainsod, *Smolensk Under Soviet Rule* (London: Macmillan, 1958); and
     John A. Armstrong, *The Soviet Bureaucratic Elite: A Case Study of the Ukrainian
     Apparatus* (London: Atlantic Books, 1959).

16   See, for example, L. G. Churchward, 'Some Aspects of Republican and Local
     Government Before the Decentralization', *Soviet Studies* [*Sov. Studs.*], vol. IX, no. 1
     (1957) pp. 84–91; 'Continuity and Change in Soviet Local Government', *Sov.
     Studs.*, vol. IX. no. 3 (1958) pp. 256–85; 'To Divide or Not to Divide', *Sov. Studs.*,
     vol. XVII, no. 1 (1965) pp. 93–6; and 'Soviet Local Government Today', *Sov. Studs.*,
     vol. XVII, no. 4 (1966) pp. 431–52.

17   See Everett M. Jacobs, 'The Composition of Local Soviets, 1959–1969', *Government
     and Opposition*, vol. 7, no. 4 (1972) pp. 503–19, 'Soviet Local Elections: What They
     Are, and What They Are Not', *Sov. Studs.*, vol. XXII, no. 1 (1970) pp. 61–76; and
     Jerome M. Gilison, 'Soviet Elections as a Measure of Dissent: The Missing One
     Percent', *APSR*, vol. LXII, no. 3 (1968) pp. 814–26.

18   See Max E. Mote, *Soviet Local and Republic Elections* (Stanford, Calif.: Hoover
     Institution, Stanford University, 1965), and Howard R. Swearer, 'The Functions
     of Soviet Local Elections', *Midwest Journal of Political Science*, vol. V, no. 2 (1961)
     pp. 129–49.

19   David T. Cattell, *Leningrad: A Case Study of Soviet Urban Government* (New York:
     Praeger, 1968).

20   T. H. Rigby, 'The Selection of Leading Personnel in the Soviet State and
     Communist Party', PhD thesis, unpublished, London University, 1954.

21   See, for example, Frolic's articles, 'Decision-Making in Soviet Cities', *APSR*, vol.
     LXVI, no. 1 (1972) pp. 38–52, 'Soviet Urban Political Leaders', *Comparative Political
     Studies*, vol. 2, no. 4 (1970) pp. 443–64, 'Municipal Administrations, Departments,

Commissions and Organizations', *Sov. Studs.*, vol. XXII, no. 3 (1971) pp. 376–93; also William Taubman, *Governing Soviet Cities: Bureaucratic Politics and Urban Development in the USSR* (New York: Praeger, 1973).

22  As Frolic has noted, 'detailed examination of Soviet municipal politics invariably becomes an analysis of the politics of Moscow or Leningrad': see 'Soviet Urban Political Leaders', p. 453.

23  For precise figures, see *Itogi Vsesoyuznoi perepisi naseleniya 1959 goda: RSFSR* [*1959 Census: RSFSR*] (Moscow: Gosstatizdat, 1963). Both of these studies were limited, incidentally, by the tendency to concentrate on one of the two main structures: the Leningrad state apparatus, and the Stalingrad oblast party committee.

24  Figures calculated from *Itogi Vsesoyuznoi perepisi naseleniya 1970 goda. Tom I: chislennost' naseleniya SSSR, soyuznykh i avtonomnykh respublik, kraev i oblastei* [*1970 Census, vol. I*], (Moscow: Statistika, 1972).

25  For a brief historical survey of the town, and discussion of its typicality in the context of Soviet urban centres, see chapter 2 below.

26  See Alex Inkeles, 'Models and Issues in the Analysis of Soviet Society', *Survey*, no. 60 (1966) pp. 3–17 (p. 16).

27  At least one western student of Soviet urban politics (B. Michael Frolic) has been more successful than myself in gaining useful interviews with Soviet officials in ten Soviet cities: see his articles cited in note 21 above, in particular 'Decision-Making in Soviet Cities'.

28  The best studies of policy-making and implementation at the local level are Hough's *The Soviet Prefects* and Taubman's *Governing Soviet Cities*, both of which deal admirably with aspects of local politics for which information is not available for Tiraspol. Taubman's concept of the 'company town' (a city dominated by the major industrial enterprises, which hold effective power against the soviet and even the party committee) is an interesting one. In view of the nature of my evidence, it is not certain that it could be applied to Tiraspol. The press reports of the debates that I examined (see chapter 5) gave no indication of conflict between the interests of the town authorities and those of industry, although an article by the then *gorplan* chairman complained in 1971 that reforms involving the transfer of enterprises to the town soviet were being but slowly introduced, and such enterprises continued to operate without taking local needs into consideration in collaboration with the planning commission – precisely the kind of problem identified by Taubman: see K. Popodnyak, 'Doverie umnozhaet sily', *Sovetskaya Moldaviya*, 18 November 1971, p. 3. We shall see in later chapters how far local industry was involved in the political institutions of the town.

29  This was normally *Dnestrovskaya pravda*, although it changed its title and formal status a number of times during the period covered by this study; it was published 3–4 times weekly (see chapter 2). For a brief discussion of some of the problems involved in basing this kind of study on the Soviet provincial press, see Joel C. Moses, *Regional Party Leadership and Policy-Making in the USSR* (New York: Praeger, 1974) pp. 45–8. It remains the case, nevertheless, that there is at the moment no alternative source of comparable information.

30  See Frederic J. Fleron, Jr, 'Note on the Explication of the Concept "Elite" in the Study of Soviet Politics', *Canadian Slavic Studies*, vol. II, no. 1 (1968) pp. 111–15, especially p. 111.

31  See, for example, Geraint Parry, *Political Elites* (London: Allen and Unwin, 1969) p. 13; Harold D. Lasswell, 'The Study of Political Elites', in Harold D. Lasswell and Daniel Lerner (eds) *World Revolutionary Elites: Studies in Coercive Ideological Movements* (Cambridge, Mass.: MIT Press, 1965) pp. 3–28 (p. 4); Harold D. Lasswell and Abraham Kaplan, *Power and Society: A Framework for Political Inquiry* (New Haven, Conn.: Yale University Press, 1950) pp. 201–3.

32 Fleron, 'Note on the Explication of the Concept "Elite"', pp. 112–14. This is a major criticism of the 'positional' approach to local elite study: see Charles M. Bonjean and David M. Olson, 'Community Leadership: Directions of Research', reprinted in Michael Aiken and Paul E. Mott (eds) *The Structure of Community Power* (New York: Random House, 1970) pp. 203–15, especially p. 204.

33 See Frederic J. Fleron, 'Career Types in the Soviet Political Leadership', in R. Barry Farrell (ed.) *Political Leadership in Eastern Europe and the Soviet Union* (London: Butterworths, 1970) pp. 108–39 (p. 124).

34 See Suzanne Keller, 'Elites', in David L. Sills (ed.) *The International Encyclopedia of the Social Sciences*, vol. 5 (New York: Macmillan and The Free Press, 1968) pp. 26–9 (p. 26). Compare Lasswell: 'Elite analysis distinguishes between members and nonmembers of a group in the context under study' ('The Study of Political Elites', p. 5); also Bottomore: 'functional, mainly occupational, groups which have high status . . . in a society' (see T. B. Bottomore, *Elites and Society*, Pelican edition, Harmondsworth: Penguin Books, 1966, p. 14).

35 See T. H. Rigby, 'The Soviet Political Elite 1917–1922', *BJPolS*, vol. 1, no. 4 (1971) pp. 415–36 (p. 416). On this view the concept of 'elitism' (implying relativity) is perhaps more valuable than 'elite'. Compare William A. Welsh's view that in concentrating simply on a restricted institutional elite (say, the *politburo*) one ignores the 'nonactive' and 'political' elites – who may serve as a recruiting ground for subsequent elites: see his article, 'Toward a Multiple-Strategy Approach to Research on Comparative Communist Political Elites: Empirical and Quantitative Problems', in Frederic J. Fleron, Jr (ed.) *Communist Studies and the Social Sciences: Essays on Methodology and Empirical Theory* (Chicago: Rand McNally, 1969) pp. 318–56 (pp. 327–8). The significance of my insistence on the relativism of the concept will become apparent particularly in chapter 6 below.

CHAPTER 2

1 *Ocherki istoriya Tiraspolya*, (Kishinev: Kartya Moldovenyaske, 1967) p. 19. Much of the historical detail in this chapter derives from that book.

2 *Entsiklopedicheskii slovar'* (St. Petersburg, 1890–1904) vol. 65 (1901).

3 Ye. Zlatova and V. V. Kotel'nikov, *Puteshestvie po Moldavii* (Moscow: Molodaya gvardiya, 1957) p. 238.

4 A. Surilov, *Istoriya gosudarstva i prava Moldavskoi SSR (1917–1959 gg.)* (Kishinev: Kartya Moldovenyaske, 1963) p. 97. In attributing capital status to Tiraspol from 1924, the *Bol'shaya Sovetskaya Entsiklopediya* is clearly wrong. See also *Istoriya Moldavskoi SSR* (Kishinev: Kartya Moldovenyaske, 1968) vol. 11, p. 805, which gives 29 June 1929 as the date on which a decision on the transfer was taken.

5 See *Istoriya Moldavskoi SSR*, vol. 11, chapter x, especially pp. 345–61.

6 See N. A. Pobeda, 'Nekotorye osobennosti formirovaniya kul'tury sovremennykh gorodov Moldavii', in V. N. Yermuratskii, A. I. Babii and G. S. Yentelis (eds) *Filosofskie i sotsiologicheskie issledovaniya v Moldavii* (Kishinev: AN MSSR, 1970) pp. 161–80 (p. 173).

7 Figures from *ibid.*, p. 165.

8 *Ibid.*, p. 172.

9 For figures see *Sovetskaya Moldaviya k 50-letiyu Velikogo Oktyabrya: Statisticheskii sbornik* (Kishinev: Statistika, 1967) p. 264.

10 M. Bazin, *Soyuz zemledeliya i promyshlennosti: o nekotorykh formakh soedineniya sel'skokhozyaistvennogo proizvodstva s promyshlennym v usloviyakh Moldavii* (Kishinev:

Kartya Moldovenyaske, 1969) p. 170. It had over 700 students by 1969 (*ibid.*).

11  I. A. Krupenikov, D. A. Mirskii and M. M. Radul (eds) *Sovetskii Soyuz: Moldaviya* (Moscow: Mysl', 1970) p. 221.

12  *Ibid.*, p. 220.

13  *Ibid.*, p. 223.

14  *Pravda*, 4 January 1971; *Sovetskaya Moldaviya*, 5 January 1971.

15  See Chauncy D. Harris, *Cities of the Soviet Union: Studies in their Functions, Size, Density, and Growth* (Chicago: Rand McNally, 1970) especially pp. 89–90, 113.

16  See A. A. Gudym, *Dinamichnost' ekonomiki Moldavskoi SSR* (Kishinev: Kartya Moldovenyaske, 1969) p. 88.

17  'Polozhenie o gorodskom Sovete deputatov trudyashchikhsya Moldavskoi SSR' [Statute on Town Soviets in the Moldavian SSR], adopted 29 November 1957, Article 5. The text of this statute is reprinted in *Sbornik normativtnykh aktov: v pomoshch' rabotnikam mestnykh Sovetov* (Kishinev: Kartya Moldovenyaske, 1968) pp. 79–94. This statute has been superseded by a similar statute adopted 8 December 1971 (for text, see *Sovetskaya Moldaviya*, 14 December 1971).

18  See, for example, George Barr Carson, Jr, *Electoral Practices in the USSR* (London: Atlantic Press, 1956); Mote, *Soviet Local and Republic Elections*; Swearer, 'The Functions of Soviet Local Elections'; Gilison, 'Soviet Elections as a Measure of Dissent'; Jacobs, 'Soviet Local Elections'; Ronald J. Hill, 'Continuity and Change in USSR Supreme Soviet Elections', *BJPolS*, vol. 2, no. 1 (1972) pp. 47–67. In addition, most textbooks on Soviet government also deal at greater or lesser length with elections.

19  Churchward, for example, has cited cases where Soviet periodicals report instances of soviets disputing appointments to executive committees of individuals selected by higher party committees: see his review in *Sov. Studs.*, vol. xx, no. 4 (1969) pp. 555–6 (p. 556), citing three issues of the journal *Sovety deputatov trudyashchikhsya* for 1960.

20  Formerly these departments were listed in the constitutions of the union republics, thus necessitating a constitutional amendment after every administrative reorganisation. For this reason in a number of republics (including Moldavia) this section was deleted (Articles 69 and 72 of the USSR Constitution, referring respectively to rural district and urban soviets): see P. T. Vasilenkov, *Organy sovetskogo gosudarstva i ikh sistema na sovremennom etape* (Moscow: Izdatel'stvo Moskovskogo universiteta, 1967) p. 244. For examples of the departmental structure in Soviet city administrations see Frolic, 'Municipal Administrations'.

21  'Polozhenie o planovoi komissii ispolnitel'nogo komiteta gorodskogo (raionnogo) Soveta deputatov trudyashchikhsya' [Statute on Planning Commission] adopted 2 June 1965; Russian text in *Sbornik normativnykh aktov*, pp. 208–11. The *political* nature of the work of the planning authorities in dealing with industrial enterprises is admirably demonstrated in Taubman, *Governing Soviet Cities*.

22  Jerry F. Hough, 'Soviet Urban Politics and Comparative Urban Theory', *Journal of Comparative Administration*, vol. 4, no. 3 (1972) pp. 311–34 (p. 320); Taubman refers to the party as 'supermayor': see *Governing Soviet Cities*, chapter 6.

23  Theodore H. Friedgut, 'Community Structure, Political Participation, and Soviet Local Government: The Case of Kutaisi', in Henry W. Morton and Rudolf L. Tökés (eds), *Soviet Politics and Society in the 1970s* (New York: The Free Press, 1974) pp. 261–96 (p. 273); according to Friedgut, a second deputy chairman is frequently responsible for housing. This was never specified in Tiraspol.

24  'Polozhenie o postoyannykh komissiyakh raionnykh, gorodskikh, sel'skikh i poselkovykh Sovetov deputatov trudyashchikhsya Moldavskoi SSR' [Statute on Permanent Commissions] adopted 8 July 1957; Russian text in *Sbornik normativnykh aktov*, pp. 108–22.

25  Barabashev, writing in D. S. Karev (ed.) *Yuridicheskii spravochnik deputata mestnogo Soveta* (Moscow: Izdatel'stvo Moskovskogo universiteta, 1962) p. 56.

26  See for example the collection of articles edited by Ye. F. Butko, '*Tekhnologiya' raboty postoyannykh komissii* (Moscow: Izvestiya, 1970); the deputy's handbook, V. I. Vasil'ev, *Rabota deputata sel'skogo, poselkovogo Soveta v postoyannoi komissii i izbiratel'nom okruge*, in the series 'Bibliotechka dlya rabotnikov sel'skikh i poselkovykh Sovetov' (Moscow: Yuridicheskaya literatura, 1969); and a further series 'Bibliotechka dlya postoyannykh komissii mestnykh Sovetov' (Moscow: Yuridicheskaya literatura, 1970) aimed at members of specific commissions. Other handbooks also contain special advice for the members of these bodies.

27  The dates on which elections to the Tiraspol town soviet were held during the period under study were as follows (dates in brackets indicate the date on which the full list of candidates or election results was published in the local newspaper):
      24 December 1950 (27 December 1950)
      22 February 1953 (5 March and 6 March 1953)
      27 February 1955 (6 March 1955)
      3 March 1957 (15 February and 6 March 1957)
      1 March 1959 (6 March 1959)
      5 March 1961 (22 February 1961)
      3 March 1963 (17 February and 8 March 1963)
      14 March 1965 (2 March and 18 March 1965)
      12 March 1967 (1 March, 2 March and 21 March 1967)

28  See *Istoriya Moldavskoi SSR*, vol. II, p. 622.

29  This is a literal translation from the Russian word *byt*, which refers to everything concerned with the daily life of citizens, but is applied in particular to the provision of repair and other services to the population.

30  Statute on Town Soviets, Article 34.

31  Jeremy R. Azrael, 'The Legislative Process in the USSR', reprinted in Richard Cornell (ed.) *The Soviet Political System: A Book of Readings* (Englewood Cliffs: Prentice-Hall, 1970) pp. 205–17 (pp. 206 and 214).

32  The party has been governed by several sets of rules since its founding congress of 1898: see Leonard Schapiro, 'The New Rules of the CPSU' in Leonard Schapiro (ed.) *The USSR and the Future: An Analysis of the New Program of the CPSU* (New York: Praeger, 1963) pp. 179–94 (p. 179). For a Soviet account, see Yu. G. Turishchev, *Istoriya Ustava KPSS* (Moscow: Vysshaya shkola, 1971). The relevant rules for the period covered in this study were adopted at the XIX Congress (1952) and amended slightly in 1956, and a new set adopted at the XXII Congress (1961). The 1952 rules are reprinted in *KPSS v rezolyutsiyakh i resheniyakh s"ezdov, konferentsii i plenumov TsK, tom 6* [*KPSS v rez.*, vol. 6] (Moscow: Politizdat, 1971) pp. 367–83; the 1961 rules, amended slightly at the XXIII Congress (1966) have been published in various editions, and appear in English in L. G. Churchward, *Contemporary Soviet Government* (London: Routledge and Kegan Paul, 1968) pp. 315–33, and in Lane, *Politics and Society*, pp. 517–34; the original version, as adopted in 1961, appears in *KPSS v rez.*, vol. 8, pp. 306–25; both 1952 and 1961 rules (amended to 1966) appear in *Programmy i Ustavy KPSS* (Moscow: Politizdat, 1969) pp. 344–67 and 368–96. In the present study, reference is to the 1952 and 1961 rules, the 1952 version preceding that of 1961, except where stated otherwise.

33  See *Spravochnik sekretarya pervichnoi partiinoi organizatsii* (Moscow: Politizdat, 1967) pp. 219–22. The frequency of these meetings is prescribed in Rule 54/55; in large PPOs, which are subdivided into smaller units, such general meetings are held every second month.

34  See *Spravochnik sekretarya*, p. 247; this book goes on to discuss the technicalities of these party elections in considerable detail (pp. 247–52).

35 M. A. Gogichaishvili says that this attendance is obligatory: see his *Partiinoe sobranie – shkola ideinogo vospitaniya kommunistov* (Moscow: Politizdat, 1969) p. 35. However, in reply to the question whether such a representative *must* attend, a handbook on the party rules states that it is merely a valuable custom: see *Organizatsionno-ustavnye voprosy KPSS: 1972* (Moscow: Politizdat, 1972) p. 110.

36 *Organizatsionno-ustavnye voprosy*, pp. 110–11. This custom obviously gives much power to the higher bodies.

37 See G. F. Yudin, *Partiinoe khozyaistvo v partiinykh organakh i pervichnykh partiinykh organizatsiyakh* (Moscow: Mysl', 1966) p. 3 and *passim*.

38 For a discussion of this practice, see N. A. Voronovskii, *Leninskie printsipy podbora, rasstanovki i vospitaniya kadrov* (Moscow: Mysl', 1967) especially pp. 30–32; for a reference to the party's prerogative in nominating non-party persons to such positions, see *Raionnyi komitet partii* (Moscow: Politizdat, 1972) p. 99. The most thorough recent exposition of the principle is the article by Bohdan Harasymiw, '*Nomenklatura*: The Soviet Communist Party's Leadership Recruitment System', *Canadian JPolS*, vol. 2, no. 3 (1969) pp. 493–512; see also Stewart, *Political Power*, especially pp. 120–27, and Hough, *The Soviet Prefects*, pp. 29–30, 115–16, and especially 149–77 (Chapter VII).

39 Abdurakhman Avtorkhanov, *The Communist Party Apparatus* (Chicago: Henry Regnery, 1966) p. 134.

40 On the analogy of the central committee this is the standard interpretation and is perhaps the most likely working rule. However, while clear in the case of the CPSU central committee (Rule 33/37), the rules are obscure on this point as far as all lower party organs are concerned; indeed, they make no mention of a category of candidate membership, although such a category certainly does exist. This is one example (we shall encounter more) where local bodies copy the central committee on uncertain points of procedure.

41 For lists of the normal complement of departments, see Avtorkhanov, *The Communist Party Apparatus*, p. 142; G. I. Shitarev (ed.) *Partiinoe stroitel'stvo (uchebno-metodicheskoe posobie)*, 2nd edition (Moscow: Mysl', 1968) p. 124. For discussions of their work, see *Raionnyi komitet partii*, pp. 117–81, and Hough. *The Soviet Prefects*, pp. 17–19 and 22–5.

42 For reference to the duties of the central auditing commission, see Rule 39/36; for a brief discussion of the auditing commission at the district level, see *Raionnyi komitet partii*, pp. 38–40; a fuller discussion of the formation and duties of these commissions at all levels is to be found in *Zapisnaya knizhka partiinogo aktivista: 1972* (Moscow: Politizdat, 1971) pp. 158–9.

43 Shitarev (ed.) *Partiinoe stroitel'stvo*, p. 124.

44 *Ibid.*, pp. 123–4; *Raionnyi komitet partii*, p. 210.

45 See chapter 7 below; also Ronald J. Hill, 'Participation in the Central Committee Plenums in Moldavia', *Sov. Studs.*, vol. XXI, no. 2 (1969) pp. 193–207 (pp. 205–6).

46 On the work of the aktiv in Moscow, see L. V. Petrov, *Partiinyi aktiv* (Moscow: Moskovskii rabochii, 1968); for Tiraspol, see chapter 7 below.

47 Figures from Shitarev (ed.) *Partiinoe stroitel'stvo*, p. 122. By 1973, the number of gorkomy had risen to 780: see 'KPSS v tsifrakh', *Partiinaya zhizn'*, 1973, no. 14, pp. 9–26 (p. 23). Comparative figures for other years are as follows:

| 1952 | 1956 | 1961 | 1966 | 1971 | 1972 |
|------|------|------|------|------|------|
| 531 | 554 | 596 | 739 | 760 | 763 |

See *Kommunisticheskaya partiya Sovetskogo soyuza – naglyadnoe posobie*, V. I. Strukov, compiler (Moscow: Politizdat, 1973) p. 53.

48   1966 figure given by Ya. Fomenko in his article, 'Gorkom i malochislennye partorganizatsii', *Partiinaya zhizn'*, 1967, no. 1, pp. 30–34 (p. 30); the 1953 figure appears in Z. G. Romanova, *Deyatel'nost' Kommunisticheskoi partii Moldavii po razvitiyu promyshlennosti respubliki (1924–1965 gg.)* (Kishinev: Kartya Moldoven-yaske, 1970), p. 96; by December 1970, the figure had risen to 7122 (*Sovetskaya Moldaviya*, 29 December 1970, p. 2).

49   *Ocherki istorii Kommunisticheskoi partii Moldavii [Ocherki istorii KPM]*, 2nd edition (D. S. Kornovan *et al.*, eds, Kishinev: Kartya Moldovenyaske, 1968) p. 463. With a population of 62,676 in 1959, Tiraspol accounted for 2.2% of Moldavia's population of 2,884,477 (figures from *1959 Census*); the party strength of 6.7% of Tiraspol's population compares with 10% in Leningrad: see Cattell, *Leningrad*, p. 39.

50   For 1945: *Ocherki istorii Tiraspolya*, p. 121; for 1953: Romanova, *Deyatel'nost' Kommunisticheskoi partii Moldavii*, p. 96.

51   This and other changes were perhaps in response to a CPSU central committee decree of 11 December 1957, 'On a Certain Simplification in the Structure of the Staffs of Gorkoms and Urban Raikoms of the Party', which proposed a reduction in staffs of 10–15% and limited the number of secretaries to three (two for small towns): see the Russian text reprinted in *Spravochnik partiinogo rabotnika*, 2nd edition (Moscow: Politizdat, 1959) p. 546. The example of Tiraspol suggests that Avtorkhanov's list of departments, including one for work among women, was superseded (see Avtorkhanov, *The Communist Party Apparatus*, p. 142).

52   Reference is to the version adopted by the XIV Komsomol Congress, slightly amended at the XV Congress: *Ustav Vsesoyuznogo leninskogo kommunisticheskogo soyuza molodezhi* (Moscow: Molodaya gvardiya, 1968) [Komsomol Rules].

53   Throughout this study, 'gorkom' will refer to the *party* town committee; the town committees of other institutions (including the Komsomol) will be identified.

54   *Dnestrovskaya pravda*, 28 October 1960 and 25 August 1965.

55   These phrases are taken from A. M. Korolëv, *Partiya i komsomol* (Moscow: Mysl', 1967) p. 4, and Party Rule 62/61.

56   On Soviet trade unions, see in particular Emily Clarke Brown, *Soviet Trade Unions and Labor Relations* (Cambridge, Mass.: Harvard University Press, 1966); she gives the figure of 94% of the labour force unionised (p. 66).

57   1964 figure from *Spravochnaya kniga o professional'nykh soyuzakh SSSR* (Moscow: Profizdat, 1965) p. 50; 1972 figure from *Pravda*, 21 March 1972, p. 1. For figures on previous growth see Brown, *Soviet Trade Unions*, p. 48.

58   *Spravochnaya kniga o professional'nykh soyuzakh*, pp. 5–6. The political role of trade unions is expounded in Ye. A. Ivanov, *Profsoyuzy v politicheskoi sisteme sotsializma* (Moscow: Profizdat, 1974); relations with the party are discussed in Chapter IV, and with the state in Chapter V.

59   For a diagrammatic representation of this structure, see Brown, *Soviet Trade Unions*, p. 67; this is elaborated in pp. 66–71.

60   The new institution was inaugurated by a CPSU central committee plenum in December 1965, and in Moldavia by decree of the republican central committee, dated 22 December 1965: see the relevant document, 'On the Transformation of the Organs of Party–State Control'; Russian text reprinted in P. V. Voronin *et al.* (eds.) *Leninskii narodnyi kontrol' v Moldavskoi SSR: sbornik dokumentov i materialov (1924–1969 gg.)* (Kishinev: Izdatel'stvo TsK KP Moldavii, 1970) pp. 359–62. See also Grey Hodnett, 'Khrushchev and Party–State Control', in Alexander Dallin and Alan F. Westin (eds) *Politics in the Soviet Union: 7 Cases* (New York: Harcourt, Brace and World, 1966) pp. 113–64.

61   See V. I. Turovtsev (ed.) *Narodnyi kontrol' v SSSR* (Moscow: Nauka, 1967) Chapter 4, especially pp. 157, 160.

62 *Ibid*, p. 157.
63 See Jerry Hough, 'Groups and Individuals', *PoC*, vol. XVI, no. 1 (1967) pp. 28–35 (p. 35). Nevertheless, when the chairman of the Tiraspol committee was replaced in 1967, it was the party gorkom plenum that relieved the outgoing chairman of his duties (*Dnestrovskaya pravda*, 21 February 1967: see below, chapter 6).
64 Voronin *et al.*, *Leninskii narodnyi kontrol'*, p. 364.

CHAPTER 3

1 See in particular Jacobs' articles 'Soviet Local Elections' and 'The Composition of Local Soviets'.
2 See Azrael, 'The Legislative Process in the USSR', p. 207.
3 Ronald J. Hill, 'Patterns of Deputy Selection to Local Soviets', *Sov. Studs.*, vol. XXV, no. 2 (1973) pp. 196–212. Some of the material in this chapter and the next originally appeared in that article, and is reproduced by permission of the editors.
4 Here and throughout this chapter, comparative statistics for soviets in Moldavia and the USSR derived from the following sources: for 1967, *Itogi vyborov i sostav deputatov mestnykh Sovetov deputatov trudyashchikhsya 1967 g. (Statisticheskii sbornik)* (Moscow: Izvestiya, 1967); for 1965, *Sostav deputatov mestnykh Sovetov deputatov trudyashchikhsya, izbrannykh v marte 1965 g. (Statisticheskii sbornik)* (Moscow: Izvestiya, 1965); for 1963, *Itogi vyborov i sostav deputatov Verkhovnykh Sovetov soyuznykh, avtonomnykh respublik i mestnykh Sovetov deputatov trudyashchikhsya 1963 g. (Statisticheskii sbornik)* (Moscow: Izvestiya, 1963); for 1961, *Itogi vyborov i sostav deputatov mestnykh Sovetov deputatov trudyashchikhsya 1961 g. (Statisticheskii sbornik)* (Moscow: Izvestiya, 1961); for 1959, *Sostav deputatov Verkhovnykh Sovetov soyuznykh, avtonomnykh respublik i mestnykh Sovetov deputatov trudyashchikhsya 1959 g. (Statisticheskii sbornik)* (Moscow: Izvestiya, 1959); for 1957, A. I. Lepëshkin, *Sovety – vlast' naroda, 1936–1967 gg.* (Moscow: Yuridicheskaya literatura, 1967), p. 137; for 1955, *Izvestiya*, 4 March 1955.
5 Jacobs, 'The Composition of Local Soviets', p. 516.
6 Lepëshkin, *Sovety – vlast' naroda*, p. 249.
7 See Pobeda, 'Nekotorye osobennosti formirovaniya kul'tury', p. 172.
8 I have no direct evidence about party strength in Moldavia's country towns; however, the weakness of the party in rural areas is discussed by, among others, Rigby in *Communist Party Membership*, pp. 486–92, and Vernon V. Aspaturian in 'The Soviet Union', in Roy C. Macridis and Robert E. Ward (eds), *Modern Political Systems: Europe*, 2nd edition (Englewood Cliffs: Prentice-Hall, 1968) pp. 451–596, especially pp. 552–4.
9 See Jacobs, 'The Composition of Local Soviets', pp. 508–9.
10 For this distinction, see Scott, *Russian Political Institutions*, p. 97.
11 See Hill, 'Patterns', pp. 206–7.
12 For the Moldavian central committee, see Ronald J. Hill, 'The Composition and Functioning of the Central Committee of the Communist Party of Moldavia, December 1963 – March 1966', M.A. dissertation, unpublished, University of Essex, 1967, pp. 21–4; for the CPSU central committee, Levytsky, *The Soviet Political Elite*, p. 23, and Michael P. Gehlen and Michael McBride, 'The Soviet Central Committee: An Elite Analysis', *APSR*, vol. LXII, no. 4 (1968) pp. 1232–41 (p. 1233).
13 See Lane, *Politics and Society*, p. 401.

14 See Rigby, *Communist Party Membership*, pp. 359–63; also Fainsod, *How Russia is Ruled*, Chapter 8.

15 See, for example, Lepëshkin, *Sovety – vlast' naroda*, p. 245; M. Saifulin (ed.) *The Soviet Parliament* (Moscow: Progress Publishers, 1967) p. 37.

16 On this point see A. H. Brown, *Soviet Politics and Political Science* (London: Macmillan, 1974) pp. 115–16, note 137.

17 Lepëshkin, *Sovety – vlast' naroda*, p. 247.

18 See Jacobs, 'The Composition of Local Soviets', p. 510.

19 See, for example, Fainsod, *How Russia is Ruled*, pp. 301–6. An interesting account of attitudes among politically conscious students in Moscow in the mid-sixties appears in William Taubman, *The View From Lenin Hills: Soviet Youth in Ferment* (London: Hamish Hamilton, 1968) especially Chapters 15 and 16.

20 See 'The 1961 Party Programme' in Schapiro (ed.) *The USSR and the Future*, pp. 255–312 (p. 299); a Russian text of the programme is reprinted in *Programmy i Ustavy KPSS*, pp. 63–224.

21 See, for example, Borys Lewytzkyj, 'Generations in Conflict', *PoC*, vol. xvi, no. 1 (1967) pp. 36–40; Jerry Hough, 'In Whose Hands the Future?', *PoC*, vol. xvi, no. 2 (1967) pp. 18–25; Tatu also stresses the ageing of the central committee (*Power in the Kremlin*, pp. 538–9); see also Levytsky, *The Soviet Political Elite*, pp. 25–8.

22 See Tatu, *Power in the Kremlin*, pp. 181–4; Schapiro, 'The New Rules of the CPSU', pp. 191–2.

23 Turishchev, *Istoriya Ustava KPSS*, pp. 215–16.

24 S. S. Kravchuk (ed.) *Gosudarstvennoe pravo SSSR* (Moscow: Yuridicheskaya literatura, 1967) p. 499.

25 See A. Nikitin, 'Grani torgovogo servisa', *Sovetskaya Moldaviya*, 3 September 1971, p. 4.

26 See Lepëshkin, *Sovety – vlast' naroda*, pp. 278–9.

27 Witness the following decisions taken within a short space of time:

   1. A Law (15 July 1964) to raise the wages of workers in education, health, housing provision, trade and public catering;
   2. A Decree (13 March 1965) on improving trade and public catering in the country;
   3. A Decree (15 May 1965) on improving the work of repair and service establishments in the country.

   Texts reprinted in *Spravochnik partiinogo rabotnika*, 6th edition (1966) pp. 261, 303–14, 321–8. See also the central committee declaration 'On the Work of the Local Soviets in Poltava Oblast' (16 November 1965) reprinted in *ibid.*, pp. 392–6; see especially p. 393.

28 See Pierre Sorlin, *The Soviet People and Their Society: From 1917 to the Present* (London: Praeger, 1969) p. 226; Lane, *Politics and Society*, p. 355; for figures on female saturation of the teaching profession in 1968, see 'Zhenshchiny v SSSR', *Vestnik statistiki*, 1968, no. 1, pp. 82–96 (p. 90). For an estimate of the general desirability etc. of the teaching profession compared with other occupations in the USSR, see Alex Inkeles and Peter H. Rossi, 'Multidimensional Ratings of Occupations', reprinted in Alex Inkeles, *Social Change in Soviet Russia* (Cambridge, Mass.: Harvard University Press, 1968) pp. 192–210.

29 On the low status of medical workers, see Sorlin, *The Soviet People and Their Society*, p. 233. However, see the study by Inkeles and Rossi (previous note) which suggests a high general desirability for the occupation of doctors; compare Lane (*Politics and Society*, p. 417): 'control over life itself, exercised by doctors, gives honour', and hence raises their *social* prestige; the same may not apply to

nurses and medical technicians (radiographers, anaesthetists etc.); nor can it necessarily be extended to political prestige. According to official statistics, in 1967, 73% of Soviet medical workers were women (see 'Zhenshchiny v sssr', p. 89).

30  See Churchward, 'Soviet Local Government Today', p. 451.

31  Stewart, *Political Power*, p. 40.

32  Hill, 'The Composition and Functioning...', p. 32.

33  Hough, 'Groups and Individuals', p. 28.

34  Stewart, *Political Power*, p. 41, Table 3, quoting *Partiinaya zhizn'*, 1962, no. 1, p. 53.

35  *Ibid.*, p. 42, Table 4.

36  Computed from Gehlen and McBride, 'The Soviet Central Committee', p. 1234, Table 5, by adding the post-1953 figures for the following groups: party *apparatchiki*, other bureaucrats, military officers, trade union officers.

37  Jacobs, 'The Composition of Local Soviets', p. 517.

38  See Stewart, *Political Power*, pp. 38–40, for a discussion of the nature of representation in the context of Soviet party committees. For further discussion of the effects of this representation, see pp. 47–9 of the same work.

39  See Schapiro, *The USSR and the Future*, p. 297; *Programmy i Ustavy*, p. 178.

40  For detailed analysis of this episode, see Roger Pethybridge, *A Key to Soviet Politics: The Crisis of the 'Anti-Party' Group* (London: Allen and Unwin, 1962); also Carl A. Linden, *Khrushchev and the Soviet Leadership, 1957–1964* (Baltimore, Maryland: Johns Hopkins Press, 1966) especially Chapter 3.

41  *1961 Rules*, Rule 25. For a discussion of the significance of these regulations see Schapiro, 'The New Rules of the cpsu', pp. 191–2. The requirement was repealed at the xxiii Congress (1966) and replaced by a further sentence added to Rule 24, calling for the preservation of the principle of systematic renewal in their composition and succession in their leadership: see *Spravochnik partiinogo rabotnika*, 6th edition, p. 26.

42  See *Ocherki istorii KPM*, 1st edition (Ye. S. Postovoi *et al.*, eds, Kishinev: Partiinoe izdatel'stvo TsK KP Moldavii, 1964) pp. 337–8; 2nd edition, pp. 358–9. For Romanova, this declaration played 'an exceptionally important role in the ideological growth of the network of (industrial) works and construction site ppos': see *Deyatel'nost' Kommunisticheskoi partii Moldavii*, p. 93.

43  Tatu discusses ways in which the crisis dominated Soviet politics for a number of years: see *Power in the Kremlin*, Part ii.

44  For a full account of this crisis and the pre-Congress purge, see Tatu, *Power in the Kremlin*, Part ii, especially pp. 127–40; the political clash at the Congress is also discussed in Linden, *Khrushchev and the Soviet Leadership*, Chapter 7.

## CHAPTER 4

1  *Dnestrovskaya pravda*, 4 January 1951..

2  For the case of the ussr supreme soviet, see Hill, 'Continuity and Change...'; in the cpsu central committee, 'occupational role associations' are an important determinant in recruitment, according to Gehlen and McBride: see 'The Soviet Central Committee', p. 1240; my study of the Moldavian central committee showed a definite connection between tenancy of specific offices and committee membership: see 'The Composition and Functioning...', Part iv; see also, for the Kazakhstan central committee, J. W. Cleary, 'Elite Career Patterns in a Soviet Republic', *BJPolS*, vol. 4, no. 3 (1974) pp. 323–44.

3  Cattell, *Leningrad*, p. 38.

4 See Hill, 'Participation in the Central Committee Plenums', especially pp. 204, 207.

5 Gehlen and McBride, 'The Soviet Central Committee', p. 1236.

6 V. P. Kazimirchuk and N. K. Adamyan, 'Sotsiologicheskie aspekty sostava deputatov mestnykh Sovetov (na materialakh Armyanskoi SSR)' in *Organizatsiya i deyatel'nost' Sovetov i organov gosudarstvennogo upravleniya Armyanskoi SSR* (Yerevan: Izdatel'stvo AN Arm SSR, 1970) pp. 109–23.

7 R. A. Safarov, *Raionnye Sovety deputatov trudyashchikhsya v gorodakh* (Moscow: Gosyurizdat, 1961) pp. 19–20, quoted in Frolic, 'The Soviet Study of Soviet Cities', p. 688, note 29.

8 Frolic, *ibid.*, p. 688.

9 Hill, 'Continuity and Change' especially pp. 57–62.

10 Stewart, *Political Power*, Chapter 6.

11 Gehlen and McBride, 'The Soviet Central Committee', pp. 1235–6.

12 Hill, 'The Composition and Functioning...', especially p. 97.

13 See Stewart, *Political Power*, Chapter 4, especially p. 48.

14 For the full Russian text of this resolution, 'On Improving the Activity of the Soviets and Strengthening their links with the Masses', see *KPSS v rez.*, vol. 7, pp. 237–48; this point is made on p. 247.

15 See V. A. Perttsik, 'Puti sovershenstvovaniya deyatel'nosti deputatov mestnykh Sovetov', *Sovetskoe gosudarstvo i pravo*, 1967, no. 7, pp. 16–21; Kazimirchuk and Adamyan, 'Sotsiologicheskie aspekty sostava deputatov'.

16 *Raionnyi komitet partii*, pp. 29–30. This instruction was slightly amended in 1973, to change the frequency of elections in accordance with changes in the party rules introduced in 1971; also to abolish the practice of electing non-voting delegates to conferences and congresses (hence, reference to non-voting delegates here is now no longer relevant). The reasons for these amendments are given in *Partiinaya zhizn'*, 1974, no. 2, pp. 49–50.

17 *Raionnyi komitet partii*, p. 29.

18 See 'Otchëty i vybory v pervichnykh partorganizatsiyakh', *Partiinaya zhizn'*, 1973, no. 18, pp. 5–10, especially p. 9.

19 See Hill, 'Patterns of Deputy Selection', especially pp. 209–11.

20 Kazimirchuk and Adamyan, 'Sotsiologicheskie aspekty sostava deputatov', p. 120.

21 For example, Peter Nettl reports that even Soviet party leaders 'have often bemoaned the inevitable lack of interest in the affairs of local and regional soviets'; the lack of interest is 'inevitable', in Nettl's view, because 'The real locus of authority legitimation is within the party': see J. P. Nettl, *Political Mobilization: A Sociological Analysis of Methods and Concepts* (London: Faber, 1967) p. 146. Compare David Apter's comment on the effect of what he calls the mobilisation system in creating political cynicism, 'which may threaten the consummatory legitimacy of the state': see David E. Apter, *The Politics of Modernization*, Phoenix edition (Chicago and London: University of Chicago Press, 1967) p. 306. Many of the characteristics that these writers and others associate with mobilisation can be identified in Soviet society: see chapter 9 below.

CHAPTER 5

1 It should be noted that although I refer to this activity as 'public', in the case of the gorkom it is technically the party's private business, and becomes public in that it deals with questions of great social importance, and in so far as publicity is given to the proceedings. Furthermore, even in the case of soviet

sessions, the public has no right of admission, and is allowed to know only what the press reports.

2   The death of Stalin, for example, in March 1953, almost coincided with local elections, and few details were given of the identity of deputies, or on what transpired at the first session of the new soviet, where the gorispolkom members and various officials were elected and appointed. Occasionally complete meetings failed to be recorded in the press: *Dnestrovskaya pravda* contained no account of a gorkom plenum between the seventh (18 February 1967) and ninth (16 June 1967).

3   V. I. Vasil'ev (ed.) *V pomoshch' deputatu mestnogo Soveta (prakticheskoe posobie)* (Moscow: Yuridicheskaya literatura, 1968) p. 72; Karev (ed.) *Yuridicheskii spravochnik*, p. 49.

4   The change is referred to by Lepëshkin (*Sovety – vlast' naroda*, p. 165); it was incorporated into the new statutes on lower soviets adopted in Moldavia in November 1957; the change was written of approvingly in 1965 by Yu. A. Tikhomirov, in D. A. Gaidukov and N. G. Starovoitov (eds) *Mestnye Sovety na sovremennom etape* (Moscow: Nauka, 1965) p. 146.

5   See Surilov, *Istoriya gosudarstva i prava Moldavskoi SSR*, p. 49.

6   Writing in Karev (ed.) *Yuridicheskii spravochnik*, p. 49.

7   Ye. I. Kozlova, *Mestnye organy gosudarstvennoi vlasti v SSSR* (Moscow: Mysl', 1967) p. 37; see also Vasil'ev (ed.) *V pomoshch' deputatu*, p. 72.

8   See Kunaev, 'Kollektivnost' – vysshyi printsip partiinogo rukovodstva', *Partiinaya zhizn'*, 1966, no. 19, reprinted in M. I. Khaldeev, K. I. Zarodov and Ye. I. Bugaev (eds) *Voprosy partiinoi zhizni: v pomoshch' izuchayushchim partiinoe stroitel'stvo* (Moscow: Pravda, 1967) pp. 141–55 (pp. 144–5, emphasis added); see also *Raionnyi komitet partii*, p. 31. On the frequency of cpsu central committee meetings, see Churchward, *Contemporary Soviet Government*, p. 214; for Stalingrad obkom, see Stewart, *Political Power*, p. 55; for the Moldavian central committee, see Hill, 'Participation in the Central Committee Plenums', p. 194.

9   See *Sovetskaya Moldaviya*, 15 July 1971, p. 4.

10  See *Partiinaya zhizn'*, 1973, no. 6, p. 37.

11  For fuller discussion of planning and budget formulation in Soviet cities see Frolic, 'Decision-Making in Soviet Cities', pp. 39–44; Taubman, *Governing Soviet Cities*, pp. 118–19; for a Soviet account, N. I. Khimicheva, *Byudzhetnye prava raionnogo, gorodskogo Soveta* (Moscow: Yuridicheskaya literatura, 1973).

12  See, for example, V. Afanas'ev, 'Krug voprosov na sessii', reprinted in V. I. Vasil'ev et al. (eds) *Voprosy raboty Sovetov deputatov trudyashchikhsya* (Moscow: Izvestiya, 1968) pp. 455–69.

13  Stewart, *Political Power*, pp. 58–9. Moses, however, presents data on obkom plenums that suggest that 'the regional parties demonstrate fairly wide-ranging and autonomous "effective competence" from central dictate in the timing and in the selection of topics for their plenums': see *Regional Party Leadership*, pp. 22–6.

14  Romanova, *Deyatel'nost' Kommunisticheskoi partii Moldavii*, p. 96.

15  See A. A. Bezuglov, *Sovetskii deputat: gosudarstvennopravovoi status* (Moscow: Yuridicheskaya literatura, 1971) pp. 57–9; see also Safarov, who writes of 'duty orators' who speak repeatedly, in Vasil'ev (ed.) *V pomoshch' deputatu*, p. 79; Tikhomirov also writes of the ispolkom chairman and his deputy as 'monopoly rapporteurs' in Gaidukov and Starovoitov (eds) *Mestnye Sovety*, p. 149.

16  See Gaidukov and Starovoitov (eds) *Mestnye Sovety*, p. 151.

17  See V. K. Vasenin, *Deputat mestnogo Soveta* (Moscow: Yuridicheskaya literatura, 1967) p. 15.

18  I. V. Pavlov and V. P. Kazimirchuk (eds) *Upravlenie, sotsiologiya, pravo* (Moscow: Yuridicheskaya literatura, 1971) p. 198, Table 17.

19  Vasenin, *Deputat mestnogo Soveta*, p. 15.
20  See Hill, 'Participation in the Central Committee Plenums', p. 201.
21  Stewart, *Political Power*, Chapter 5, especially p. 83.
22  Vasenin, *Deputat mestnogo Soveta*, p. 15.
23  Bezuglov, *Sovetskii deputat*, p. 58.
24  See in particular I. Kalits, A. Laumets and Kh. Shneider, 'Izuchenie deyatel'nosti Sovetov s pomoshch'yu konkretno-sotsiologicheskogo metoda', *Sovetskoe gosudarstvo i pravo*, 1965, no. 9, pp. 65–70; Perttsik, 'Puti sovershenstvovaniya deyatel'nosti deputatov', especially p. 19; Kazimirchuk and Adamyan, 'Sotsiologicheskie aspekty sostava deputatov', especially pp. 121–2; also Pavlov and Kazimirchuk (eds) *Upravlenie, sotsiologiya, pravo*, pp. 176–206, especially p. 185, Table 15.
25  Kunaev, 'Kollektivnost' – vysshyi printsip', pp. 143–4; also, for a discussion of this practice and its effects on the Moldavian central committee, Hill, 'Participation in the Central Committee Plenums'.
26  Pavlov and Kazimirchuk, *Upravlenie, sotsiologiya, pravo*, pp. 195–7.
27  A. Kryachek, 'Na sessiyakh peremeny', *Sovety deputatov trudyashchikhsya*, 1969, no. 5, pp. 67–9 (p. 68).
28  Hill, 'Participation in the Central Committee Plenums', p. 201; Stewart, *Political Power*, pp. 83–5.
29  See Stewart, *Political Power*, p. 83.
30  See Vasil'ev (ed.) *V pomoshch' deputatu*, p. 78; Gaidukov and Starovoitov (eds) *Mestnye Sovety*, p. 150, note 2.
31  See B. N. Gabrichidze, *Gorodskie Sovety deputatov trudyashchikhsya* (Moscow: Yuridicheskaya literatura, 1968) p. 163; Kozlova, *Mestnye organy*, pp. 39–40, calls it 'a very interesting initiative'; also Safarov, in Vasil'ev (ed.) *V pomoshch' deputatu*, p. 82; and *Izvestiya*, 19 February 1966.
32  See A. Moskalev and V. Rostovtsev, 'Komissiya na sessii', reprinted in Butko (ed.) '*Tekhnologiya' raboty postoyannykh komissii*, pp. 61–70 (p. 65).
33  For an interesting discussion of these criticisms, see Vasenin, *Deputat mestnogo Soveta*, pp. 13–18; also Tikhomirov, in Gaidukov and Starovoitov (eds) *Mestnye Sovety*, p. 151.
34  R. M. Punnett, *British Government and Politics*, 2nd edition (London: Heinemann, 1971) p. 387.

CHAPTER 6

1  See Fainsod, *Smolensk*, p. 93; on a similar point, see Leonard Schapiro, 'The Party and the State', *Survey*, no. 38, pp. 111–16. This view, perhaps naturally, is not shared by Soviet writers: writing for a western readership, N. Veselov states that 'The political organization of socialist society in the USSR is ... distinguished by the clarity and unambiguousness of relations between the Communist Party, on the one hand, and the state together with the mass organizations of working people, on the other.' He explains that 'These relations are based on the recognition of the CPSU as the leading force of society, the political leader of the people and all its organizations': see N. Veselov, *The Communist Party and Mass Organizations in the USSR* (Moscow: Novosti Press Agency, 1973) pp. 5–6.
2  See Brown, *Soviet Politics and Political Science*, pp. 52–70, and especially pp. 52–6, for a discussion of various approaches to studying Soviet political institutions; his reference to the Webbs' book is on pp. 54–5.
3  A. I. Luk'yanov and B. M. Lazarev, *Sovetskoe gosudarstvo i obshchestvennye organizatsii*, 2nd edition (Moscow: Gosyurizdat, 1961) p. 212.

4    Swearer, 'The Functions', p. 137; Lane, *Politics and Society*, p. 222. We also have
     the testimony of at least one Soviet writer that the key coordinating role in
     selection to the soviets lies with the district party committee (raikom); in the case
     of Tiraspol, whose authorities are directly subordinated to the republican govern-
     ment, and which has no subordinate district structure, this role would devolve on
     the gorkom, and specifically its organisation and instruction department. The
     Soviet writer in question is Yu. Shabanov, whose work is discussed in my article
     'The cpsu in a Soviet Election Campaign', *Sov. Studs.*, vol. xxviii, no. 4 (1976)
     pp. 590–8.

5    For an account of their work, see the article 'Partiinye gruppy v mestnykh
     Sovetakh', *Partiinaya zhizn'*, 1973, no. 8, pp. 48–52.

6    For a discussion, with diagrams, of the structure and role of party organisations
     within state administrations, see Frolic, 'Municipal Administrations', pp. 387–93,
     and 'Decision-Making in Soviet Cities', especially pp. 43 and 45; for a Soviet
     account, see 'Partorganizatsiya apparata ispolkoma Soveta', *Partiinaya zhizn'*,
     1973, no. 12, pp. 50–4.

7    Punnett, *British Government and Politics*, p. 387; also the British Labour Party's
     booklet, *Guide for the New Councillor and Candidate* (London: The Labour Party,
     1973) especially pp. 16–17.

8    See Hough, *The Soviet Prefects*, p. 115; Frolic, 'Decision-Making in Soviet Cities',
     pp. 48–50; and especially Harasymiw, '*Nomenklatura*'.

9    John A. Armstrong, *Ideology, Politics and Government in the Soviet Union: An Intro-
     duction*, 3rd edition (London: Nelson, 1973) p. 157; the same phrase appeared on
     p. 102 of the 1st edition (New York: Praeger, 1962).

10   See Thomas Remeikis, 'The Administration of Power: The Communist Party and
     the Soviet Government', in V. Stanley Vardys (ed.) *Lithuania Under the Soviets:
     Portrait of a Nation, 1940–65* (New York: Praeger, 1965) pp. 111–40 (p. 111).

11   See Churchward, *Contemporary Soviet Government*, Chapter 15, especially pp. 223–4.
     Taubman, using a very different approach from my own, also argues that the
     political position of the party is not simply one of dominance over all other
     institutions and interests: see *Governing Soviet Cities*, especially Chapter 11.

12   See 'Report of the Central Committee of the cpsu to the xxiii Congress', reprinted
     in *XXIII s"ezd Kommunisticheskoi partii Sovetskogo Soyuza: Stenograficheskii otchët*
     (Moscow: Politizdat, 1966) vol. I, pp. 18–109 (p. 92).

13   See S. Sabaneev and G. Konovalov, 'Ruka ob ruku', *Izvestiya*, 16 May 1967,
     reprinted in Vasil'ev *et al.* (eds) *Voprosy raboty Sovetov*, pp. 527–34 (p. 530).

14   Vasenin, *Deputat mestnogo Soveta*, p. 4.

15   G. Guza, in *Sovetskaya Moldaviya*, 5 December 1972, p. 2.

16   G. Tsarik, 'Kommunist-deputat', *Partiinaya zhizn'*, 1970, no. 10, pp. 50–53
     (p. 50). It is not clear from the writer's account whether he was unaware that he
     had been considered for recommendation as a candidate, or merely surprised and
     delighted at being chosen against the competition of others.

17   In practice this sanction might not be difficult for the authorities to obtain, but
     the whole principle raises interesting legal questions, in part related to the prin-
     ciples of subordination and democratic centralism: see Bezuglov, *Sovetskii deputat*,
     pp. 174–80. The English translation of this work – *Soviet Deputy (Legal Status)*
     (Moscow: Progress Publishers, 1973) – omits this discussion, and notes simply that
     'Jurists are now making comprehensive research into the problem of invio-
     lability of the deputy since it touches the legal regulations concerning state,
     criminal, labour and collective farm laws' (p. 131).

18   See 'Zakon o statuse deputatov Sovetov deputatov trudyashchikhsya v sssr'
     [Statute on Deputy's Status], Article 31 (*Pravda*, 22 September 1972).

19   See G. Ustinov (ed.) *We're the Soviets* (Moscow: Novosti Press Agency, 1973)

illustrations. This enhanced social life is perhaps a mixed blessing, since it can disrupt personal life and interfere with work as a deputy. Perttsik reports that about 40% of deputies interviewed in his survey had two or more extra 'public assignments': see 'Puti sovershenstvovaniya deyatel'nosti deputatov', p. 19.

20 Statute on Deputy's Status, Article 35; formerly the wearing of these badges was restricted to supreme soviet deputies, who also enjoyed the use of luxury waiting rooms at airports and railway stations, and free travel within the USSR.

21 V. Sadchikov, 'Povyshaem rol' chlenov gorkoma partii', *Partiinaya zhizn'*, 1970, no. 10, pp. 25–9; see also V. Zhitkov, 'Gorkom informiruet o svoei rabote', *Partiinaya zhizn'*, 1970, no. 3, pp. 38–40.

22 Yu. Derevskoi, writing about I. Konoptsev, in 'Chlen vybornogo partiinogo organa', *Partiinaya zhizn'*, 1971, no. 2, pp. 35–7 (p. 35).

23 The distinction between real and potential influence is the important point in Fleron's discussion of the concept of 'elite': see his 'Note on the Explication of the Concept "Elite"'. For a discussion of influence in the obkom, see Stewart, *Political Power*, Chapter 9, especially pp. 199–213.

24 Given that gorkom membership lists are not available for analysis in three instances, the total number of persons passing through various grades of elite membership in this period was probably about 1400.

25 For fuller details, see my PhD thesis, 'Tiraspol: A Study of a Soviet Town's Political Elite', unpublished, University of Essex, 1973, p. 211, Table 6.1.

26 Schapiro, 'The Party and the State', p. 112.

27 Jerry F. Hough, 'Reforms in Government and Administration', in Alexander Dallin and Thomas B. Larson (eds) *Soviet Politics Since Khrushchev* (Englewood Cliffs: Prentice-Hall, 1968) pp. 23–40 (p. 24); George A. Brinkley, 'Khrushchev Remembered: On the Theory of Soviet Statehood', *Sov. Studs.*, vol. XXIV, no. 3 (1973) pp. 387–401 (p. 398); Churchward, 'Soviet Local Government Today', pp. 433–8.

28 This ignores 104 individuals in Group B whose sex has not been identified: even if all were males, women would still account for 41.1% of the non-overlapping grades.

29 See Vasil'ev (ed.) *V pomoshch' deputatu*, p. 79.

30 The vigilantes, or *druzhinniki*, are volunteers, organised under the auspices of local soviets, who patrol the streets in the evenings, in groups distinguished by their red arm-bands, to prevent hooliganism and maintain public order. For a description of how they are formed and operate, see 'Narodnye druzhiny: kak oni sozdayutsya i deistvuyut', *Sovety deputatov trudyashchikhsya*, 1971, no. 7, pp. 95–9.

31 For a full discussion of the composition and role of the party committee executive at oblast level, see Stewart, *Political Power*, Chapter 6.

32 See V. Kask, 'Sodeistvie khozyaistvennika', *Sovety deputatov trudyashchikhsya*, 1970, no. 1, pp. 55–8 (pp. 56–7).

## CHAPTER 7

1 Korolëv, *Partiya i komsomol*, p. 4.

2 See 'Declaration of the XXIV CPSU Congress on Partial Changes in the CPSU Rules', adopted 9 April 1971; Russian text reprinted in *Spravochnik partiinogo rabotnika*, 11th edition (1971) pp. 30–1.

3 Stewart, *Political Power*, p. 33.

4 Peter Frank reports that in the late 1960s a total of 68% of obkom first secretaries were members of the CPSU central bodies – the central committee and the central auditing commission: see Frank, 'The CPSU Obkom First Secretary',

pp. 188–90. For RSFSR oblasti alone the proportion was even higher.

5  Stewart, *Political Power*, p. 32.

6  See Hill, 'Participation in the Central Committee Plenums', pp. 205–6. One reason given for the development of the aktiv in recent years is the need to provide an outlet for the talents and expertise of the high-calibre new party recruits: see Petrov, *Partiinyi aktiv*, pp. 6–7.

7  Meeting of 26 May 1964, reported in *Leninskoe znamya*, 28 and 30 May 1964.

8  DOSAAF: the initials in Russian for the 'All-Union Voluntary Society for Assistance to the Army, Air Force and Navy of the USSR', a 'para-military civilian defense agency which serves the various branches of the armed services' (Fainsod, *How Russia is Ruled*, p. 299). It involves mainly young people in militarily oriented sports and hobbies such as rifle-shooting, orienteering, amateur radio etc. In this study DOSAAF employees were classified as security personnel.

9  Petrov, making this point, gives detailed examples of programmes for training and instruction for party aktiv members, running through the year: see *Partiinyi aktiv*, pp. 9–30 and 38–48. Moses speculates from data for obkomy in 1970 that 'the only real difference between plenums and meetings of the Party aktiv on the same theme is the formal ability of plenums to act on personnel assignments' (*Regional Party Leadership*, p. 28). My data would support this interpretation, and identify it at a lower level and several years previously.

10  *Dnestrovskaya pravda*, 6 September 1950; *Znamya pobedy*, 7 September 1950.

11  The Russian text of this resolution 'On immediate measures for the further development of agriculture in the USSR', dated 26 March 1965, appears in *Spravochnik partiinogo rabotnika*, 6th edition, pp. 104–7. That volume contains the texts of several other measures introduced at that time with a view to improving various branches of agriculture.

12  This phrase is used by Cattell in the context of Leningrad, to refer to 'top leaders of the Party and government in the city and province' who 'jointly control politics': see *Leningrad*, p. 41.

13  For this chapter and the next, evidence of membership of the Moldavian central committee and supreme soviet was taken from lists published in *Sovetskaya Moldaviya* as follows:

Central committees:   III (1951):  3 April 1951
                       IV (1952):  23 September 1952
                        V (1954):  19 February 1954
                       VI (1956):  21 January 1956
                      VII (1958):  30 January 1958
                       IX (1960):  30 January 1960
                        X (1961):  30 September 1961
                       XI (1963):  27 December 1963
                      XII (1966):  2 March 1966
                     XIII (1971):  27 February 1971
Supreme soviets:  1951: 21 January 1951
                  1955: 3 March 1955
                  1959: 7 March 1959
                  1963: 7 March 1963
                  1967: 16 March 1967
                  1971: 17 June 1971
The extraordinary VIII Congress (1959) elected no fresh central committee.

14  See Perttsik, 'Puti sovershenstvovaniya deyatel'nosti deputatov', pp. 19–20.

15  Hill, 'The Composition and Functioning', *passim*.

16  Hough, 'Groups and Individuals', p. 28.

CHAPTER 8

1   Petrov, *Partiinyi aktiv*, p. 8.
2   *Dnestrovskaya pravda*, 23 July 1950; *Sovetskaya Moldaviya*, 6 November 1965.
3   *Sovetskaya Moldaviya*, 7 March 1963.
4   *Dnestrovskaya pravda*, 1 May 1967.
5   *Ibid.*, 25 March 1960.
6   *Ibid.*, 4 August and 5 November 1965, 18 January 1966.
7   The *okrug* was an intermediate administrative unit between the republic and the
    raion. Four such units were established in Moldavia by a decree of the republican
    supreme soviet presidium dated 31 January 1952, including one centred on
    Tiraspol: see Surilov, *Istoriya gosudarstva i prava*, pp. 261–2. An okrug soviet was
    elected on 22 February 1953, consisting of 85 deputies, including 19 who con-
    currently or subsequently had connections with the town elite (the full list of
    okrug soviet deputies appeared in *Stalinskii put'*, 27 January 1953). This election
    was preceded by the election of a party committee (list of members published in
    *Stalinskii put'*, 5 September 1952), comprising 61 full and 15 candidate members,
    plus an 11-man auditing commission: 34 of these 87 individuals became members
    of the town elite. However, these institutions did not survive long after the death
    of Stalin: the okrugi were abolished some time during 1953, and by February–
    March 1954 a cpsu central committee plenum criticised the Moldavian party
    organisation for failure to send the redundant leading workers in the okrug
    administrations to help strengthen party and soviet organs in the raiony: see
    *Ocherki istorii KPM*, 1st edition, p. 369.
8   *Dnestrovskaya pravda*, 23 September 1960.
9   Scott, *Russian Political Institutions*, p. 140.
10  Stewart, *Political Power*, p. 133. For Hough, these secretaries and their party organs
    enjoy not only *influence*, but 'very clear-cut formal and legal authority' in bearing
    complete responsibility for running their territory: see his 'Soviet Urban Politics',
    p. 320, and his major study of their 'prefectural' role, *The Soviet Prefects*.
11  *Dnestrovskaya pravda*, 23 July 1950; no date was given for the plenum.
12  Philip D. Stewart, Robert L. Arnett, William T. Ebert, Raymond E. McPhail,
    Terence L. Rich and Craig E. Schopmeyer, 'Political Mobility and the Soviet
    Political Process: A Partial Test of Two Models', *APSR*, vol. LXVI, no. 4 (1972)
    pp. 1269–90 (p. 1280).
13  He was identified in his central committee position in *Sovetskaya Moldaviya*, 24
    January 1964; also in *Leninskoe znamya*, 25 January 1964, in an account of a
    Tiraspol gorkom plenum for which he came back to read a report; his minis-
    terial appointment was announced in *Sovetskaya Moldaviya*, 19 October 1965; his
    relief from the party post in *Sovetskaya Moldaviya*, 22 December 1965.
14  A similar case identified by Friedgut is the director of the Kutaisi (Georgia) truck
    factory, who was 'involved in every body of any importance locally, and many
    nationally': see 'Community Structure, Political Participation, and Soviet Local
    Government', pp. 270–1.
15  See Jerry Hough, 'In Whose Hands the Future?', *PoC*, vol. XVI, no. 2 (1967)
    pp. 18–25, especially p. 23. Compare Schapiro in 1961: '... Khrushchev has tried
    to diminish rivalry between two administrations [party and state] by insisting on
    technical training for the party officials' ('The Party and the State', p. 112).
16  Hough, 'Reforms in Government and Administration', p. 36.
17  Article 44 of the Statute on Town Soviets clearly states that the executive com-
    mittee is elected 'from among the deputies of the soviet'. The statute contained

no provision for the election of non-deputies, and the press carried no report of a by-election at which Yulin had been elected. His appointment as deputy chairman was in replacement of V. I. Slogotskii, relieved of that position in June 1964 'in connection with his transfer to other work' (*Leninskoe znamya*, 30 June 1964).

18  Tiraspol appears to differ in this respect from Kutaisi (Georgia), where a 'locally known and experienced replacement' was usually available to take over from leaders promoted to republic level: see Friedgut, 'Community Structure, Political Participation, and Soviet Local Government', p. 271.

19  Armstrong, *The Soviet Bureaucratic Elite*, pp. 144–5.

20  Laird, *The Soviet Paradigm*, p. 95.

21  *Ibid.*, p. 122.

22  Stewart *et al.*, 'Political Mobility and the Soviet Political Process', p. 1279. For an illuminating study of recruitment and training of top party executives, see George Fischer, *The Soviet System and Modern Society* (New York: Atherton Press, 1968).

23  Fleron, 'Career Types in the Soviet Political Leadership', pp. 123–4; for his usage of the term 'political elite' see above, chapter 1.

24  Michael P. Gehlen, 'The Soviet Apparatchiki', in Farrell (ed.) *Political Leadership in Eastern Europe and the Soviet Union*, pp. 140–56 (p. 155); Gehlen adds (p. 156) that this trend became established in the period 1952–66.

25  Frolic, 'Decision-Making in Soviet Cities', p. 51; he adds that this tendency is more pronounced in large cities. Elsewhere, however, Frolic has written that 'Generally, crossover between party and nonparty posts was common in most Soviet cities', with the exception of Moscow: see 'Soviet Urban Political Leaders', p. 444.

26  In his thesis, 'The Selection of Leading Personnel'.

## CHAPTER 9

1  Seweryn Bialer, 'Soviet Political Elite: Concept, Sample, Case Study', PhD thesis, unpublished, Columbia University, 1966, p. 42, quoted in Cornell (ed.) *The Soviet Political System*, Introduction, p. 3, note 3.

2  Frolic, 'Soviet Urban Political Leaders', p. 450; Cleary also argues for identifying an elite within a party committee ('Elite Career Patterns in a Soviet Republic', pp. 323–6), and quotes Bialer ('How Russians Rule Russia', *PoC*, vol. XIII, no. 5 (1964) pp. 45–52 [p. 46]) in support of his view. An example similar to Antosyak, this time at the USSR supreme soviet level, adds further doubt about the validity of identifying Soviet elites in terms of party committee membership: I. G. Petrovskii, professor and rector of Moscow University since 1951, was not a party member in 1966, and hence was ineligible for membership of any party organs. Yet it is scarcely conceivable that a person in such an important administrative position should be identified as not part of the 'elite' with influence in at least educational policy-making. If the concept is extended to cover the state organs, however, Petrovskii can (like Antosyak) be accommodated: he was elected to the supreme soviet in 1962, 1966 and 1970, and to its presidium in 1966 and 1970: see *Deputaty Verkhovnogo Soveta SSSR: sed'moi sozyv* (Moscow: Izvestiya, 1966), p. 349, and *Pravda*, 17 June 1970.

3  This raises again the whole significance of the concept of elite. Lester G. Seligman has suggested that 'the dichotomy of elites and nonelites perhaps does us no service, because it obscures the differentiations among those in positions of influence and those who are less influential': see his review article 'Political Elites Reconsidered: Process, Consequences, and Values', *Comparative Politics*, vol. VI,

no. 2 (1974) pp. 299–314 (p. 312). I would concur with Seligman: my relativistic approach is an attempt to overcome this difficulty.

4    See Martin Page and David Burg, *Unpersoned: The Fall of Nikita Sergeyevitch Khrushchev* (London: Chapman and Hall, 1966).

5    Frolic, 'Decision-Making in Soviet Cities', p. 38.

6    Frolic, 'Soviet Urban Political Leaders', p. 444.

7    See, for example, David Lane, *The End of Inequality? Stratification Under State Socialism* (Harmondsworth: Penguin, 1971), especially pp. 120–8; Armstrong, *The Soviet Bureaucratic Elite*, especially pp. 142–50; Frederic J. Fleron, Jr., 'Toward a Reconceptualization of Political Change in the Soviet Union: The Political Leadership System', reprinted in Fleron (ed.) *Communist Studies and the Social Sciences*, pp. 223–43; Fischer, *The Soviet System and Modern Society*; Stewart *et al.*, 'Political Mobility and the Soviet Political Process'. This and related questions have been explored in the work of Hough: note especially his stimulating article, 'The Soviet System: Petrification or Pluralism?' *PoC*, vol. xxi, no. 2 (1972) pp. 25–45.

8    Harry Eckstein, 'The Determinants of Pressure Group Politics', reprinted in Mattei Dogan and Richard Rose (eds) *European Politics: A Reader* (London: Macmillan, 1971) pp. 314–32 (p. 315).

9    A recent attempt to analyse and categorise career patterns in Kazakhstan is the article by Cleary, 'Elite Career Patterns in a Soviet Republic'.

10   See, in particular, Alex Inkeles, 'Models and Issues', especially pp. 5–9. The point is made explicitly in a comparative study of the USSR and a new African state: see Robert E. Dowse, *Political Modernization in Ghana and the USSR: A Comparative Study* (London: Routledge and Kegan Paul, 1969); Dowse argues that the USSR and Ghana 'faced a variety of similar problems and that their responses to these had a great deal in common' (Preface). Other writers who stress this aspect of Soviet society include Alec Nove, 'Soviet Political Organization and Development', in Colin Leys (ed.) *Politics and Change in Developing Countries: Studies in the Theory and Practice of Development* (Cambridge: Cambridge University Press, 1969) pp. 65–84; John A. Armstrong, 'Communist Political Systems as Vehicles for Modernization', in Monty Palmer and Larry Stern (eds) *Political Development in Changing Societies: An Analysis of Modernization* (Lexington, Mass.: D. C. Heath, 1971) pp. 127–58; and John A. Kautsky, *The Political Consequences of Modernization* (New York: Wiley, 1972).

11   Apter, *The Politics of Modernization*, p. 404.

12   T. H. Rigby, 'Traditional, Market, and Organizational Societies and the USSR', reprinted in Fleron (ed.) *Communist Studies and the Social Sciences*, pp. 170–87 (p. 183).

13   Karl W. Deutsch, 'Social Mobilization and Political Development', first published in *APSR*, September 1961, reprinted in abridged form in Roy C. Macridis and Bernard E. Brown (eds) *Comparative Politics: Notes and Readings*, revised edition (Homewood, Ill.: The Dorsey Press, 1964) pp. 641–8; Nettl, *Political Mobilization*.

14   Deutsch, in Macridis and Brown, *Comparative Politics*, p. 641.

15   Nettl, *Political Mobilization*, p. 70.

16   Robert C. Tucker, 'Culture, Political Culture, and Communist Society', *Political Science Quarterly*, vol. 88, no. 2 (1973) pp. 173–90.

17   Dennis Kavanagh, *Political Culture* (London: Macmillan, 1972) p. 40. The 'dominant political culture' of the Soviet system has been explored by Barghoorn: see *Politics in the USSR*, Chapter 1.

18   The formulation is that of A. E. Siegel and S. Siegel, in their article 'Reference Groups, Membership Groups and Attitude Change', reprinted in Marie Jahoda and Neil Warren (eds) *Attitudes: Selected Readings* (Harmondsworth: Penguin, 1966) pp. 187–95 (p. 187). Compare the following statement from a primer in social

psychology: 'The group affiliations of the individual play a vital role in the formation of his attitudes. Both the membership groups with which the individual affiliates and the nonmembership groups to which he aspires to belong are important in shaping his attitudes': David Krech, Richard S. Crutchfield and Egerton L. Ballachey, *Individual in Society: A Textbook of Social Psychology* (New York: McGraw-Hill, 1962) p. 197. In the case in point, the 'membership group' refers to the body of deputies, but the same principle could equally well be applied to the communist party. The principle is well expressed in the familiar adage, first applied to French politics, that 'two deputies, one of whom is a communist, have more in common than two communists, one of whom is a deputy'. Compare Kavanagh, *Political Culture*, p. 44, for a similar view of political participation in Cuba and China.

19  C. H. Dodd, *Political Development* (London: Macmillan, 1972) p. 27.
20  'O chëm rasskazala anketa', *Sovety deputatov trudyashchikhsya*, 1966, no. 10, pp. 41-7 (pp. 44-5).
21  Lucian W. Pye, *Aspects of Political Development* (Boston, Mass.: Little, Brown, 1966) pp. 94-5.
22  George McT. Kahin, Guy J. Pauker and Lucian W. Pye distinguish between the more clearly defined and specific roles of political actors in western societies and the more diffuse and uncertain roles performed by politicians in other systems: see their article 'Comparative Politics of Non-Western Countries', in Macridis and Brown (eds) *Comparative Politics*, pp. 611-18 (p. 616).
23  'Partorganizatsiya apparata ispolkoma Soveta', p. 50 (emphasis added).
24  For a fuller discussion of this point, see Hill, 'Recent Developments', pp. 172-3.
25  For a strong appeal for greater examination of (among other aspects) the sociological dimension of local government institutions in measuring their efficiency, see K. F. Sheremet, *Kompetentsiya mestnykh Sovetov* (Moscow: Izdatel'stvo Moskovskogo universiteta, 1968) Chapter 3.
26  This proposal, cited in B. N. Gabrichidze, *Apparat upravleniya mestnykh Sovetov* (Moscow: Yuridicheskaya literatura, 1971) p. 15, was made by N. A. Kudinov in 1969; Gabrichidze dismisses the suggestion as 'premature', but it indicates the direction of thinking in some quarters in the USSR on the subject of local government.
27  Perttsik, 'Puti sovershenstvovaniya deyatel'nosti deputatov', p. 19.
28  Kazimirchuk and Adamyan, 'Sotsiologicheskie aspekty sostava deputatov', p. 114.
29  This proposal was made by A. V. Moshak, in 'Nakazy izbiratelei i status deputata Soveta', *Sovetskoe gosudarstvo i pravo*, 1971, no. 2, pp. 93-6 (p. 95). Moshak criticised the fact that incompetent deputies were often re-elected, but from a fresh constituency, which meant that his dissatisfied former constituents were deprived of any means of controlling his re-election. This was perhaps an oblique criticism of the procedure whereby deputies are chosen for a specific constituency not by their electors, but by authorised ('public') nominating bodies.
30  See Kalits, Laumets and Shneider, 'Izuchenie deyatel'nosti deputatov'; also 'O chëm rasskazala anketa'.
31  See Hough, 'Reforms in Government and Administration', p. 25. Compare Richard Little: 'Soviet legislative committees have not yet achieved an important position in the policy-making process, but the next few years may well see some further improvement in this direction'. See D. Richard Little, 'Soviet Parliamentary Committees After Khrushchev: Obstacles and Opportunities', *Sov. Studs.*, vol. XXIV, no. 1 (1972) pp. 41-60 (p. 60).
32  Thus, Vasenin writes, 'The centre of all the work of a deputy is his constituency [where he] meets the workers, learns of their needs and requirements, organises the population for fulfilling the decisions of the soviet and the electors' mandates,

and here too the deputy reports back to his electors': see *Deputat mestnogo Soveta*, p. 53. Other Soviet sociologists have studied the amount of time spent by deputies on various aspects of their work: see, for example, the work of Pavlov, Kazimirchuk and their associates, reported in *Upravlenie, sotsiologiya, pravo*, pp. 183 and 194, Tables 14 and 16; and of Kazimirchuk and Adamyan, 'Sotsiologicheskie aspekty sostava deputatov', p. 115. See also Bezuglov, *Sovetskii deputat*, pp. 101-45, for a full discussion of the deputy's work among the population.

33 Fainsod, *How Russia is Ruled*, pp. 382-3.

# Bibliography

REFERENCE SOURCES

*Newspapers and journals* (note: the place of publication appears in brackets after the title of the periodical)

*Dnestrovskaya pravda* (Tiraspol)
*Drapelul Leninist* (Tiraspol)
*Izvestiya Sovetov deputatov trudyashchikhsya* (Moscow)
*Leninskoe znamya* (Tiraspol)
*Partiinaya zhizn'* (Moscow)
*Pravda* (Moscow)
*Sovetskaya Moldaviya* (Kishinev)
*Sovety deputatov trudyashchikhsya* (Moscow)
*Stalinskii put'* (Tiraspol)
*Znamya pobedy* (Tiraspol)

*Legal documents*

*Constitution (Fundamental Law) of the Union of Soviet Socialist Republics* (Moscow: Foreign Languages Publishing House, 1962).

*Konstitutsiya (osnovnoi zakon) Moldavskoi Sovetskoi sotsialisticheskoi respubliki* (Kishinev: Kartya Moldovenyaske, 1967).

'Ob osnovnykh pravakh i obyazannostyakh gorodskikh i raionnykh v gorodakh Sovetov deputatov trudyashchikhsya' (Ukaz Prezidiuma Verkhovnogo Soveta SSSR), 19 March 1971, reprinted in *Sovety deputatov trudyashchikhsya*, 1971, no. 4, pp. 23–9.

'O povyshenii zarabotnoi platy rabotnikov ... otraslei narodnogo khozyaistva, neposredstvenno obsluzhivayushchikh naselenie' (Zakon SSR), 15 July 1964, reprinted in *Spravochnik partiinogo rabotnika, vypusk 6*, p. 261.

*Polozhenie ob organakh narodnogo kontrolya v SSSR* (Moscow: Politizdat, 1969).

'Polozhenie o gorodskom Sovete deputatov trudyashchikhsya Moldavskoi SSR' (1957), reprinted in *Sbornik normativnykh aktov*, pp. 79–94.

'Polozhenie o planovoi komissii ispolnitel'nogo komiteta gorodskogo (raionnogo) Soveta deputatov trudyashchikhsya', reprinted in *Sbornik normativnykh aktov*, pp. 208–11.

'Polozhenie o postoyannykh komissiyakh raionnykh, gorodskikh, sel'skikh i poselkovykh Sovetov deputatov trudyashchikhsya Moldavskoi SSR', reprinted in *Sbornik normativnykh aktov*, pp. 108–22.

'Polozhenie o vyborakh v raionnye, gorodskie, sel'skie i poselkovye Sovety deputatov trudyashchikhsya Moldavskoi SSR', reprinted in *Sbornik normativnykh aktov*, pp. 40–57.

'Ustav Kommunisticheskoi partii Sovetskogo Soyuza' (1952), reprinted in *Programmy i Ustavy KPSS*, pp. 344–67.

'Ustav Kommunisticheskoi partii Sovetskogo Soyuza' (1961), reprinted in *Programmy i Ustavy KPSS*, pp. 368–96.

*Ustav Vsesoyuznogo leninskogo kommunisticheskogo soyuza molodezhi* (Moscow: Molodaya gvardiya, 1968).

'Zakon o gorodskom, raionnom v gorode Sovete deputatov trudyashchikhsya Moldavskoi SSR' (1971), in *Sovetskaya Moldaviya*, 14 December 1971.

211

'Zakon o statuse deputatov Sovetov deputatov trudyashchikhsya v sssr' (1972), in *Pravda*, 22 September 1972.

*Official statements, speeches etc.*

Khrushchev, N. S., 'On the Cult of the Personality and its Consequences' ('Secret Speech'), reprinted in Henry M. Christman (ed.) *Communism in Action: A Documentary History* (New York: Bantam Books, 1969) pp. 158–228.
'Ob uluchshenii deyatel'nosti Sovetov deputatov trudyashchikhsya i usilenii ikh svyazei s massami', reprinted in *KPSS v rezolyutsiyakh i resheniyakh s"ezdov, konferentsii i plenumov TsK, tom 6 (1941–1956)* (Moscow: Politizdat, 1971) pp. 237–48.
'Ob uluchshenii torgovli i obshchestvennogo pitaniya v strane' (Postanovlenie Soveta Ministrov sssr), reprinted in *Spravochnik partiinogo rabotnika, vypusk 6*, pp. 303–14.
'O merakh po dal'neishemu uluchsheniyu raboty raionnykh i gorodskikh Sovetov deputatov trudyashchikhsya' (Postanovlenie TsK kpss), reprinted in *Sovety deputatov trudyashchikhsya*, 1971, no. 4, pp. 11–15.
'O merakh po ukrepleniyu material'no-finansovoi bazy ispolkomov raionnykh i gorodskikh Sovetov deputatov trudyashchikhsya' (Postanovlenie Soveta Ministrov sssr), reprinted in *Sovety deputatov trudyashchikhsya*, 1971, no. 4, pp. 30–1.
'O merakh po uluchsheniyu raboty predpriyatii bytovogo obsluzhivaniya naseleniya' (Postanovlenie Soveta Ministrov sssr), reprinted in *Spravochnik partiinogo rabotnika, vypusk 6*, pp. 321–8.
'O nekotorom uproshenii struktury apparata i sokrashchenii shtatov gorkomov i gorodskikh raikomov partii' (Postanovlenie TsK kpss), reprinted in *Spravochnik partiinogo rabotnika, vypusk 2*, p. 546.
'O neotlozhnykh merakh po dal'neishemu razvitiyu sel'skogo khozyaistva sssr' (Postanovlenie Plenuma TsK kpss, 26 March 1965), reprinted in *Spravochnik partiinogo rabotnika, vypusk 6*, pp. 104–7.
'O rabote mestnykh Sovetov deputatov trudyashchikhsya Poltavskoi oblasti' (Postanovlenie TsK kpss), reprinted in *Spravochnik partiinogo rabotnika, vypusk 6*, pp. 392–6.
'Otchëtnyi doklad Tsentral'nogo komiteta kpss xxiii s"ezdu Kommunisticheskoi partii Sovetskogo Soyuza', in *XXIII s"ezd Kommunisticheskoi partii Sovetskogo Soyuza: Stenograficheskii otchët*, vol. 1, pp. 18–109.
'Postanovlenie xxiii s"ezda Kommunisticheskoi partii Sovetskogo Soyuza o chastichnykh izmeneniyakh v Ustave kpss', reprinted in *Spravochnik partiinogo rabotnika, vypusk 6*, pp. 25–7.
'Postanovlenie xxiv s"ezda Kommunisticheskoi partii Sovetskogo Soyuza o chastichnykh izmeneniyakh v Ustave kpss', reprinted in *Spravochnik partiinogo rabotnika, vypusk 11*, pp. 30–1.
*Programma KPSS* (1961), reprinted in *Programmy i Ustavy KPSS*, pp. 63–224.
'Rezolyutsiya xxiii s"ezda Kommunisticheskoi partii Sovetskogo Soyuza po otchëtnomu dokladu Tsentral'nogo Komiteta kpss', reprinted in *Spravochnik partiinogo rabotnika, vypusk 6*, pp. 7–25.
*XXIII s"ezd Kommunisticheskoi partii Sovetskogo Soyuza: Stenograficheskii otchët*, 2 vols. (Moscow: Politizdat, 1966).
*XXIV s"ezd Kommunisticheskoi partii Sovetskogo Soyuza: Stenograficheskii otchët*, 2 vols. (Moscow: Politizdat, 1971).

*Statistical handbooks etc.*

*Itogi Vsesoyuznoi perepisi naseleniya 1959 goda: Moldavskaya SSR* (Moscow: Gosstatizdat, 1963).
*Itogi Vsesoyuznoi perepisi naseleniya 1959 goda: RSFSR* (Moscow: Gosstatizdat, 1963).

*Itogi Vsesoyuznoi perepisi naseleniy a 1970 goda. Tom I: chislennost' naseleniya SSSR, soyuznykh i avtonomnykh respublik, kraev i oblastei* (Moscow: Statistika, 1972).

*Itogi vyborov i sostav deputatov mestnykh Sovetov deputatov trudyashchikhsya 1961 goda (Statisticheskii sbornik)* (Moscow: Izvestiya, 1961).

*Itogi vyborov i sostav deputatov Verkhovnykh Sovetov soyuznykh, avtonomnykh respublik i mestnykh Sovetov deputatov trudyashchikhsya 1963 g. (Statisticheskii sbornik)* (Moscow: Izvestiya, 1963).

*Itogi vyborov i sostav deputatov mestnykh Sovetov deputatov trudyashchikhsya 1967 g. (Statisticheskii sbornik)* (Moscow: Izvestiya, 1967).

*Itogi vyborov i sostav deputatov mestnykh Sovetov deputatov trudyashchikhsya 1969 g. (Statisticheskii sbornik)* (Moscow: Izvestiya, 1969).

*Narodnoe khozyaistvo Moldavskoi SSR 1970 (Statisticheskii sbornik)* (Kishinev: Statistika, 1971).

*Sostav deputatov Verkhovnykh Sovetov soyuznykh, avtonomnykh respublik i mestnykh Sovetov deputatov trudyashchikhsya 1959 g. (Statisticheskii sbornik)* (Moscow: Izvestiya, 1959).

*Sostav deputatov mestnykh Sovetov deputatov trudyashchikhsya, izbrannykh v marte 1965 g. (Statisticheskii sbornik)* (Moscow: Izvestiya, 1965).

*Sovetskaya Moldaviya k 50-letiyu Velikogo Oktyabrya: Statisticheskii sbornik* (Kishinev: Statistika, 1967).

'Zhenshchiny v SSSR', *Vestnik statistiki*, 1968, no. 1, pp. 82–96.

*Other reference works*

*Bol'shaya Sovetskaya Entsiklopediya*, 2nd edition, in 51 vols (Moscow, 1949–58); vol. 42, 1956.

*Deputaty Verkhovnogo Soveta SSSR: sed'moi sozyv* (Moscow: Izvestiya, 1966).

*Entsiklopedicheskii slovar'*, in 82 vols (St. Petersburg, 1890–1904); vol. 65, 1901.

*Kommunisticheskaya Partiya Sovetskogo Soyuza – naglyadnoe posobie po partiinomu stroitel'stvu* (V. I. Strukov, compiler) (Moscow: Politizdat, 1973).

*KPSS v rezolyutsiyakh i resheniyakh s"ezdov, konferentsii i plenumov TsK*, 8th edition, in 10 vols (Moscow: Politizdat, 1970–72); vol. 6 (1941–56), 1971; vol. 7 (1955–9), 1971; vol. 8 (1959–65), 1971.

Levytsky, Borys, *The Soviet Political Elite*, xeroxed manuscript distributed by the Hoover Institution on War, Revolution and Peace, for Stanford University Press (Stanford, Calif., 1970).

*Organizatsionno-ustavnye voprosy KPSS: 1972* (Moscow: Politizdat, 1972).

*Programmy i Ustavy KPSS* (Moscow: Politizdat, 1969).

*Sbornik normativnykh aktov (v pomoshch' rabotnikam mestnykh Sovetov)* (Kishinev: Kartya Moldovenyaske, 1968).

*Spravochnaya kniga o professional'nykh soyuzakh SSSR* (Moscow: Profizdat, 1965).

*Spravochnik partiinogo rabotnika*, various issues (Moscow: Politizdat; no. 2, 1959; no. 6, 1966; no. 11, 1971).

Vigor, P. H. (ed.) *Books on Communism and the Communist Countries* (London: Ampersand, 1971).

Voronin, P. V., Bibileishvili, N. K., Laptënok, M. Ye., Oleinik, K. Ye. and Terekhina, I. I. (eds) *Leninskii narodnyi kontrol' v Moldavskoi SSR: Sbornik dokumentov i materialov (1924–1969 gg.)* (Kishinev: Izdatel'stvo TsK KP Moldavii, 1970).

*Zapisnaya knizhka partiinogo aktivista: 1972* (Moscow: Politizdat, 1971).

SECONDARY SOURCES

*Soviet*

AFANAS'EV, V., 'Krug voprosov na sessii', in Vasil'ev *et al.* (eds) *Voprosy raboty Sovetov deputatov trudyashchikhsya*, pp. 455–69.

BAZIN, M., *Soyuz zemledeliya i promyshlennosti: o nekotorykh formakh soedineniya sel'skokhozyaistvennogo proizvodstva s promyshlennym v usloviyakh Moldavii* (Kishinev: Kartya Moldovenyaske, 1969).

BEZUGLOV, A. A., *Sovetskii deputat: gosudarstvennopravovoi status* (Moscow: Yuridicheskaya literatura, 1971).

BEZUGLOV, A. A., *Soviet Deputy (Legal Status)* (Moscow: Progress Publishers, 1973).

BUTKO, YE. F. (ed.) '*Tekhnologiya' raboty postoyannykh komissii* (Moscow: Izvestiya, 1970).

CHEREPNIN, L. V. *et al.* (eds) *Istoriya Moldavskoi SSR*, 2 vols (Kishinev: Kartya Moldovenyaske, 1968).

'Chlen gorkoma partii', *Dnestrovskaya pravda*, 19 May 1960.

DEREVSKOI, YU., 'Chlen vybornogo partiinogo organa', *Partiinaya zhizn*', 1971, no. 2, pp. 35–7.

FOMENKO, YA., 'Gorkom i malochislennye partorganizatsii', *Partiinaya zhizn*', 1967, no. 1, pp. 30–4.

GABRICHIDZE, B. N., *Gorodskie Sovety deputatov trudyashchikhsya* (Moscow: Yuridicheskaya literatura, 1968).

GABRICHIDZE, B. N., *Apparat upravleniya mestnykh Sovetov* (Moscow: Yuridicheskaya literatura, 1971).

GAIDUKOV, D. A. and STAROVOITOV, N. G. (eds) *Mestnye Sovety na sovremennom etape* (Moscow: Nauka, 1965).

GOGICHAISHVILI, M. A., *Partiinoe sobranie – shkola ideinogo vospitaniya kommunistov* (Moscow: Politizdat, 1969).

GUDYM, A. A., *Dinamichnost' ekonomiki Moldavskoi SSR* (Kishinev: Kartya Moldovenyaske, 1969).

IVANOV, YE. A., *Profsoyuzy v politicheskoi sisteme sotsializma* (Moscow: Profizdat, 1974).

KALITS, I., LAUMETS, A. and SHNEIDER, KH., 'Izuchenie deyatel'nosti deputatov s pomoshch'yu konkretno-sotsiologicheskogo metoda', *Sovetskoe gosudarstvo i pravo*, 1965, no. 9, pp. 65–70.

KAREV, D. S. (ed.) *Yuridicheskii spravochnik deputata mestnogo Soveta* (Moscow: Izdatel'stvo Moskovskogo universiteta, 1962).

KASK, V., 'Sodeistvie khozyaistvennika', *Sovety deputatov trudyashchikhsya*, 1970, no. 1, pp. 55–8.

KAZIMIRCHUK, V. P. and ADAMYAN, N. K., 'Sotsiologicheskie aspekty sostava deputatov mestnykh Sovetov (na materialakh Armyanskoi SSR)', in *Organizatsiya i deyatel'nost' Sovetov i organov gosudarstvennogo upravleniya Armyanskoi SSR* (Yerevan: Izdatel'stvo Akademii Nauk Armyanskoi SSR, 1970) pp. 109–23.

KHALDEEV, M. I., ZARODOV, K. I. and BUGAEV, YE. I. (eds) *Voprosy partiinoi zhizni: v pomoshch' izuchayushchim partiinoe stroitel'stvo* (Moscow: Pravda, 1967).

KHIMICHEVA, N. I., *Byudzhetnye prava raionnogo, gorodskogo Soveta* (Moscow: Yuridicheskaya literatura, 1973).

KOROLËV, A. M., *Partiya i komsomol* (Moscow: Mysl', 1967).

KOZLOVA, YE. I., *Mestnye organy gosudarstvennoi vlasti v SSSR* (Moscow: Mysl', 1967).

KRAVCHUK, S. S. (ed.) *Gosudarstvennoe pravo SSSR* (Moscow: Yuridicheskaya literatura, 1967).

KRUPENIKOV, I. A., MIRSKII, D. A. and RADUL, M. M. (eds) *Sovetskii Soyuz: Moldaviya* (Moscow: Mysl', 1970).
KRYACHEK, A., 'Na sessiyakh peremeny', *Sovety deputatov trudyashchikhsya*, 1969, no. 5, pp. 67–9.
KUNAEV, D. A., 'Kollektivnost' – vysshyi printsip partiinogo rukovodstva', reprinted in Khaldeev *et al.* (eds) *Voprosy partiinoi zhizni*, pp. 141–55.
LEPËSHKIN, A. I., *Sovety – vlast' naroda, 1936–1967 gg.* (Moscow: Yuridicheskaya literatura, 1967).
LUK'YANOV, A. I. and LAZAREV, B. M., *Sovetskoe gosudarstvo i obshchestvennye organizatsii*, 2nd edition (Moscow: Gosyurizdat, 1961).

MIRONOVA, A. (ed.) *Ocherki istorii Tiraspolya* (Kishinev: Kartya Moldovenyaske, 1967).
MOSHAK, A. V., 'Nakazy izbiratelei i status deputata Soveta', *Sovetskoe gosudarstvo i pravo*, 1971, no. 2, pp. 93–6.
MOSKALEV, A. and ROSTOVTSEV, V., 'Komissiya na sessii', in Butko (ed.) *'Tekhnologiya' raboty postoyannykh komissii*, pp. 61–70.

NAIDA, S. F. *et al.* (eds) *Sovety za 50 let* (Moscow: Mysl', 1967).
'Narodnye druzhiny: kak oni sozdayutsya i deistvuyut', *Sovety deputatov trudyashchikhsya*, 1971, no. 7, pp. 95–9.
NEBYLITSA, V., 'Litso raionnogo tsentra', *Sovetskaya Moldaviya*, 12 November 1971, p. 2.
NIKITIN, A., 'Grani torgovogo servisa', *Sovetskaya Moldaviya*, 3 September 1971, p. 4.

'O chëm rasskazala anketa', *Sovety deputatov trudyashchikhsya*, 1966, no. 10, pp. 41–7.
*Ocherki istorii Kommunisticheskoi partii Moldavii*, 1st edition (Ye. S. Postovoi *et al.*, eds) (Kishinev: Partiinoe izdatel'stvo TsK KP Moldavii, 1964); 2nd edition (D. S. Kornovan *et al.*, eds) (Kishinev: Kartya Moldovenyaske, 1968).
'Otchëty i vybory v pervichnykh partorganizatsiyakh', *Partiinaya zhizn'*, 1973, no. 18, pp. 5–10.

'Partiinye gruppy v mestnykh Sovetakh', *Partiinaya zhizn'*, 1973, no. 8, pp. 48–52.
'Partorganizatsiya apparata ispolkoma Soveta', *Partiinaya zhizn'*, 1973, no. 12, pp. 50–4.
PAVLOV, I. V. and KAZIMIRCHUK, V. P. (eds) *Upravlenie, sotsiologiya, pravo* (Moscow: Yuridicheskaya literatura, 1971).
'Perevod iz kandidatov v chleny partiinogo komiteta', *Partiinaya zhizn'*, 1973, no. 6, p. 37.
PERTTSIK, V. A., 'Puti sovershenstvovaniya deyatel'nosti deputatov mestnykh Sovetov', *Sovetskoe gosudarstvo i pravo*, 1967, no. 7, pp. 16–21.
PETROV, L. V., *Partiinyi aktiv* (Moscow: Moskovskii rabochii, 1968).
POBEDA, N. A., 'Nekotorye osobennosti formirovaniya kul'tury sovremennykh gorodov Moldavii', in Yermuratskii *et al.* (eds) *Filosofskie i sotsiologicheskie issledovaniya v Moldavii*, pp. 161–80.

*Raionnyi komitet partii* (Moscow: Politizdat, 1972).
ROMANOVA, Z. G., *Deyatel'nost' Kommunisticheskoi partii Moldavii po razvitiyu promyshlennosti respubliki (1924–1965 gg.)* (Kishinev: Kartya Moldovenyaske, 1970).

SABANEEV, S. and KONOVALOV, G., 'Ruka ob ruku', *Izvestiya*, 16 May 1967, reprinted in Vasil'ev *et al.* (eds) *Voprosy raboty Sovetov deputatov trudyashchikhsya*, pp. 527–34.
SADCHIKOV, V., 'Povyshaem rol' chlenov gorkoma partii', *Partiinaya zhizn'*, 1970, no. 10, pp. 25–9.
SAIFULIN, M. (ed.) *The Soviet Parliament* (Moscow: Progress Publishers, 1967).
SHEREMET, K. F., *Kompetentsiya mestnykh Sovetov* (Moscow: Izdatel'stvo Moskovskogo universiteta, 1968).

SHITAREV, G. I. (ed.) *Partiinoe stroitel'stvo (uchebno-metodicheskoe posobie)*, 2nd edition (Moscow: Mysl', 1968).

*Spravochnik sekretarya pervichnoi partiinoi organizatsii* (Moscow: Politizdat, 1967).

SURILOV, A., *Istoriya gosudarstva i prava Moldavskoi SSR (1917–1959 gg.)* (Kishinev: Kartya Moldovenyaske, 1963).

TSARIK, G., 'Kommunist-deputat', *Partiinaya zhizn'*, 1970, no. 10, pp. 50–3.

TURISHCHEV, YU. G., *Istoriya Ustava KPSS* (Moscow: Vysshaya shkola, 1971).

TUROVTSEV, V. I. (ed.) *Narodnyi kontrol' v SSSR* (Moscow: Nauka, 1967).

USTINOV, G. (ed.) *We're the Soviets* (Moscow: Novosti Press Agency, 1973).

VASENIN, V. K., *Deputat mestnogo Soveta* (Moscow: Yuridicheskaya literatura, 1967).

VASILENKOV, P. T., *Organy sovetskogo gosudarstva i ikh sistema na sovremennom etape* (Moscow: Izdatel'stvo Moskovskogo universiteta, 1967).

VASIL'EV, V. I. (ed.) *V pomoshch' deputatu mestnogo Soveta (prakticheskoe posobie)* (Moscow: Yuridicheskaya literatura, 1968).

VASIL'EV, V. I., *Rabota deputata sel'skogo, poselkovogo Soveta v postoyannoi komissii i izbiratel'nom okruge* (Moscow: Yuridicheskaya literatura, 1969).

VASIL'EV, V. I., MOTYSHEVA, A. T., PIGALEV, P. F., SEVRIKOV, K. I. and STREPUKHOV, M. F. (eds) *Voprosy raboty Sovetov deputatov trudyashchikhsya* (Moscow: Izvestiya, 1968).

VESELOV, N., *The Communist Party and Mass Organizations in the USSR* (Moscow: Novosti Press Agency, 1973).

VORONOVSKII, N. A., *Leninskie printsipy podbora, rasstanovki i vospitaniya kadrov* (Moscow: Mysl', 1967).

YERMURATSKII, V. N., BABII, A. I. and YENTELIS, G. S. (eds) *Filosofskie i sotsiologcheskie issledovaniya v Moldavii* (Kishinev: Izdatel'stvo Akademii Nauk Moldavskoi SSR, 1970).

YUDIN, G. F., *Partiinoe khozyaistvo v partiinykh organakh i pervichnykh partiinykh organizatsiyakh* (Moscow: Mysl', 1966).

ZHITKOV, V., 'Gorkom informiruet o svoei rabote', *Partiinaya zhizn'*, 1970, no. 3, pp. 38–40.

ZLATOVA, YE. and KOTEL'NIKOV, V. V., *Puteshestvie po Moldavii* (Moscow: Molodaya gvardiya, 1957).

*Non-Soviet*

ALLILUYEVA, SVETLANA, *Twenty Letters to a Friend* (London: Hutchinson, 1967).

APTER, DAVID E., *The Politics of Modernization*, Phoenix edition (Chicago and London: University of Chicago Press, 1967).

ARMSTRONG, JOHN A., *The Soviet Bureaucratic Elite: A Case Study of the Ukrainian Apparatus* (London: Atlantic Books, 1959).

ARMSTRONG, JOHN A., *Ideology, Politics and Government in the Soviet Union: An Introduction*, 1st edition (New York: Praeger, 1962); 3rd edition (London: Nelson, 1973).

ARMSTRONG, JOHN A., 'Party Bifurcation and Elite Interests', *Soviet Studies*, vol. XVII, no. 4 (1966) pp. 417–30.

ARMSTRONG, JOHN A., 'Communist Political Systems as Vehicles for Modernization', in Monty Palmer and Larry Stern (eds) *Political Development in Changing Societies: An Analysis of Modernization* (Lexington, Mass.: D. C. Heath, 1971) pp. 127–58.

ASPATURIAN, VERNON V., 'The Soviet Union', in Roy C. Macridis and R. E. Ward (eds) *Modern Political Systems: Europe*, 2nd edition (Englewood Cliffs: Prentice-Hall, 1968) pp. 451–596.

AVTORKHANOV, ABDURAKHMAN, *The Communist Party Apparatus* (Chicago: Henry Regnery, 1966).

AZRAEL, JEREMY R., 'The Legislative Process in the USSR', reprinted under the title 'Decision-Making in the USSR', in Cornell (ed.) *The Soviet Political System: A Book of Readings*, pp. 205–17.

BARGHOORN, FREDERICK C., *Politics in the USSR* (Boston and Toronto: Little, Brown, 1966).

BELL, DANIEL, 'Ten Theories in Search of Reality: The Prediction of Soviet Behavior', reprinted in Daniel Bell, *The End of Ideology: On the Exhaustion of Political Ideas in the Fifties*, revised edition (New York: The Free Press, 1962) pp. 315–52.

BIALER, SEWERYN, 'How Russians Rule Russia', *Problems of Communism*, vol. XIII, no. 5 (1964) pp. 45–52.

BLACKWELL, ROBERT E., Jr, 'Elite Recruitment and Functional Change: An Analysis of the Soviet Obkom Elite, 1950–1968', *Journal of Politics*, vol. 34, no. 1 (1972) pp. 124–52.

BONJEAN, CHARLES M. and OLSON, DAVID M., 'Community Leadership: Directions of Research', reprinted in Michael Aiken and Paul E. Mott (eds) *The Structure of Community Power* (New York: Random House, 1970) pp. 203–15.

BOTTOMORE, T. B., *Elites and Society* (Harmondsworth: Penguin, 1966).

BRINKLEY, GEORGE A., 'Khrushchev Remembered: On the Theory of Soviet State-hood', *Soviet Studies*, vol. XXIV, no. 3 (1973) pp. 387–401.

BROWN, A. H., *Soviet Politics and Political Science* (London: Macmillan, 1974).

BROWN, EMILY CLARKE, *Soviet Trade Unions and Labor Relations* (Cambridge, Mass.: Harvard University Press, 1966).

CARSON, GEORGE BARR, Jr, *Electoral Practices in the USSR* (London: Atlantic Press, 1956).

CATTELL, DAVID T., *Leningrad: A Case Study of Soviet Urban Government* (New York: Praeger, 1968).

CHURCHWARD, L. G., 'Some Aspects of Republican and Local Government Before the Decentralization', *Soviet Studies*, vol. IX, no. 1 (1957) pp. 84–91.

CHURCHWARD, L. G., 'Continuity and Change in Soviet Local Government, 1947–1957', *Soviet Studies*, vol. IX, no. 3 (1958) pp. 256–85.

CHURCHWARD, L. G., 'To Divide or Not to Divide', *Soviet Studies*, vol. XVII, no. 1 (1965) pp. 93–6.

CHURCHWARD, L. G., 'Soviet Local Government Today', *Soviet Studies*, vol. XVII, no. 4 (1966) pp. 431–52.

CHURCHWARD, L. G., *Contemporary Soviet Government* (London: Routledge and Kegan Paul, 1968).

CHURCHWARD, L. G., Review in *Soviet Studies*, vol. XX, no. 4 (1969) pp. 555–6.

CLEARY, J. W., 'Elite Career Patterns in a Soviet Republic', *British Journal of Political Science*, vol. 4, no. 3 (1974) pp. 323–44.

CONQUEST, ROBERT, *Power and Policy in the USSR: The Study of Soviet Dynastics* (London: Macmillan, 1961).

CONQUEST, ROBERT, 'In Defence of Kremlinology', *Survey*, no. 50 (1964) pp. 163–73.

CONQUEST, ROBERT, *Russia After Khrushchev* (New York: Praeger, 1965).

CORNELL, RICHARD (ed.) *The Soviet Political System: A Book of Readings* (Englewood Cliffs: Prentice-Hall, 1970).

DALLIN, ALEXANDER and LARSON, THOMAS B. (eds) *Soviet Politics Since Khrushchev* (Englewood Cliffs: Prentice-Hall, 1968).

DEUTSCH, KARL W., 'Social Mobilization and Political Development', reprinted in Roy C. Macridis and Bernard E. Brown (eds) *Comparative Politics: Notes and Readings*, pp. 641–8.

DJILAS, MILOVAN, *Conversations With Stalin* (London: Rupert Hart-Davis, 1962).

DODD C. H., *Political Development* (London: Macmillan, 1972).

DOWSE, ROBERT E., *Political Modernization in Ghana and the USSR: A Comparative Study* (London: Routledge and Kegan Paul, 1969).

ECKSTEIN, HARRY, 'The Determinants of Pressure Group Politics', reprinted in Mattei Dogan and Richard Rose (eds) *European Politics: A Reader* (London: Macmillan, 1971) pp. 314–32.

FAINSOD, MERLE, *Smolensk Under Soviet Rule* (London: Macmillan, 1958).

FAINSOD, MERLE, *How Russia is Ruled*, 2nd edition (Cambridge, Mass.: Harvard University Press, 1965).

FARRELL, R. BARRY (ed.) *Political Leadership in Eastern Europe and the Soviet Union* (London: Butterworths, 1970).

FISCHER, GEORGE, *The Soviet System and Modern Society* (New York: Atherton Press, 1968).

FLERON, FREDERIC J., Jr, 'Note on the Explication of the Concept "Elite" in the Study of Soviet Politics', *Canadian Slavic Studies*, vol. II, no. 1 (1968) pp. 111–15.

FLERON, FREDERIC J., Jr (ed.) *Communist Studies and the Social Sciences: Essays on Methodology and Empirical Theory* (Chicago: Rand McNally, 1969).

FLERON, FREDERIC J., Jr, 'Toward a Reconceptualization of Political Change in the Soviet Union: The Political Leadership System', reprinted in Fleron (ed.) *Communist Studies and the Social Sciences*, pp. 222–43.

FLERON, FREDERIC J., Jr, 'Career Types in the Soviet Political Leadership', in Farrell (ed.) *Political Leadership in Eastern Europe and the Soviet Union*, pp. 108–39.

FRANK, PETER, 'The CPSU Obkom First Secretary: A Profile', *British Journal of Political Science*, vol. 1, no. 2 (1971) pp. 173–90.

FRIEDGUT, THEODORE H., 'Community Structure, Political Participation, and Soviet Local Government: The Case of Kutaisi', in Henry W. Morton and Rudolf L. Tökés (eds) *Soviet Politics and Society in the 1970s* (New York: The Free Press, 1974) pp. 261–96.

FROLIC, B. MICHAEL, 'Soviet Urban Political Leaders', *Comparative Political Studies*, vol. 2, no. 4 (1970) pp. 443–64.

FROLIC, B. MICHAEL, 'The Soviet Study of Soviet Cities', *Journal of Politics*, vol. 32, no. 3 (1970) pp. 675–95.

FROLIC, B. MICHAEL, 'Municipal Administrations, Departments, Commissions and Organizations', *Soviet Studies*, vol. XXII, no. 3 (1971) pp. 376–93.

FROLIC, B. MICHAEL, 'Decision-Making in Soviet Cities', *American Political Science Review*, vol. LXVI, no. 1 (1972) pp. 38–52.

GEHLEN, MICHAEL P., *The Communist Party of the Soviet Union: A Functional Analysis* (Bloomington and London: Indiana University Press, 1969).

GEHLEN, MICHAEL P., 'The Soviet Apparatchiki', in Farrell (ed.) *Political Leadership in Eastern Europe and the Soviet Union*, pp. 140–56.

GEHLEN, MICHAEL P. and MCBRIDE, MICHAEL, 'The Soviet Central Committee: An Elite Analysis', *American Political Science Review*, vol. LXII, no. 4 (1968) pp. 1232–41.

GILISON, JEROME M., 'Soviet Elections as a Measure of Dissent: The Missing One Percent', *American Political Science Review*, vol. LXII, no. 3 (1968) pp. 814–26.

*Guide for the New Councillor and Candidate*, published by the Labour Party (London: The Labour Party, 1973).

HARASYMIW, BOHDAN, '*Nomenklatura*: The Soviet Communist Party's Leadership Recruitment System', *Canadian Journal of Political Science*, vol. 2, no. 3 (1969) pp. 493–512.

HARRIS, CHAUNCY D., *Cities of the Soviet Union: Studies in their Functions, Size, Density, and Growth* (Chicago: Rand McNally, 1970).

HILL, RONALD J., 'The Composition and Functioning of the Central Committee of the Communist Party of Moldavia, December 1963 – March 1966', MA dissertation, unpublished, University of Essex, 1967.

HILL, RONALD J., 'Participation in the Central Committee Plenums in Moldavia', *Soviet Studies*, vol. XXI, no. 2 (1969) pp. 193–207.

HILL, RONALD J., 'Continuity and Change in USSR Supreme Soviet Elections', *British Journal of Political Science*, vol. 2, no. 1 (1972) pp. 47–67.

HILL, RONALD J., 'Recent Developments in Soviet Local Government', *Community Development Journal*, vol. 7, no. 3 (1972) pp. 169–75.

HILL, RONALD J., 'Tiraspol: A Study of a Soviet Town's Political Elite', PhD thesis, unpublished, University of Essex, 1973.

HILL, RONALD J., 'Patterns of Deputy Selection to Local Soviets', *Soviet Studies*, vol. XXV, no. 2 (1973) pp. 196–212.

HILL, RONALD J., 'The CPSU in a Soviet Election Campaign', *Soviet Studies*, vol. XXVIII, no. 4 (1976) pp. 590–8.

HODNETT, GREY, 'Khrushchev and Party–State Control', in Alexander Dallin and Alan F. Westin (eds) *Politics in the Soviet Union: 7 Cases* (New York: Harcourt, Brace and World, 1966) pp. 113–64.

HOUGH, JERRY, 'Groups and Individuals', *Problems of Communism*, vol. XVI, no. 1 (1967) pp. 28–35.

HOUGH, JERRY, 'In Whose Hands the Future?', *Problems of Communism*, vol. XVI, no. 2 (1967) pp. 18–25.

HOUGH, JERRY, 'Reforms in Government and Administration', in Dallin and Larson (eds) *Soviet Politics Since Khrushchev*, pp. 23–40.

HOUGH, JERRY, *The Soviet Prefects: The Local Party Organs in Industrial Decision-Making* (Cambridge, Mass.: Harvard University Press, 1969).

HOUGH, JERRY, 'The Soviet System: Petrification or Pluralism?', *Problems of Communism*, vol. XXI, no. 2 (1972) pp. 25–45.

HOUGH, JERRY, 'Soviet Urban Politics and Comparative Urban Theory', *Journal of Comparative Administration*, vol. 4, no. 3 (1972) pp. 311–34.

INKELES, ALEX, 'Models and Issues in the Analysis of Soviet Society', *Survey*, no. 60 (1966) pp. 3–17.

INKELES, ALEX and ROSSI, PETER H., 'Multidimensional Ratings of Occupations', reprinted in Alex Inkeles, *Social Change in Soviet Russia* (Cambridge, Mass.: Harvard University Press, 1968) pp. 192–210.

JACOBS, EVERETT M., 'Soviet Local Elections: What They Are, and What They Are Not', *Soviet Studies*, vol. XXII, no. 1 (1970) pp. 61–76.

JACOBS, EVERETT M., 'The Composition of Local Soviets, 1959–1969', *Government and Opposition*, vol. 7, no. 4 (1972) pp. 503–19.

KAHIN, GEORGE McT., PAUKER, GUY J. and PYE, LUCIAN W., 'Comparative Politics of Non-Western Countries', in Roy C. Macridis and Bernard E. Brown (eds) *Comparative Politics: Notes and Readings*, pp. 611–18.

KATZ, ZEV, 'Sociology in the Soviet Union', *Problems of Communism*, vol. xx, no. 3 (1971) pp. 22–40.

KAUTSKY, JOHN A., *The Political Consequences of Modernization* (New York: Wiley, 1972).

KAVANAGH, DENNIS, *Political Culture* (London: Macmillan, 1972).

KELLER, SUZANNE, 'Elites', in the *International Encyclopedia of the Social Sciences* (David L. Sills, ed.) (New York: Macmillan and The Free Press, 1968) vol. 5, pp. 26–9.

KHRUSHCHEV, NIKITA, *Khrushchev Remembers*, 2 vols (London: Andre Deutsch, 1970 and 1974).

KRECH, DAVID, CRUTCHFIELD, RICHARD S. and BALLACHEY, EGERTON L., *Individual in Society: A Textbook of Social Psychology* (New York: McGraw-Hill, 1962).

LAIRD, ROY D., *The Soviet Paradigm: An Experiment in Creating a Monohierarchical Polity* (New York: The Free Press, 1970).

LANE, DAVID, *Politics and Society in the USSR* (London: Weidenfeld and Nicolson, 1970).

LANE, DAVID, *The End of Inequality? Stratification Under State Socialism* (Harmondsworth: Penguin, 1971).

LASSWELL, HAROLD D., 'The Study of Political Elites', in Harold D. Lasswell and Daniel Lerner (eds) *World Revolutionary Elites: Studies in Coercive Ideological Movements* (Cambridge, Mass.: MIT Press, 1965) pp. 3–28.

LASSWELL, HAROLD D. and KAPLAN, ABRAHAM, *Power and Society: A Framework for Political Inquiry* (New Haven, Conn.: Yale University Press, 1950).

LEWYTZKJ (LEVYTSKY), BORYS, 'Generations in Conflict', *Problems of Communism*, vol. xvi, no. 1 (1967) pp. 36–40.

LINDEN, CARL A., *Khrushchev and the Soviet Leadership, 1957–1964* (Baltimore: Johns Hopkins Press, 1966).

LITTLE, D. RICHARD, 'Soviet Parliamentary Committees After Khrushchev: Obstacles and Opportunities', *Soviet Studies*, vol. xxiv, no. 1 (1972) pp. 41–60.

MACRIDIS, ROY C. and BROWN, BERNARD E. (eds) *Comparative Politics: Notes and Readings*, revised edition (Homewood, Ill.: The Dorsey Press, 1964).

MAXWELL, BERTRAM W., *The Soviet State* (London: Selwyn and Blount, 1935).

MOSES, JOEL C., *Regional Party Leadership and Policy-Making in the USSR* (New York: Praeger, 1974).

MOTE, MAX E., *Soviet Local and Republic Elections* (Stanford, Calif.: Hoover Institution, 1965).

NETTL, J. P., *Political Mobilization: A Sociological Analysis of Methods and Concepts* (London: Faber, 1967).

NOVE, ALEC, 'Soviet Political Organization and Development', in Colin Leys (ed.) *Politics and Change in Developing Countries: Studies in the Theory and Practice of Development* (Cambridge: Cambridge University Press, 1969) pp. 65–84.

PAGE, MARTIN and BURG, DAVID, *Unpersoned: The Fall of Nikita Sergeyevitch Khrushchev* (London: Chapman and Hall, 1966).

PARRY, GERAINT, *Political Elites* (London: Allen and Unwin, 1969).

PETHYBRIDGE, ROGER, *A Key to Soviet Politics: The Crisis of the 'Anti-Party' Group* (London: Allen and Unwin, 1962).

PLOSS, SIDNEY I., *Conflict and Decision-Making in Soviet Russia: A Case Study of Agricultural Policy, 1953–1963* (Princeton, N.J.: Princeton University Press, 1965).

POWELL, DAVID E. and SHOUP, PAUL, 'The Emergence of Political Science in Communist Countries', *American Political Science Review*, vol. LXIV, no. 2 (1970) pp. 572–88.

PUNNETT, R. M., *British Government and Politics*, 2nd edition (London: Heinemann, 1971).

PYE, LUCIAN W., *Aspects of Political Development* (Boston, Mass.: Little, Brown, 1966).

REMEIKIS, THOMAS, 'The Administration of Power: The Communist Party and the Soviet Government', in Vardys (ed.) *Lithuania Under the Soviets*, pp. 111–40.

RIGBY, T. H., 'The Selection of Leading Personnel in the Soviet State and Communist Party', PhD thesis, unpublished, University of London, 1954.

RIGBY, T. H., *Communist Party Membership in the Soviet Union, 1917–1967* (Princeton, N.J.: Princeton University Press, 1968).

RIGBY, T. H., 'Traditional, Market, and Organizational Societies and the USSR', reprinted in Fleron (ed.) *Communist Studies and the Social Sciences*, pp. 170–87.

RIGBY, T. H., 'The Soviet Political Elite 1917–1922', *British Journal of Political Science*, vol. I, no. 4 (1971) pp. 415–36.

SCHAPIRO, LEONARD, 'The Party and the State', *Survey*, no. 38 (1961) pp. 111–16.

SCHAPIRO, LEONARD, 'The New Rules of the CPSU', in Schapiro (ed.) *The USSR and the Future: An Analysis of the New Program of the CPSU* (New York: Praeger, 1963).

SCOTT, DEREK J. R., *Russian Political Institutions*, 4th edition (London: Allen and Unwin, 1969).

SELIGMAN, LESTER G., 'Political Elites Reconsidered: Process, Consequences, and Values', *Comparative Politics*, vol VI, no. 2 (1974) pp. 299–314.

SIEGEL, A. E. and SIEGEL, S., 'Reference Groups, Membership Groups and Attitude Change', reprinted in Marie Jahoda and Neil Warren (eds) *Attitudes: Selected Readings* (Harmondsworth: Penguin, 1966) pp. 187–95.

SORLIN, PIERRE, *The Soviet People and Their Society: From 1917 to the Present* (London: Praeger, 1969).

STEWART, PHILIP D., *Political Power in the Soviet Union: A Study of Decision-Making in Stalingrad* (Indianapolis and New York: Bobbs-Merrill, 1968).

STEWART, PHILIP D., ARNETT, ROBERT L., EBERT, WILLIAM T., McPHAIL, RAYMOND E., RICH, TERENCE L. and SCHOPMEYER, CRAIG E., 'Political Mobility and the Soviet Political Process: A Partial Test of Two Models', *American Political Science Review*, vol. LXVI, no. 4 (1972) pp. 1269–90.

SWEARER, HOWARD R., 'The Functions of Soviet Local Elections', *Midwest Journal of Political Science*, vol. V, no. 2 (1961) pp. 129–49.

TATU, MICHEL, *Power in the Kremlin: From Khrushchev's Decline to Collective Leadership* (London: Collins, 1969).

TAUBMAN, WILLIAM, *The View from Lenin Hills: Soviet Youth in Ferment* (London: Hamish Hamilton, 1968).

TAUBMAN, WILLIAM, *Governing Soviet Cities: Bureaucratic Politics and Urban Development in the USSR* (New York: Praeger, 1973).

THEEN, ROLF H. W., 'Political Science in the USSR: "To Be Or Not To Be?" ...', *World Politics*, vol. XXIII, no. 4 (1971) pp. 684–703.

TUCKER, ROBERT C., 'Culture, Political Culture, and Communist Society', *Political Science Quarterly*, vol. 88, no. 2 (1973) pp. 173–90.

VARDYS, V. STANLEY (ed.) *Lithuania Under the Soviets: Portrait of a Nation, 1940–65* (New York: Praeger, 1965).

VORONTSYN, SERGEI, 'Oblast and Krai First Secretaries', *Studies on the Soviet Union*, vol. VIII, no. 4 (1968–9) pp. 32–5.

WEBB, SIDNEY and WEBB, BEATRICE, *Soviet Communism – a New Civilisation?* (London: Longmans, Green, 1935–7).

WELSH, WILLIAM A., 'Toward a Multiple-Strategy Approach to Research on Comparative Communist Political Elites: Empirical and Quantitative Problems', in Fleron (ed.) *Communist Studies and the Social Sciences*, pp. 318–56.

# Index of Names

*This index only includes names referred to in the text.*

# Subject Index